UNDERSTANDING THE TIMES SERIES

UNDERSTANDING THE CULTURE

A SURVEY OF SOCIAL ENGAGEMENT

STUDENT MANUAL

UNDERSTANDING THE CULTURE STUDENT MANUAL
Published by Summit Ministries
P.O. Box 207
Manitou Springs, CO 80829

Contributors: Amanda Bridger, Jason Graham, Mike Hamel, Harley Ihm, David Knopp, Jeff Myers, Travis Satterfield, and Stephen Sutherland

Editors: Louise Betelli, Linda Harris, Tisha Martin, and Rachel Newman

LCCN: 2017962858
ISBN-13: 978-0-936163-65-9
ISBN-10: 0-936163-65-8

Printed in India
Second Printing 2019

CONTENTS

Using Understanding the Culture Curriculum

Curriculum Overview

Culture happens when humans interact with the natural world. Everyone participates in culture, and some people even help create or change it. *Understanding the Culture* is a guidebook for learning what culture is and how Christians can work to influence it for the better.

Despite stunning advances in technology and medicine, most people think our culture has gotten worse. But should Christians have anything to do with trying to fix it? Haven't so many culture-change efforts ended badly? Won't there always be legitimate disagreements?

It is a daunting task to apply a biblical worldview to the challenges of our times, but *Understanding the Culture* effectively does so by helping students understand:

- What culture is, how it is made, and how Christians in the past have shaped it.
- What biblical principles look like applied to tough issues such as technology, amusement, abortion, euthanasia, bio-ethics, same-sex attraction, feminism, marriage, politics, creation care, poverty, community development, diversity, justice, and the use of force.
- How we can become cultural change agents.

Understanding the Culture also outlines in great detail how Christians in the past have positively influenced nearly every aspect of Western culture, and other cultures around the world. Now it's our turn. This hands-on manual will equip Christians to heal a broken world and restore God's original design for culture.

Curriculum Sections

Before beginning this curriculum, it will be helpful to understand its structure and components.

1. **Syllabus:** What occurs each day and when assignments are due.

2. **Objectives:** Main learning goals for each chapter.

3. **Chapter Discussion Questions:** A review of the material read in each chapter.

4. **Classroom Activities:** Activities designed to reinforce content from each chapter.

5. **Readings:** Primary source materials, sometimes from non-Christian sources.

6. **Reading Discussion Questions:** A review of the material from the primary source readings.

7. **Reading Quizzes:** Multiple-choice and true/false questions for each primary source reading.

8. **Videos:** Lectures from experts, which dive deeper into key subjects.

9. **Video Outlines:** Notes from each video.

10. **Video Discussion Questions: A review of the material covered in each video.**

11. **Video Quizzes:** Multiple-choice and true/false questions for each video.

12. **Key Points:** Includes key questions, terms, verses, players, and works from each chapter reading.

13. **Writing Assignments:** Essay questions to answer at the end of each chapter.

14. **Tests:** A mixture of questions (matching, multiple choice, true/false, fill-in-the-blank, short answer, and essay) taken from each chapter's content.

College Credit

If you are interested in learning more about college credit for this course, please take visit summit.org/college-credit for more information.

Summit Alumni Network

This is a fabric of Christian thinkers and doers woven together by Summit Ministries' conference and curriculum grads. We gather—online and in-person—for ongoing study, strengthening community, and serving the cities in which we live. Join the network at summit.org/alumni.

WEEK 1

DAY	5-Day	ASSIGNMENT	PG
1	In Class	**ASSIGN** UTC Chapter 01 Assignment (p. 17)	
	In Class	**VIEW** UTC Chapter 01 Objectives	1
	At Home	**READ** UTC Chapter 01	
2	In Class	**DISCUSS** UTC Chapter 01 Questions	2
	In Class	**EXPLORE** UTC Chapter 01 Activities	2
3	In Class	**DISCUSS** UTC Chapter 01 Questions	2
	In Class	**EXPLORE** UTC Chapter 01 Activities	2
4	In Class	**DISCUSS** UTC Chapter 01 Questions	2
	In Class	**EXPLORE** UTC Chapter 01 Activities	2
5	In Class	**DISCUSS** UTC Chapter 01 Questions	2
	In Class	**EXPLORE** UTC Chapter 01 Activities	2

WEEK 2

DAY	5-Day	ASSIGNMENT	PG
6	In Class	**DISCUSS** UTC Chapter 01 Questions	2
	In Class	**EXPLORE** UTC Chapter 01 Activities	2
	At Home	**WATCH** "Culture Making" Part 1	8
7	In Class	**GIVE** "Culture Making" Part 1 Quiz	CD
	In Class	**DISCUSS** "Culture Making" Part 1 Questions	10
	At Home	**WATCH** "Culture Making" Part 2	12
8	In Class	**GIVE** "Culture Making" Part 2 Quiz	CD
	In Class	**DISCUSS** "Culture Making" Part 2 Questions	14
9	In Class	**STUDY FOR** UTC Chapter 01 Test	
10	In Class	**COLLECT** UTC Chapter 01 Assignment	CD
	In Class	**GIVE** UTC Chapter 01 Test	CD
	At Home	**READ** UTC Chapter 02	

WEEK 3

DAY	5-Day	ASSIGNMENT	PG
11	In Class	**REVIEW** UTC Chapter 01 Test	
	In Class	**REVIEW** UTC Chapter 01 Assignment	
	In Class	**ASSIGN** UTC Chapter 02 Assignment (p. 41)	
	In Class	**VIEW** UTC Chapter 02 Objectives	19
	At Home	**READ** UTC Chapter 02	
12	In Class	**DISCUSS** UTC Chapter 02 Questions	20
	In Class	**EXPLORE** UTC Chapter 02 Activities	20
13	In Class	**DISCUSS** UTC Chapter 02 Questions	20
	In Class	**EXPLORE** UTC Chapter 02 Activities	20
14	In Class	**DISCUSS** UTC Chapter 02 Questions	20
	In Class	**EXPLORE** UTC Chapter 02 Activities	20
15	In Class	**DISCUSS** UTC Chapter 02 Questions	20
	In Class	**EXPLORE** UTC Chapter 02 Activities	20

WEEK 4

DAY	5-Day	ASSIGNMENT	PG
16	In Class	**DISCUSS** UTC Chapter 02 Questions	20
	In Class	**EXPLORE** UTC Chapter 02 Activities	20
	At Home	**READ** "What Is Culture?"	26
17	In Class	**GIVE** "What Is Culture?" Quiz	CD
	In Class	**DISCUSS** "What Is Culture?" Questions	34
	At Home	**WATCH** "A Christian Perspective of Art"	36
18	In Class	**GIVE** "A Christian Perspective of Art" Quiz	CD
	In Class	**DISCUSS** "A Christian Perspective of Art" Questions	38
19	In Class	**STUDY FOR** UTC Chapter 02 Test	
20	In Class	**COLLECT** UTC Chapter 02 Assignment	CD
	In Class	**GIVE** UTC Chapter 02 Test	CD
	At Home	**READ** UTC Chapter 03	

WEEK 5

DAY	5-Day	ASSIGNMENT	PG
21	In Class	**REVIEW** UTC Chapter 02 Test	
	In Class	**REVIEW** UTC Chapter 02 Assignment	
	In Class	**ASSIGN** UTC Chapter 03 Assignment (p. 59)	
	In Class	**VIEW** UTC Chapter 03 Objectives	43
	At Home	**READ** UTC Chapter 03	
22	In Class	**DISCUSS** UTC Chapter 03 Questions	44
	In Class	**EXPLORE** UTC Chapter 03 Activities	44
23	In Class	**DISCUSS** UTC Chapter 03 Questions	44
	In Class	**EXPLORE** UTC Chapter 03 Activities	44
24	In Class	**DISCUSS** UTC Chapter 03 Questions	44
	In Class	**EXPLORE** UTC Chapter 03 Activities	44
25	In Class	**DISCUSS** UTC Chapter 03 Questions	44
	In Class	**EXPLORE** UTC Chapter 03 Activities	44

WEEK 6

DAY	5-Day	ASSIGNMENT	PG
26	In Class	**DISCUSS** UTC Chapter 03 Questions	44
	In Class	**EXPLORE** UTC Chapter 03 Activities	44
	At Home	**WATCH** "J-Shaped Cultures"	50
27	In Class	**GIVE** "J-Shaped Cultures" Quiz	CD
	In Class	**DISCUSS** "J-Shaped Cultures" Questions	52
	At Home	**WATCH** "How to Move Ideas"	54
28	In Class	**GIVE** "How to Move Ideas" Quiz	CD
	In Class	**DISCUSS** "How to Move Ideas" Questions	56
29	In Class	**STUDY FOR** UTC Chapter 03 Test	
30	In Class	**COLLECT** UTC Chapter 03 Assignment	CD
	In Class	**GIVE** UTC Chapter 03 Test	CD
	At Home	**READ** UTC Chapter 04	

WEEK 7

DAY	5-Day	ASSIGNMENT	PG
31	In Class	**REVIEW** UTC Chapter 03 Test	
	In Class	**REVIEW** UTC Chapter 03 Assignment	
	In Class	**ASSIGN** UTC Chapter 04 Assignment (p. 78)	
	In Class	**VIEW** UTC Chapter 04 Objectives	61
	At Home	**READ** UTC Chapter 04	
32	In Class	**DISCUSS** UTC Chapter 04 Questions	62
	In Class	**EXPLORE** UTC Chapter 04 Activities	62
33	In Class	**DISCUSS** UTC Chapter 04 Questions	62
	In Class	**EXPLORE** UTC Chapter 04 Activities	62
34	In Class	**DISCUSS** UTC Chapter 04 Questions	62
	In Class	**EXPLORE** UTC Chapter 04 Activities	62
35	In Class	**DISCUSS** UTC Chapter 04 Questions	62
	In Class	**EXPLORE** UTC Chapter 04 Activities	62

WEEK 8

DAY	5-Day	ASSIGNMENT	PG
36	In Class	**DISCUSS** UTC Chapter 04 Questions	62
	In Class	**EXPLORE** UTC Chapter 04 Activities	62
	At Home	**READ** "Cultural Issues in the Coming Years"	67
37	In Class	**GIVE** "Cultural Issues in the Coming Years" Quiz	CD
	In Class	**DISCUSS** "Cultural Issues in the Coming ..." Questions	71
	At Home	**WATCH** "Engaging the Culture"	73
38	In Class	**GIVE** "Engaging the Culture" Quiz	CD
	In Class	**DISCUSS** "Engaging the Culture" Questions	75
39	In Class	**STUDY FOR** UTC Chapter 04 Test	
40	In Class	**COLLECT** UTC Chapter 04 Assignment	CD
	In Class	**GIVE** UTC Chapter 04 Test	CD
	At Home	**READ** UTC Chapter 05	

WEEK 9

DAY	5-Day	ASSIGNMENT	PG
41	In Class	**REVIEW** UTC Chapter 04 Test	
	In Class	**REVIEW** UTC Chapter 04 Assignment	
	In Class	**ASSIGN** UTC Chapter 05 Assignment (p. 104)	
	In Class	**VIEW** UTC Chapter 05 Objectives	81
	At Home	**READ** UTC Chapter 05	
42	In Class	**DISCUSS** UTC Chapter 05 Questions	82
	In Class	**EXPLORE** UTC Chapter 05 Activities	82
43	In Class	**DISCUSS** UTC Chapter 05 Questions	82
	In Class	**EXPLORE** UTC Chapter 05 Activities	82
44	In Class	**DISCUSS** UTC Chapter 05 Questions	82
	In Class	**EXPLORE** UTC Chapter 05 Activities	82
45	In Class	**DISCUSS** UTC Chapter 05 Questions	82
	In Class	**EXPLORE** UTC Chapter 05 Activities	82

WEEK 10

DAY	5-Day	ASSIGNMENT	PG
46	In Class	**DISCUSS** UTC Chapter 05 Questions	82
	In Class	**EXPLORE** UTC Chapter 05 Activities	82
	At Home	**READ** "The Christian Mind"	88
47	In Class	**GIVE** "The Christian Mind" Quiz	CD
	In Class	**DISCUSS** "The Christian Mind" Questions	97
	At Home	**WATCH** "Critical Thinking"	99
48	In Class	**GIVE** "Critical Thinking" Quiz	CD
	In Class	**DISCUSS** "Critical Thinking" Questions	101
49	In Class	**STUDY FOR** UTC Chapter 05 Test	
50	In Class	**COLLECT** UTC Chapter 05 Assignment	CD
	In Class	**GIVE** UTC Chapter 05 Test	CD
	At Home	**READ** UTC Chapter 06	

WEEK 11

DAY	5-Day	ASSIGNMENT	PG
51	In Class	**REVIEW** UTC Chapter 05 Test	
	In Class	**REVIEW** UTC Chapter 05 Assignment	
	In Class	**ASSIGN** UTC Chapter 06 Assignment (p. 126)	
	In Class	**VIEW** UTC Chapter 06 Objectives	107
	At Home	**READ** UTC Chapter 06	
52	In Class	**DISCUSS** UTC Chapter 06 Questions	108
	In Class	**EXPLORE** UTC Chapter 06 Activities	108
53	In Class	**DISCUSS** UTC Chapter 06 Questions	108
	In Class	**EXPLORE** UTC Chapter 06 Activities	108
54	In Class	**DISCUSS** UTC Chapter 06 Questions	108
	In Class	**EXPLORE** UTC Chapter 06 Activities	108
55	In Class	**DISCUSS** UTC Chapter 06 Questions	108
	In Class	**EXPLORE** UTC Chapter 06 Activities	108

WEEK 12

DAY	5-Day	ASSIGNMENT	PG
56	In Class	**DISCUSS** UTC Chapter 06 Questions	108
	In Class	**EXPLORE** UTC Chapter 06 Activities	108
	At Home	**READ** "Connectivity and Its Disconnects"	114
57	In Class	**GIVE** "Connectivity and Its Disconnects" Quiz	CD
	In Class	**DISCUSS** "Connectivity and Its ..." Questions	119
	At Home	**WATCH** "Bioethics"	121
58	In Class	**GIVE** "Bioethics" Quiz	CD
	In Class	**DISCUSS** "Bioethics" Questions	123
59	In Class	**STUDY FOR** UTC Chapter 06 Test	
60	In Class	**COLLECT** UTC Chapter 06 Assignment	CD
	In Class	**GIVE** UTC Chapter 06 Test	CD
	At Home	**READ** UTC Chapter 07	

WEEK 13

DAY	5-Day	ASSIGNMENT	PG
61	In Class	**REVIEW** UTC Chapter 06 Test	
	In Class	**REVIEW** UTC Chapter 06 Assignment	
	In Class	**ASSIGN** UTC Chapter 07 Assignment (p. 150)	
	In Class	**VIEW** UTC Chapter 07 Objectives	129
	At Home	**READ** UTC Chapter 07	
62	In Class	**DISCUSS** UTC Chapter 07 Questions	130
	In Class	**EXPLORE** UTC Chapter 07 Activities	130
63	In Class	**DISCUSS** UTC Chapter 07 Questions	130
	In Class	**EXPLORE** UTC Chapter 07 Activities	130
64	In Class	**DISCUSS** UTC Chapter 07 Questions	130
	In Class	**EXPLORE** UTC Chapter 07 Activities	130
65	In Class	**DISCUSS** UTC Chapter 07 Questions	130
	In Class	**EXPLORE** UTC Chapter 07 Activities	130

WEEK 14

DAY	5-Day	ASSIGNMENT	PG
66	In Class	**DISCUSS** UTC Chapter 07 Questions	130
	In Class	**EXPLORE** UTC Chapter 07 Activities	130
	At Home	**READ** "The Impact of the Net"	135
67	In Class	**GIVE** "The Impact of the Net" Quiz	CD
	In Class	**DISCUSS** "The Impact of the Net" Questions	143
	At Home	**WATCH** "Amusing Ourselves to Death"	145
68	In Class	**GIVE** "Amusing Ourselves to Death" Quiz	CD
	In Class	**DISCUSS** "Amusing Ourselves to Death" Questions	147
69	In Class	**STUDY FOR** UTC Chapter 07 Test	
70	In Class	**COLLECT** UTC Chapter 07 Assignment	CD
	In Class	**GIVE** UTC Chapter 07 Test	CD
	At Home	**READ** UTC Chapter 08	

WEEK 15

DAY	5-Day	ASSIGNMENT	PG
71	In Class	**REVIEW** UTC Chapter 07 Test	
	In Class	**REVIEW** UTC Chapter 07 Assignment	
	In Class	**ASSIGN** UTC Chapter 08 Assignment (p. 169)	
	In Class	**VIEW** UTC Chapter 08 Objectives	153
	At Home	**READ** UTC Chapter 08	
72	In Class	**DISCUSS** UTC Chapter 08 Questions	154
	In Class	**EXPLORE** UTC Chapter 08 Activities	154
73	In Class	**DISCUSS** UTC Chapter 08 Questions	154
	In Class	**EXPLORE** UTC Chapter 08 Activities	154
74	In Class	**DISCUSS** UTC Chapter 08 Questions	154
	In Class	**EXPLORE** UTC Chapter 08 Activities	154
75	In Class	**DISCUSS** UTC Chapter 08 Questions	154
	In Class	**EXPLORE** UTC Chapter 08 Activities	154

WEEK 16

DAY	5-Day	ASSIGNMENT	PG
76	In Class	**DISCUSS** UTC Chapter 08 Questions	154
	In Class	**EXPLORE** UTC Chapter 08 Activities	154
	At Home	**WATCH** "The Case for the Pro-Life Position P1"	160
77	In Class	**GIVE** "The Case for the Pro-Life Position P1" Quiz	CD
	In Class	**DISCUSS** "The Case for the ... P1" Questions	162
	At Home	**WATCH** "The Case for the Pro-Life Position P2"	164
78	In Class	**GIVE** "The Case for the Pro-Life Position P2" Quiz	CD
	In Class	**DISCUSS** "The Case for the ... P2" Questions	166
79	In Class	**STUDY FOR** UTC Chapter 08 Test	
80	In Class	**COLLECT** UTC Chapter 08 Assignment	CD
	In Class	**GIVE** UTC Chapter 08 Test	CD
	At Home	**READ** UTC Chapter 09	

WEEK 17

DAY	5-Day	ASSIGNMENT	PG
81	In Class	**REVIEW** UTC Chapter 08 Test	
	In Class	**REVIEW** UTC Chapter 08 Assignment	
	In Class	**ASSIGN** UTC Chapter 09 Assignment (p. 188)	
	In Class	**VIEW** UTC Chapter 09 Objectives	171
	At Home	**READ** UTC Chapter 09	
82	In Class	**DISCUSS** UTC Chapter 09 Questions	172
	In Class	**EXPLORE** UTC Chapter 09 Activities	172
83	In Class	**DISCUSS** UTC Chapter 09 Questions	172
	In Class	**EXPLORE** UTC Chapter 09 Activities	172
84	In Class	**DISCUSS** UTC Chapter 09 Questions	172
	In Class	**EXPLORE** UTC Chapter 09 Activities	172
85	In Class	**DISCUSS** UTC Chapter 09 Questions	172
	In Class	**EXPLORE** UTC Chapter 09 Activities	172

WEEK 18

DAY	5-Day	ASSIGNMENT	PG
86	In Class	**DISCUSS** UTC Chapter 09 Questions	172
	In Class	**EXPLORE** UTC Chapter 09 Activities	172
	At Home	**WATCH** "The Hermeneutics of Sexuality"	178
87	In Class	**GIVE** "The Hermeneutics of Sexuality" Quiz	CD
	In Class	**DISCUSS** "The Hermeneutics of Sexuality" Questions	181
	At Home	**WATCH** "The Worldview behind Porn"	183
88	In Class	**GIVE** "The Worldview behind Porn" Quiz	CD
	In Class	**DISCUSS** "The Worldview behind Porn" Questions	185
89	In Class	**STUDY FOR** UTC Chapter 09 Test	
90	In Class	**COLLECT** UTC Chapter 09 Assignment	CD
	In Class	**GIVE** UTC Chapter 09 Test	CD
	At Home	**READ** UTC Chapter 10	

WEEK 19

DAY	5-Day	ASSIGNMENT	PG
91	In Class	**REVIEW** UTC Chapter 09 Test	
	In Class	**REVIEW** UTC Chapter 09 Assignment	
	In Class	**ASSIGN** UTC Chapter 10 Assignment (p. 208)	
	In Class	**VIEW** UTC Chapter 10 Objectives	191
	At Home	**READ** UTC Chapter 10	
92	In Class	**DISCUSS** UTC Chapter 10 Questions	192
	In Class	**EXPLORE** UTC Chapter 10 Activities	192
93	In Class	**DISCUSS** UTC Chapter 10 Questions	192
	In Class	**EXPLORE** UTC Chapter 10 Activities	192
94	In Class	**DISCUSS** UTC Chapter 10 Questions	192
	In Class	**EXPLORE** UTC Chapter 10 Activities	192
95	In Class	**DISCUSS** UTC Chapter 10 Questions	192
	In Class	**EXPLORE** UTC Chapter 10 Activities	192

WEEK 20

DAY	5-Day	ASSIGNMENT	PG
96	In Class	**DISCUSS** UTC Chapter 10 Questions	192
	In Class	**EXPLORE** UTC Chapter 10 Activities	192
	At Home	**WATCH** "Same-Sex Marriage"	198
97	In Class	**GIVE** "Same-Sex Marriage" Quiz	CD
	In Class	**DISCUSS** "Same-Sex Marriage" Questions	200
	At Home	**WATCH** "Why Marriage Matters"	202
98	In Class	**GIVE** "Why Marriage Matters" Quiz	CD
	In Class	**DISCUSS** "Why Marriage Matters" Questions	205
99	In Class	**STUDY FOR** UTC Chapter 10 Test	
100	In Class	**COLLECT** UTC Chapter 10 Assignment	CD
	In Class	**GIVE** UTC Chapter 10 Test	CD
	At Home	**READ** UTC Chapter 11	

WEEK 21

DAY	5-Day	ASSIGNMENT	PG
101	In Class	**REVIEW** UTC Chapter 10 Test	
	In Class	**REVIEW** UTC Chapter 10 Assignment	
	In Class	**ASSIGN** UTC Chapter 11 Assignment (p. 236)	
	In Class	**VIEW** UTC Chapter 11 Objectives	211
	At Home	**READ** UTC Chapter 11	
102	In Class	**DISCUSS** UTC Chapter 11 Questions	212
	In Class	**EXPLORE** UTC Chapter 11 Activities	212
103	In Class	**DISCUSS** UTC Chapter 11 Questions	212
	In Class	**EXPLORE** UTC Chapter 11 Activities	212
104	In Class	**DISCUSS** UTC Chapter 11 Questions	212
	In Class	**EXPLORE** UTC Chapter 11 Activities	212
105	In Class	**DISCUSS** UTC Chapter 11 Questions	212
	In Class	**EXPLORE** UTC Chapter 11 Activities	212

WEEK 22

DAY	5-Day	ASSIGNMENT	PG
106	In Class	**DISCUSS** UTC Chapter 11 Questions	212
	In Class	**EXPLORE** UTC Chapter 11 Activities	212
	At Home	**READ** "A Christian Environmental Ethic"	218
107	In Class	**GIVE** "A Christian Environmental Ethic" Quiz	CD
	In Class	**DISCUSS** "A Christian Environmental ..." Questions	229
	At Home	**WATCH** "Energy and the Environment"	231
108	In Class	**GIVE** "Energy and the Environment" Quiz	CD
	In Class	**DISCUSS** "Energy and the Environment" Questions	233
109	In Class	**STUDY FOR** UTC Chapter 11 Test	
110	In Class	**COLLECT** UTC Chapter 11 Assignment	CD
	In Class	**GIVE** UTC Chapter 11 Test	CD
	At Home	**READ** UTC Chapter 12	

WEEK 23

DAY	5-Day	ASSIGNMENT	PG
111	In Class	**REVIEW** UTC Chapter 11 Test	
	In Class	**REVIEW** UTC Chapter 11 Assignment	
	In Class	**ASSIGN** UTC Chapter 12 Assignment (p. 262)	
	In Class	**VIEW** UTC Chapter 12 Objectives	239
	At Home	**READ** UTC Chapter 12	
112	In Class	**DISCUSS** UTC Chapter 12 Questions	240
	In Class	**EXPLORE** UTC Chapter 12 Activities	240
113	In Class	**DISCUSS** UTC Chapter 12 Questions	240
	In Class	**EXPLORE** UTC Chapter 12 Activities	240
114	In Class	**DISCUSS** UTC Chapter 12 Questions	240
	In Class	**EXPLORE** UTC Chapter 12 Activities	240
115	In Class	**DISCUSS** UTC Chapter 12 Questions	240
	In Class	**EXPLORE** UTC Chapter 12 Activities	240

WEEK 24

DAY	5-Day	ASSIGNMENT	PG
116	In Class	**DISCUSS** UTC Chapter 12 Questions	240
	In Class	**EXPLORE** UTC Chapter 12 Activities	240
	At Home	**READ** "The Golden Triangle of Freedom"	246
117	In Class	**GIVE** "The Golden Triangle of Freedom" Quiz	CD
	In Class	**DISCUSS** "The Golden Triangle of ..." Questions	255
	At Home	**WATCH** "Political Animal"	257
118	In Class	**GIVE** "Political Animal" Quiz	CD
	In Class	**DISCUSS** "Political Animal" Questions	259
119	In Class	**STUDY FOR** UTC Chapter 12 Test	
120	In Class	**COLLECT** UTC Chapter 12 Assignment	CD
	In Class	**GIVE** UTC Chapter 12 Test	CD
	At Home	**READ** UTC Chapter 13	

WEEK 25

DAY	5-Day	ASSIGNMENT	PG
121	In Class	**REVIEW** UTC Chapter 12 Test	
	In Class	**REVIEW** UTC Chapter 12 Assignment	
	In Class	**ASSIGN** UTC Chapter 13 Assignment (p. 289)	
	In Class	**VIEW** UTC Chapter 13 Objectives	265
	At Home	**READ** UTC Chapter 13	
122	In Class	**DISCUSS** UTC Chapter 13 Questions	266
	In Class	**EXPLORE** UTC Chapter 13 Activities	266
123	In Class	**DISCUSS** UTC Chapter 13 Questions	266
	In Class	**EXPLORE** UTC Chapter 13 Activities	266
124	In Class	**DISCUSS** UTC Chapter 13 Questions	266
	In Class	**EXPLORE** UTC Chapter 13 Activities	266
125	In Class	**DISCUSS** UTC Chapter 13 Questions	266
	In Class	**EXPLORE** UTC Chapter 13 Activities	266

WEEK 26

DAY	5-Day	ASSIGNMENT	PG
126	In Class	**DISCUSS** UTC Chapter 13 Questions	266
	In Class	**EXPLORE** UTC Chapter 13 Activities	266
	At Home	**READ** "A World Split Apart"	271
127	In Class	**GIVE** "A World Split Apart" Quiz	CD
	In Class	**DISCUSS** "A World Split Apart" Questions	281
	At Home	**WATCH** "Religious Liberty"	283
128	In Class	**GIVE** "Religious Liberty" Quiz	CD
	In Class	**DISCUSS** "Religious Liberty" Questions	286
129	In Class	**STUDY FOR** UTC Chapter 13 Test	
130	In Class	**COLLECT** UTC Chapter 13 Assignment	CD
	In Class	**GIVE** UTC Chapter 13 Test	CD
	At Home	**READ** UTC Chapter 14	

WEEK 27

DAY	5-Day	ASSIGNMENT	PG
131	In Class	**REVIEW** UTC Chapter 13 Test	
	In Class	**REVIEW** UTC Chapter 13 Assignment	
	In Class	**ASSIGN** UTC Chapter 14 Assignment (p. 316)	
	In Class	**VIEW** UTC Chapter 14 Objectives	291
	At Home	**READ** UTC Chapter 14	
132	In Class	**DISCUSS** UTC Chapter 14 Questions	292
	In Class	**EXPLORE** UTC Chapter 14 Activities	292
133	In Class	**DISCUSS** UTC Chapter 14 Questions	292
	In Class	**EXPLORE** UTC Chapter 14 Activities	292
134	In Class	**DISCUSS** UTC Chapter 14 Questions	292
	In Class	**EXPLORE** UTC Chapter 14 Activities	292
135	In Class	**DISCUSS** UTC Chapter 14 Questions	292
	In Class	**EXPLORE** UTC Chapter 14 Activities	292

WEEK 28

DAY	5-Day	ASSIGNMENT	PG
136	In Class	**DISCUSS** UTC Chapter 14 Questions	292
	In Class	**EXPLORE** UTC Chapter 14 Activities	292
	At Home	**READ** "Living as if People Mattered"	298
137	In Class	**GIVE** "Living as if People Mattered" Quiz	CD
	In Class	**DISCUSS** "Living as if People Mattered" Questions	308
	At Home	**WATCH** "Effective Compassion"	310
138	In Class	**GIVE** "Effective Compassion" Quiz	CD
	In Class	**DISCUSS** "Effective Compassion" Questions	313
139	In Class	**STUDY FOR** UTC Chapter 14 Test	
140	In Class	**COLLECT** UTC Chapter 14 Assignment	CD
	In Class	**GIVE** UTC Chapter 14 Test	CD
	At Home	**READ** UTC Chapter 15	

WEEK 29

DAY	5-Day	ASSIGNMENT	PG
141	In Class	**REVIEW** UTC Chapter 14 Test	
	In Class	**REVIEW** UTC Chapter 14 Assignment	
	In Class	**ASSIGN** UTC Chapter 15 Assignment (p. 343)	
	In Class	**VIEW** UTC Chapter 15 Objectives	319
	At Home	**READ** UTC Chapter 15	
142	In Class	**DISCUSS** UTC Chapter 15 Questions	320
	In Class	**EXPLORE** UTC Chapter 15 Activities	320
143	In Class	**DISCUSS** UTC Chapter 15 Questions	320
	In Class	**EXPLORE** UTC Chapter 15 Activities	320
144	In Class	**DISCUSS** UTC Chapter 15 Questions	320
	In Class	**EXPLORE** UTC Chapter 15 Activities	320
145	In Class	**DISCUSS** UTC Chapter 15 Questions	320
	In Class	**EXPLORE** UTC Chapter 15 Activities	320

WEEK 30

DAY	5-Day	ASSIGNMENT	PG
146	In Class	**DISCUSS** UTC Chapter 15 Questions	320
	In Class	**EXPLORE** UTC Chapter 15 Activities	320
	At Home	**READ** "Just War Tradition"	326
147	In Class	**GIVE** "Just War Tradition" Quiz	CD
	In Class	**DISCUSS** "Just War Tradition" Questions	335
	At Home	**WATCH** "The Rules of the Game"	337
148	In Class	**GIVE** "The Rules of the Game" Quiz	CD
	In Class	**DISCUSS** "The Rules of the Game" Questions	340
149	In Class	**STUDY FOR** UTC Chapter 15 Test	
150	In Class	**COLLECT** UTC Chapter 15 Assignment	CD
	In Class	**GIVE** UTC Chapter 15 Test	CD
	At Home	**READ** UTC Chapter 16	

WEEK 31

DAY	5-Day	ASSIGNMENT	PG
151	In Class	**REVIEW** UTC Chapter 15 Test	
	In Class	**REVIEW** UTC Chapter 15 Assignment	
	In Class	**ASSIGN** UTC Chapter 16 Assignment (p. 364)	
	In Class	**VIEW** UTC Chapter 16 Objectives	345
	At Home	**READ** UTC Chapter 16	
152	In Class	**DISCUSS** UTC Chapter 16 Questions	346
	In Class	**EXPLORE** UTC Chapter 16 Activities	346
153	In Class	**DISCUSS** UTC Chapter 16 Questions	346
	In Class	**EXPLORE** UTC Chapter 16 Activities	346
154	In Class	**DISCUSS** UTC Chapter 16 Questions	346
	In Class	**EXPLORE** UTC Chapter 16 Activities	346
155	In Class	**DISCUSS** UTC Chapter 16 Questions	346
	In Class	**EXPLORE** UTC Chapter 16 Activities	346

WEEK 32

DAY	5-Day	ASSIGNMENT	PG
156	In Class	**DISCUSS** UTC Chapter 16 Questions	346
	In Class	**EXPLORE** UTC Chapter 16 Activities	346
	At Home	**READ** "Letter from a Birmingham Jail"	351
157	In Class	**GIVE** "Letter from a Birmingham Jail" Quiz	CD
	In Class	**DISCUSS** "Letter from a Birmingham Jail" Questions	357
	At Home	**WATCH** "The Struggle for Equality"	359
158	In Class	**GIVE** "The Struggle for Equality" Quiz	CD
	In Class	**DISCUSS** "The Struggle for Equality" Questions	361
159	In Class	**STUDY FOR** UTC Chapter 16 Test	
160	In Class	**COLLECT** UTC Chapter 16 Assignment	CD
	In Class	**GIVE** UTC Chapter 16 Test	CD
	At Home	**READ** UTC Chapter 17	

WEEK 33

DAY	5-Day	ASSIGNMENT	PG
161	In Class	**REVIEW** UTC Chapter 16 Test	
	In Class	**REVIEW** UTC Chapter 16 Assignment	
	In Class	**ASSIGN** UTC Chapter 17 Assignment (p. 489)	
	In Class	**VIEW** UTC Chapter 17 Objectives	367
	At Home	**READ** UTC Chapter 17	
162	In Class	**DISCUSS** UTC Chapter 17 Questions	368
	In Class	**EXPLORE** UTC Chapter 17 Activities	368
163	In Class	**DISCUSS** UTC Chapter 17 Questions	368
	In Class	**EXPLORE** UTC Chapter 17 Activities	368
164	In Class	**DISCUSS** UTC Chapter 17 Questions	368
	In Class	**EXPLORE** UTC Chapter 17 Activities	368
165	In Class	**DISCUSS** UTC Chapter 17 Questions	368
	In Class	**EXPLORE** UTC Chapter 17 Activities	368

WEEK 34

DAY	5-Day	ASSIGNMENT	PG
166	In Class	**DISCUSS** UTC Chapter 17 Questions	368
	In Class	**EXPLORE** UTC Chapter 17 Activities	368
	At Home	**READ** "A Theology of Cities"	373
167	In Class	**GIVE** "A Theology of Cities" Quiz	CD
	In Class	**DISCUSS** "A Theology of Cities" Questions	381
	At Home	**WATCH** "Christianity in Community"	383
168	In Class	**GIVE** "Christianity in Community" Quiz	CD
	In Class	**DISCUSS** "Christianity in Community" Questions	386
169	In Class	**STUDY FOR** UTC Chapter 17 Test	
170	In Class	**COLLECT** UTC Chapter 17 Assignment	CD
	In Class	**GIVE** UTC Chapter 17 Test	CD
	At Home	**READ** UTC Chapter 18	

WEEK 35

DAY	5-Day	ASSIGNMENT	PG
171	In Class	**REVIEW** UTC Chapter 17 Test	
	In Class	**REVIEW** UTC Chapter 17 Assignment	
	In Class	**VIEW** UTC Chapter 18 Objectives	391
	At Home	**READ** UTC Chapter 18	
172	In Class	**DISCUSS** UTC Chapter 18 Questions	392
173	In Class	**DISCUSS** UTC Chapter 18 Questions	392
174	In Class	**DISCUSS** UTC Chapter 18 Questions	392
175	In Class	**DISCUSS** UTC Chapter 18 Questions	392

WEEK 36

DAY	5-Day	ASSIGNMENT	PG
176	In Class	**DISCUSS** UTC Chapter 18 Questions	392
177	In Class	**STUDY FOR** UTC Chapter 18 Test	
178	In Class	**STUDY FOR** UTC Chapter 18 Test	
179	In Class	**STUDY FOR** UTC Chapter 18 Test	
180	In Class	**GIVE** UTC Chapter 18 Test	CD

UNIT 1

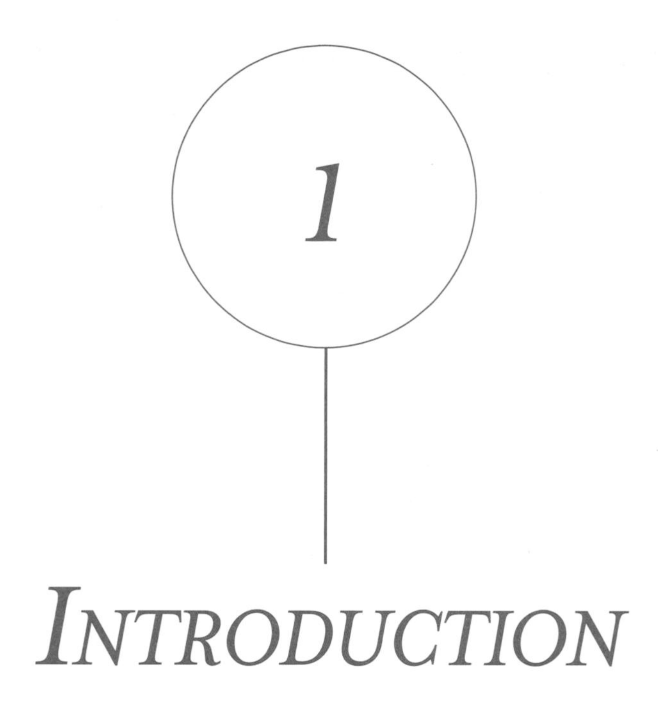

INTRODUCTION

CHAPTER 1 LEARNING OBJECTIVES

Students will be able to:

1. recognize the importance of Christians to properly care about the world around us. [1.1]
2. recognize the consequences our ideas should have on our actions, and discuss the influence of our decisions on the world around us. [1.2]
3. identify the impact our concept of "the big picture" has on our caring for the world around us. [1.3]
4. discuss the implications of living in a universe that we can observe and how that demonstrates God's concern for humanity. [1.4]
5. explain how our answers to metaphysical questions, addressing both the positive and negative aspects of human progress, often lead to cultural conflict. [1.5]
6. analyze the culture conflict in America between liberal and fundamentalist movements in the early twentieth century. [1.6]
7. discuss the responses of Christian conservatism in the latter half of the twentieth century to cultural changes. [1.7]
8. identify the multiple reasons why Christian conservatism as a cultural movement began to fracture by the end of the twentieth century. [1.8]
9. identify and discuss the biblical reasons for Christians to concern themselves with the culture around us. [1.9]
10. identify and discuss the biblical directives for the attributes Christians ought to pursue when engaging with the culture. [1.10]

Chapter 1 Discussion Questions

1. **What is the overall purpose of this book? [1:1]**

2. **How has technology enabled us to make better decisions? [1:2]**

3. **If you had to go a week without any access to information technology or social media, how would your life be different?**

4. **What is the "anthropic principle?' [1:4]**

5. **What is "metaphysics" and what questions does it seek to answer? [1:5]**

6. **Does being a citizen of heaven mean we shouldn't get involved in the things of this world? [1.6]**

7. **What factors led to the creation of the Fundamentalist movement? [1:6]**

8. **What happened to the Fundamentalist movement? [1:6]**

9. **What are some issues over which Christians should leave their churches? What are some issues where disagreement doesn't necessarily call for breaking fellowship?**

10. **Who are the New Evangelicals?** [1:7]

11. **How did the New Evangelicals impact American culture?** [1:7]

12. **Which group do you most identify with: Fundamentalists, Liberals, New Evangelicals, or something else?** [1.7]

13. What factors caused Evangelicalism to splinter in the early twenty-first century? [1:8]

14. What is "the third way" suggested by this book between Secularism and Gnosticism? [1:8]

15. What are the main things God cares about? [1:9]

16. Is the command to love our neighbor strictly a New Testament concept or can it be found in the Old Testament? [1:9]

17. How does the biblical view of humanity differ from all other worldviews? [1:9]

18. What is narcissism and how is it affecting our culture? [1:9]

19. What is involved in pursuing a life of wisdom? [1:10]

20. What does it mean to live a worthy life? [1:10]

21. What role do words play in a caring life? [1:10]

22. What are some key things you will learn in this book? [1:11]

23. What factors determine if we go through life as "givers" or "takers"? [1:12]

"Culture Making" Part 1 Video

Andy Crouch notes the dysfunctional relationship between Christianity and culture in which both parties see each other at their worst. Christianity embraced a series of postures in the last hundred years that hasn't helped very much. Christians became known for condemning, critiquing, consuming, and copying culture instead of changing and creating it.

Crouch explains why the most important chapters in the Bible for properly understanding culture are the first two (Genesis 1 and 2) and the last two (Revelation 21 and 22). The Bible starts with a good world and ends with a glorious one. Sin (Genesis 3) and judgment (Revelation 20) are part of reality but they aren't what God intended or what will prevail in the end.

To access this video, go to www.summitu.com/utc and enter the passcode found in the back of your manual.

"Culture Making" Part 1 Video Outline

The relationship between ____________________ and culture over the past century has become dysfunctional as both parties focus on the worst aspects of the other. Christians have become known for condemning, critiquing, and judging culture.

Movements like Fundamentalism have correlated holiness with what Christians *don't* do. The children of fundamentalists have reacted to their parents' **condemnation** of culture by **critiquing**, **copying**, or **consuming** culture.

What these four Cs have in common is that they are all reactions to culture but they don't add anything creative or new to it.

Twenty-first Century Prayer—"Deliver us from ____________________."

The Lord's Prayer, "deliver us from evil," has been replaced with "deliver us from culture." This assumes *evil* and *culture* are synonymous. This mindset ignores some important chapters in the Bible

Key chapters for properly understanding culture:

Genesis 1 and 2: Six times God says creation is good. It becomes "__________________" when he makes humans as his image bearers and tells them to fill and subdue—"cultivate" —the world.

Revelation 21 and 22: God's goal is not a restored garden but a____________________. A city is where the depth and diversity of culture reaches critical mass. The work of culture will be brought into the city, not swept into the lake of fire.

The Bible starts with a good world and ends with a glorious one. Sin (Genesis 3) and judgment (Revelation 20) are part of reality but they aren't what God intended or what will prevail in the end.

We have to do our part to shape the *good* into the *very good*, to move from nature to culture. Cultivation doesn't happen automatically; humans have to do it.

Examples of culture:

- Grain to bread
- Grapes to wine
- Sound to music
- Minerals to jewels

"Culture Making" Part 1 Discussion Questions

1. **What are the four Cs that have characterized the approach many Christians take to culture?**

2. **Which of the four Cs do you think characterizes the church or denomination of which you are a part?**

3. **What do the first two chapters and the last two chapters of the Bible add to our worldview?**

4. **What kind of worldview results from ignoring these important chapters?**

5. **What are some examples of how cultivation takes something "good" in nature and makes it "very good"?**

“Culture Making” Part 2 Video

The good news that frames the Bible is that creation was “good” and became “very good” with the creation of God’s image bearers. And in the end God rescues and redeems the world and gives it to his image bearers in a beautiful city they will inhabit forever.

The Bible gives two answers as to what went wrong in the middle of the story: 1) Idolatry—the putting of what God made in the place of God himself. The danger of idols is that they take over and destroy the lives of their followers. 2) Injustice—the sign that someone has tried to play God in the life of someone else. Injustice exaggerates the image of God in the powerful and debases it in the poor.

To access this video, go to www.summitu.com/utc and enter the passcode found in the back of your manual.

"Culture Making" Part 2 Video Outline

God's story, as told in the Bible, moves from "good" to "very good" to "glory." This progression gives us a sense of hope. But two things went wrong in the middle of the story.

1. **Idolatry:**

   Idolatry is the putting of what God made in the place of God himself. The image bearers, meaning to represent God in the world, make substitute images instead. They turn to created things as a substitute for their Creator.

   Every idol makes two false promises:

   1. You shall not surely ____________—the conditions of a creature will not apply to you.

   2. You shall be like ____________—you will ascend out of your creaturely status into something better.

   The danger of idols is that they take over and destroy the lives of their followers.

   All idols work at first, but they don't keep working. They demand everything in the end and deliver nothing of what they promised.

   God hates that the world is full of ________________ of himself.

   Any good thing can be an idol, such as exercise or wine.

2. **Injustice:**

   Injustice is the sign that someone is "trying to play God" in the life of someone else. Injustice exaggerates the image of God in the powerful and debases it in the poor.

   God hates idolatry and injustice for the same reason: they are the substitution of false images for the true image of God. Instead of "making" a false god (idolatry) someone is "playing" God in the lives of others (injustice).

   God does not leave us in our idolatry and injustice. He is ________________ his image in us and in creation. God is rescuing and redeeming the world and giving it to his image bearers in a beautiful city they will inhabit forever.

"Culture Making" Part 2 Discussion Questions

1. **The Bible begins and ends with good news, but what happened in the middle of the story?**

2. **What is idolatry?**

3. **Why are idols dangerous?**

4. What is injustice?

5. How are idolatry and injustice related?

Chapter 1 Key Points

Key Questions:

1. Should Christians care about culture?
2. Should Christians try to shape culture?

Key Terms:

1. Ecumenism
2. Evangelicalism
3. Fundamentalism
4. Gnosticism*
5. Imago Dei*
6. Metaphysics
7. Moral Majority
8. Moralistic Therapeutic Deism*
9. Narcissism
10. Shalom*
11. Social Gospel
12. Two-Kingdoms Theology*
13. Worldview

Key Verses:

1. Genesis 1:26–28
2. Leviticus 19:9–15
3. Matthew 22:37–40*
4. 1 Corinthians 10:31

Key Works:

1. *The Fundamentals: A Testimony to the Truth* by A. C. Dixon, R. A. Torrey, James Orr, B. B. Warfield, and C. I. Scofield
2. *Theology for the Social Gospel* by Walter Rauschenbusch

Key Players:

1. Shane Claiborne
2. Jerry Falwell
3. Johannes Gutenberg
4. Dwight L. Moody
5. Walter Rauschenbusch

Key Events:

1. *Roe v. Wade*

**Short answer or essay question on the exam*

Chapter 1 Assignment

Answer the following questions with at least one paragraph.

1. List and briefly describe the five essential questions that comprise a worldview.

2. Why is a focus on God's glory central to the Christian worldview?

3. What is the doctrine of imago Dei, how does the biblical understanding of human beings different than that of any other worldview, and how should it affect our relationships with our neighbors?

4. How is our status as image bearers of God related to our use of words?

UNIT 2

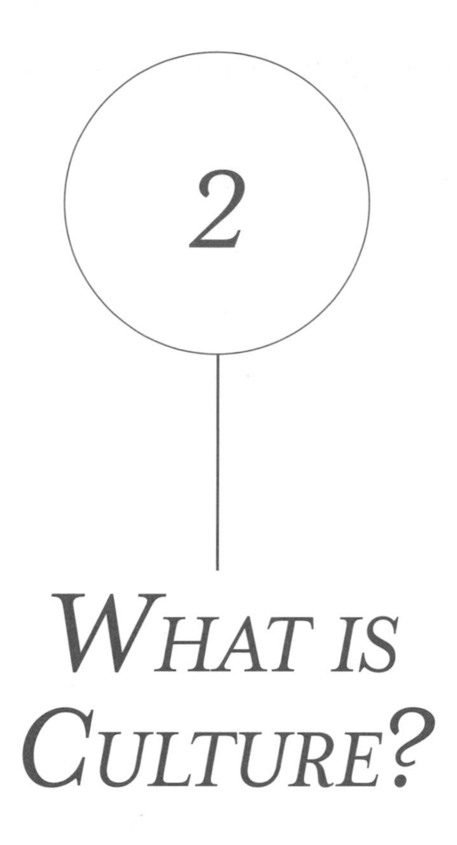

2

What Is Culture?

Chapter 2 Learning Objectives

Students will be able to:

1. express the development of culture as something that happens when humans interact with the world around them. [2.1]
2. recognize the biblical support for and proper approach in engaging culture. [2.2]
3. identify a definition of culture and important considerations for studying culture. [2.3]
4. identify six aspects of culture: artifacts, institutions, practices, beliefs, ethos, and meta-beliefs. [2.4]
5. analyze five approaches to culture that have been adopted by Christians throughout history. [2.5]
6. identify and discuss steps that Christians may take in order to participate in the transformation of culture. [2.6]
7. describe the Christian's responsibility to engage culture as obedience to God and imitation of Christ. [2.7]

CHAPTER 2 DISCUSSION QUESTIONS

1. **Does culture transform people or do people transform culture?** [2.1]

2. **Can you think of examples in history where a small group of Christians changed culture?** [2.1]

3. **Do you think American culture has gotten better or worse in the twenty-first century? Give examples to support your opinion.** [2.2]

4. **What is the "quill removal" approach to changing culture?** [2.2]

5. **What is culture? [2.3]**

6. **Who are "cultural anthropologists" and what do they do? [2.3]**

7. **In what ways does technology affect culture? [2.3]**

8. **How does language help to shape culture? [2.4]**

9. **Ken Myers of the influential Mars Hill Audio says there are six aspects of culture we must consider to both understand and influence culture. These include artifacts, institutions, practices, beliefs, moods and styles, and meta-beliefs. What are "artifacts" and why should we pay attention to them? [2.4]**

10. **What are "institutions" and why should we pay attention to them? [2.4]**

11. **What are "practices" and why should we pay attention to them? [2.4]**

12. **What are "beliefs" and why should we pay attention to them? [2.4]**

13. What are "moods and styles" and why should we pay attention to them? [2.4]

14. What are "meta-beliefs" and why should we pay attention to them? [2.4]

15. In his book *Christ and Culture*, theologian H. Richard Niebuhr outlines five approaches to culture that Christians have taken through the centuries. What is the "Christ against culture" approach? [2.5]

16. What is the "Christ of culture" approach? [2.5]

17. What is the "Christ above culture" approach? [2.5]

18. What is the "Christ and culture in paradox" approach? [2.5]

19. What is the "Christ, the transformer of culture" approach? [2.5]

20. Which of these approaches to Christ and culture seem to align more closely with what the Bible teaches? [2.6]

21. **Which of these views of Christ and culture do you personally think is the best approach?** [2.6]

22. **What does it mean to see culture as part of our Christian mission?** [2.6]

23. **What does it mean to take culture seriously?** [2.6]

24. **What's involved in creating a new culture?** [2.6]

"What Is Culture?" Reading

Roger Scruton defines culture from the perspective of anthropologists, ethnologists, and sociologists. He underscores the role of the "elite" in creating culture that is then shared by all. He also draws a distinction between culture and civilization and then focuses on Western civilization, which began as a fusion of Christianity and the Roman Empire.

Surprisingly, Scruton delves into the importance of laughter and jokes as a way to understand the "judgment" and "taste" of a culture. Reflecting on humor and amusement gives us a clear intimation of the nature and meaning of culture to a given group. The same can be said for the group's understanding and appreciation of art.

What Is Culture?

by Roger Scruton

Anthropologists write of the "culture" of the people they observe, meaning those customs and artifacts which are shared, and the sharing of which brings social cohesion. Ethnologists, on the one hand, define culture more widely, to include all intellectual, emotional, and behavioral features that are transmitted through learning and social interaction, rather than through genetic endowment. Sociologists, on the other hand, use the term more narrowly, to mean the thoughts and habits whereby people define their group identity, and stake out a claim for social territory. In all those uses, the term "culture" is associated with the human need for membership, and describes a shared asset of a social group. In this book I shall be defining "culture" in another way, to denote an acquisition that may not be shared by every member of a community, and which opens the hearts, minds, and senses of those who possess it to an intellectual and artistic patrimony. Culture, as I shall describe and defend it in this book, is the creation and creator of elites. This does not mean, however, that culture has nothing to do with membership or with the social need to define and conserve a shared way of life. Although an elite product, its meaning lies in emotions and aspirations that are common to all.

By "culture" I mean what has also been called "high culture"—the accumulation of art, literature, and humane reflection that has stood the "test of time" and established a continuing tradition of reference and allusion among educated people. That definition raises a question: whose accumulation, and which people? In response, it is useful to revisit a distinction, made in another way and for another purpose by Herder, and exploited for yet another purpose by Spengler, between culture and civilization. A civilization is a social entity that manifests religious, political, legal, and customary uniformity over an extended period, and which confers on its members the benefits of socially accumulated knowledge. Thus, we can speak of

Ancient Egyptian civilization, Roman civilization, Chinese civilization, and Western civilization. Civilizations can include each other, whether as contemporaneous or as successive parts. For example, Roman civilization includes that of Roman Gaul, and Islamic civilization that of the Abbasids.

The culture of a civilization is the art and literature through which it rises to consciousness of itself and defines its vision of the world. All civilizations have a culture, but not all cultures achieve equal heights. The stone-age civilization that produced the wall-paintings of the Lascaux caves has left a memorable icon of its world, but its one lasting cultural achievement pales beside the art and literature of Greece. Whether we can describe one culture as objectively superior to another is a question that I shall touch on later in this book. For the moment it is enough to recognize that cultures are the means through which civilizations become conscious of themselves, and are permeated by the strengths and weaknesses of their inherited form of life. There are as many cultures as there are civilizations, even though you can belong to a civilization and know little or nothing of its culture—which is the situation of most Westerners today.

Western Culture

This book is about Western culture, which means the culture of Western civilization. To say as much is to set no clear limits to my topic. Civilizations grow out of and into each other, and often divide like amoebas so as to generate two contemporaneous offshoots; hence, it is very hard to set spatial or temporal boundaries on Western civilization. It grew from the fusion of Christianity with the law and government of Rome, became conscious of itself in the high Middle Ages, passed through a period of skepticism and Enlightenment, and was simultaneously spread around the globe by the trading and colonial interests of its more adventurous members. And throughout its most flourishing periods, Western civilization has produced a culture which happily absorbs and adapts the cultures of other places, other faiths, and other times. Its basic fund of stories, its moral precepts, and its religious imagery come from the Hebrew Bible and the Greek New Testament. Onto those Judeo-Christian roots, however, has been grafted a tree of many branches, bearing many kinds of fruit. *The Thousand and One Nights*, which has a central place in Islamic culture, is equally part of the cultural heritage of the West, while the pagan literature of Greece and Rome has been taught for centuries as the fount of our literary tradition.

Those facts should not make for confusion. There is no paradox in the idea that two distinct cultures (belonging to two distinct civilizations) may nevertheless share parts of their heritage, and certainly no paradox in the idea that they can cross-fertilize each other, as Muslim, Christian, and Jewish cultures cross-fertilized each other in the great days of Averroes, Maimonides, and Peter Lombard. Indeed, it is important to understand, in the context of today's "culture wars" and the widespread advocacy of "multiculturalism," that Western culture has an unparalleled ability and willingness to assimilate other cultural traditions.

Still, it might be suggested that I have so far done very little to confine my subject matter. Are we really to consider all the art, literature, music, and philosophical reflection of the West as part of its culture, and does it all have a claim to our protection? Neither suggestion is plausible. Although new works are constantly being added to our inheritance, there is a distinction between those that "enter the canon" and those that remain on the periphery. Every culture is characterized by a central stream or tradition of works that have not merely "stood the test of time" but which continue to serve as models and inspirations for living practitioners. The process whereby an artistic, literary, or musical tradition develops and strengthens is a fascinating one, to which critics have devoted much thought. And theories of the "tradition" are invariably controversial, as critics fight to champion favorites of their own and to denigrate those of others. But this battle over the canon is itself part of the canon: a tradition is the residue of critical conflicts, that which remains when the sound and fury has dwindled to a schoolroom murmur.

Culture and Judgment

Another way of putting that point is to say that culture issues from judgment. A culture is supplied with its monuments and its durable styles by unceasing comparisons and choices, from which a canon of masterpieces emerges not as the object of a single collective choice, not even a choice that must be made anew by each generation, but as the by-product of myriad choices over centuries. Just as customs emerge over time, from the countless efforts of human beings to coordinate their conduct, so do cultural traditions emerge from the discussions, allusions, and comparisons, with which people fill their leisure hours.

Many people will be unhappy with that idea, believing either that there is no such thing as this "judgment" to which I refer or that, if there is such a thing, it is irremediably "subjective," with no inherent ability either to stand up to skeptical examination or to guarantee the survival of a culture in times of doubt. This response is expressed in a variety of ways and for a variety of purposes, and it is one aim of this book to rebut it. In all its forms, however, it rests on a confusion, long ago pointed out by Kant. It is true that our judgments of works of art are subjective in the sense that they issue from our personal experience, impressions, and tastes. But it does not follow that they are subjective in the sense of admitting no argument in their favor, or connecting with no important experiences and emotions which might be tested by life.

Still, it might be wondered, what kind of judgment is intended? In considering this question, eighteenth-century writers referred to "taste;" by which they meant a distinct rational faculty, through which we choose what is worthy of our attention. But what kind of attention? And worthy in what respect? During the course of their discussions, thinkers of the Enlightenment began to write of "aesthetic" judgment making use of a term introduced by Kant's mentor Baumgarten, though often disagreeing radically over what they meant by it. The term stuck, and today it is a commonplace to speak of aesthetic judgment as the thing that distinguishes the realm of culture from the realms of science, religion, and morality. We are, however, no nearer to a definition today than were those philosophers of the Enlightenment who, whether they stuck, like Hume and Addison, to the old idea of taste, or whether they adopted, like Kant and Schiller, the new jargon of aesthetics, were never able to satisfy one another that they were referring to a single thing.

Judgment and Laughter

Rather than tie myself in that knot, therefore, I propose to cut through it by considering one of the raw materials from which culture is built, namely laughter. All rational beings laugh—and maybe only rational beings laugh. And all rational beings benefit from laughing. As a result there has emerged a peculiar human institution—that of the joke, the repeatable performance in words or gestures that is designed as an object of laughter. Now there is a great difficulty in saying exactly what laughter is. It is not just a sound—not even a sound, since it can be silent. Nor is it just a thought, like the thought of some object as incongruous. It is a response to something, which also involves a judgment of that thing. Moreover, it is not an individual peculiarity, like a nervous tic or a sneeze. Laughter is an expression of amusement, and amusement is an outwardly directed, socially pregnant state of mind. Laughter begins as a collective condition, as when children giggle together over some absurdity. And in adulthood amusement remains one of the ways in which human beings enjoy each other's company, become reconciled to their differences, and accept their common lot. Laughter helps us to overcome our isolation and fortifies us against despair.

That does not mean that laughter is subjective in the sense that "anything goes" or that it is uncritical of its object. On the contrary, jokes are the object of fierce disputes and many are dismissed as "not funny," "in bad taste," "offensive," and so on. The habit of laughing at things is not detachable from the habit of judging things to be worthy of laughter. Indeed, amusement, although a spontaneous outflow of social emotion, is also the most frequently practiced form of judgment. To laugh at something is already to judge it, and when we refrain from laughing at what someone nevertheless believes to be funny, we may thereby show our disapproval of that person's stance. A joke in "bad taste" is not just a failure: it is an offence, and one of the most important aspects of moral education is to teach children not to commit that offense. Think about this, and you will quickly see that, however difficult it may be to define such notions as "judgment" and "taste," they are absolutely indispensable to us.

Shakespeare provides us with a telling example of what I mean in the involved subplot to *Twelfth Night*. The drunken Sir Toby Belch and his disorderly companions decide to play a practical joke on Malvolio, steward to Sir Toby's beautiful cousin Olivia, in revenge for Malvolio's justified but stuck-up disapproval of their ways. The practical joke involves persuading Malvolio that Olivia loves him and will love him yet more if he obeys various absurd recommendations concerning his costume and conduct. As a result of this prank, Malvolio is at first humiliated, then wounded, and finally locked up as mad, to be rescued at last only by the twists and turns of the somewhat farcical plot. Remorse, of a shallow kind, visits the pranksters. But the audience, which had begun by laughing with them, finds itself now looking on them with cold disdain and on Malvolio with uneasy pity. A cloud of discomfiture surrounds the play's conclusion, as the laughter which had propelled it is suddenly brought to judgment and condemned.

The Concept of Art

Those remarks do not amount to a theory of humor, or of the "judgment of taste" on which it depends. But they point to the fact that there is nothing obscure about this judgment, which is a familiar part of everybody's life, with a vital role to play in cementing human society. Maybe amusement is a species of, a cousin to, or a prelude to, aesthetic appreciation. But we don't have to determine whether that is so, in order to see that there really is a kind of judgment at the heart of culture, and that we are engaged in it all the time. Furthermore, this judgment can be educated, is in all forms morally relevant, and involves many of our deepest and most important social instincts. Reflecting on amusement and humor, and their place in our lives, you get a very clear intimation of a more general truth, at the nature and meaning of culture—namely that culture is judgment, and that judgment matters.

The example also helps us to deflect what has come to be a routine dismissal of culture and the pursuit of it—a dismissal that begins from skepticism about the concept of art. A century ago Marcel Duchamp signed a urinal, entitled it "La Fontaine," and then exhibited it as a work of art. This famous gesture has since been repeated *ad nauseam*, and insofar as students now learn anything in art schools, it consists in the ability to perform this gesture while believing it to be original—an epistemological achievement comparable to that of the White Queen who, in her youth, could believe six impossible propositions before breakfast. One immediate result of Duchamp's joke was to precipitate an intellectual industry devoted to answering the question "What is art?" The literature of this industry is as tedious and pointless as are the imitations of Duchamp's gesture, and not even the wit and intellect of Arthur Danto has served to enliven it. Nevertheless, it has left a residue of skepticism that has fueled the attack on culture. If anything can count as art, then art ceases to have a point. All that is left is the curious but unfounded fact that some people like looking at some things, others like looking at others. As for the suggestion that there is an enterprise of criticism, which searches for objective values and lasting monuments to the human spirit, this is dismissed out of hand as depending on a conception of the artwork that was washed down the drain of Duchamp's "fountain."

The argument has been rehearsed with malicious wit by John Carey, and is fast becoming orthodoxy, not least because it seems to emancipate people from the burden of culture, telling them that all those venerable masterpieces can be ignored with impunity, that reality TV is "as good as" Shakespeare and techno-rock the equal of Brahms, since nothing is better than anything else and all claims to aesthetic value are void. The argument, however, is based on the elementary mistake of thinking of art as what Mill called a "natural kind" like water, calcium carbonate, or the tiger—in other words, a kind whose essence is fixed not by human interests, but by the way things are. If, in defining art, we were attempting to isolate some feature of the natural order, then our definition would certainly have failed if we could set no limits to the concept. "Art" however, is not the name of a natural kind, but of a functional kind like "table." Anything is a table if it can be can be used as tables are used—to support things at which we sit to work or eat. A packing case can be a table; an old urinal can be a table; a human slave can be a table. This does not make the concept arbitrary, nor does it prevent us from distinguishing good tables from bad.

Return now to the example of jokes. It is as hard to circumscribe the class of jokes as it is the class of artworks. Anything is a joke if somebody says so. For "joke" names a functional kind. A joke is an artifact made to be laughed at. It may fail to perform its function, in which case it is a joke that "falls flat." Or it may perform its function, but offensively, in which case it is a joke "in bad taste." But none of this implies that the category of jokes is arbitrary, or that there is no such thing as a distinction between good jokes and bad. Nor does it in any way suggest that there is no place for the criticism of jokes, or for the kind of moral education that has a dignified and decorous sense of humor as its goal. Indeed, the first thing you might learn, in considering jokes, is that Marcel Duchamp's urinal was one—quite a good one the first time around, corny by mid-twentieth century, and downright stupid today.

Art and Aesthetic Interest

What I have said about jokes can be readily transferred to artworks too. Anything is art if somebody sincerely says so, for art is a functional kind. A work of art is something put forward as an object of aesthetic interest. It may fail to perform its function, in which case it is aesthetically empty. Or it may perform its function, but offensively, in which case it is brash, vulgar, disturbing, or whatever. But none of this implies that the category of art is arbitrary, or that there is no such thing as a distinction between good and had art. Still less does it suggest that there is no place for the criticism of art, or for the kind of aesthetic education that has a decorous and humane aesthetic understanding as its goal.

It is hardly surprising that jokes and artworks are so similar. For some artworks consist entirely of jokes: not only cheeky gestures like Duchamp's urinal, but also extended works of literature, like *Tristram Shandy* and *Through the Looking Glass*. Comedies and jokes appeal to the same emotional repertoire. And jokes, like works of art, can be endlessly repeatable. Still, in defining art as a functional kind I have introduced a new idea—that of "aesthetic interest." And the reader will want to know what kind of interest this is, and whether it is central to culture in general, or specialized to works of art. This is another knot which I propose to cut through. Aesthetic interest, I suggest, is simply the kind of interest that we take in works of art. We are all familiar with it, though we don't necessarily know how to define it. And we all know that, like amusement, aesthetic interest is inseparable from judgment.

Works of art, like jokes, are objects of perception: it is how they look, how they sound, how they appeal to our sensory perception that matters. In aesthetic interest we see the world as it really seems: in Wallace Stevens's words we "let be be finale of seem." We then encounter a unity of experience and thought, a coming together of the sensory and the intellectual for which "imagination" is the everyday name. This fact, which places the meaning of aesthetic experience outside the reach of science, explains its peculiar value. In the moment of beauty we encounter meaning in immediate and sensory form.

Aesthetic interest is of the greatest practical import to beings like us, who move on the surface of things. To engage now with those distant parts of my life which are not of immediate concern, to absorb into the present choice the full reality of a life that stretches into distant moral space, I need insight into the meaning of things. I need symbols in the present moment, of matters beyond the moment. The ability to participate imaginatively in merely possible states of affairs is one of the gifts of culture: without this ability a person may not know what it is like to achieve the goals at which he aims, and his pursuit of those goals will be to a certain measure irrational.

Aesthetic interest is an interest in appearances. But there are appearances that we ought to avoid, however much they fascinate us. By contrast, there are appearances which are not merely permissible objects of aesthetic interest, but which reward that interest with knowledge, understanding, and emotional uplift. We deplore the Roman games, at which animals are slaughtered, prisoners crucified, and innocents tormented, all for the sake of the spectacle and its gruesome meaning. And we would deplore it, even if the suffering were simulated, as in some cinematic replication, if we thought that the interest of the observer were merely one of gleeful fascination. But we praise the Greek tragedy, in which profound myths are enacted in lofty verse, in which the imagined deaths take place out of sight and unrelished by the audience. An interest in the one, we suppose, is depraved, in the other noble. And a high culture aims, or ought to aim, at preserving and enhancing experiences of the second kind, in which human life is raised to a higher level—the level of ethical reflection.

The Sphere of Culture

A culture does not compromise works of art only, nor is it directed solely to aesthetic interests. It is the sphere of intrinsically interesting artifacts, linked in the faculty of judgment to our aspirations and ideals. We appreciate jokes, works of art, arguments, works of history and literature, manners, dress, and forms of behavior. And all these things are shaped through judgment.

What should we include in the category of culture? The answer is suggested by my argument, which has pointed to a certain kind of judgment as central to the phenomenon. A culture consists of all those activities and artifacts which are organized by the "common pursuit of true judgment" as T.S. Elliot once put it. And true judgment involves the search for meaning through the reflective encounter with things made, composed, and written, with such an end in view. Some of those things will be works of art, addressed to the aesthetic interest; others will be discursive works of history or philosophy, addressed to the interest in ideas. Both kinds of work explore the meaning of the world and the life of society. And the purpose of both is to stimulate the judgments through which we understand each other and ourselves.

Artistic philosophical traditions therefore provide our paradigm of culture. And the principle that organizes a tradition also discriminates within it, creating the canon of masterpieces, the received monuments, the "touchstones" as Matthew Arnold once called them, which it is the goal of humane education to appreciate and to understand. The question now before us is how we might justify such an education, and what should be its place in the curriculum today.

Before addressing that question, however, there is an objection that must be acknowledged. Many people with no interest in high culture make moral judgments. They judge people in terms of their characters and actions, and organize their world through conceptions of right and wrong, good and bad, virtue and vice. Yet the species of judgment that I have been considering, which looks critically on the forms of human interest, and which searches the world for meanings, implications, and allusions, may hold no interest for them. Their taste in art, like their taste in jokes, may be coarse or nonexistent; their interest in ideas and arguments may be equally sparse, and the only spectacles they enjoy might be those of organized sport. Yet this says nothing about their moral worth, or their utility as members of society. Conversely, there are highly cultivated people, with a refined taste in art and consuming interest in intellectual questions, who live the lives of vicious psychopaths: Hitler and Stalin, to name but two. These evident facts, repeatedly and lamentably confirmed by history, lend a new kind of force to the cultural skeptic, who may still ask what the point is of activities and interests that leave the moral landscape seemingly so little changed. This is, I suspect, the principal reservation that educated people may have, concerning the value of culture and the purpose of teaching it. It will therefore be necessary for me to return, in the course of my argument, to the problem posed by the "evil aesthete," and the "philistine philanthropist"—the problem of the seeming disconnection between moral virtue and cultural refinement.

This essay originally appeared as a chapter in Roger Scruton, *Culture Counts: Faith and Feeling in a World Besieged* (New York, NY: Brief Encounters, 2007), 1–15. It is reproduced here with the permission of Mark Moyar, published by arrangement with Encounter Books and Writers' Representatives, LLC.

[1]Kant, *The Critique of Judgment* (1790), available in various translations, which puts aesthetic judgment for the first time clearly in the center of our modern intellectual concerns.

[2]See Frank Buckley, *The Morality of Laughter*, University of Michigan Press (2003), in which the nature of laughter, as a society-forming practice among moral beings, is admirably spelled out.

[3](1981), a work which shows how problems of ontology are intrinsic to our normal ways of describing art.

[4]John Carey, *What Good are the Arts?* London, Faber and Faber (2005).

[5]J. S. Mill, *A System of Logic*, tenth edition, London, Longmans (1879), Book 1, Chapter 7, Section 4.

[6]Failure to appreciate this point, I have argued, underlies the disaster of utilitarian and modernist architecture—an architecture that denies the tradition which has formed and educated the human eye. See *The Aesthetics of Architecture*, London and Princeton (1979).

[7]T. S. Eliot, *On the Use of Poetry and the Use of Criticism*, London (1933).

[8]Matthew Arnold, *Culture and Anarchy*, London (1869).

"What Is Culture?" Discussion Questions

1. **How is "culture" defined by the various academic disciplines?**

2. **Is there a difference between civilization and culture?**

3. **What role does tradition play in defining culture?**

4. **What can laughter teach us about a culture's value system?**

5. **What should be included in the category of culture?**

“A Christian Perspective of Art” Video

Steve Griesen and Charles Denler introduce themselves and share how they got involved in media, from humble beginnings to award-winning careers in movie scoring, documentary films, and more. They debunk the idea of “Christian” films or “Christian” music based on the simple truth that a Christian is a follower of Christ. A movie or song can't be a follower of Christ, so it can't be a Christian.

Jesus shared his message through stories known as parables. The power of story is how we communicate our values and worldview. Every movie has a worldview behind it because it's made by people with worldviews. Steve and Charles show clips from *Star Wars* and *Mr. Holmes* and point out the underlying worldviews. They also show two of their own documentaries—*The Bear Man of Eno* and *Master Designer*—and explain how they go about their craft.

To access this video, go to www.summitu.com/utc and enter the passcode found in the back of your manual.

▶ "A Christian Perspective of Art" Video Outline

Is there such a thing as "Christian" music and movies?

No, because a Christian is a follower of Christ and a movie or a song can't be a follower of Christ. But movies and music can be used to spread the gospel and share the Christian worldview.

Jesus shared his message through ____________________ i.e., parables (Matthew 13:34).

Parables were a common cultural communication. Through them, Jesus connected with his audience in a way the religious leaders did not, both touching personal needs and communicating spiritual truth.

The power of story is how we can communicate our Christian values and worldview.

Worldviews ask and answer basic questions:

- What is the existence and nature of ______________________?
- What is the nature of humans?
- What is the origin and nature of evil?
- What is the source and nature of ______________________?
- What is the meaning of human history?

All films have a worldview because they're made by people with worldviews:

Examples of worldviews behind popular movies:

- *Star Wars*: Far Eastern thought about ultimate reality. An impersonal life force is behind everything and is accessible to all.
- *Mr. Holmes*: Traditional Western (Christian) values of honoring parents, forgiving those who wronged you, being honest and compassionate.

Examples of documentary films with a Christian message:

- *The Gentle Bear Man of Eno:* Steve explained how the story of Michael took shape when he went to Canada and began shooting.
- *Master Designer*: Underscores intelligent design in nature by looking at sophisticated animal design for which evolution has no explanation.

"A Christian Perspective of Art" Discussion Questions

1. **What is a Christian movie?**

2. **What is the "Jesus model" for sharing the Christian story?**

3. **What are some of the basic questions a worldview seeks to answer?**

4. **Does every movie express a worldview?**

5. **Can you identify the worldviews behind the movies *Star Wars* and *Mr. Holmes*?**

Chapter 2 Key Points

Key Questions:

1. What is culture?
2. Can Christians change culture in any meaningful and positive way?
3. What approach should Christians take in dealing with culture?

Key Terms:

1. Artifact
2. Belief
3. Benedict Option
4. Conversionist
5. Cultural Anthropologist
6. Culture*
7. Derek
8. Ethos
9. Institution
10. Meta-beliefs
11. Practice
12. Secularization

Key Verses:

1. Acts 17:16–34*

Key Works:

1. *Notes Toward the Definition of Culture*, T. S. Eliot
2. *Christ and Culture*, H. Richard Niebuhr
3. *The Last Christian on Earth*, Os Guinness

Key Players:

1. H. Richard Niebuhr
2. Francis Schaeffer
3. Samuel Wilberforce
4. William Wilberforce

Key Organizations:

1. L'Abri

**Short answer or essay question on the exam*

Chapter 2 Assignment

Answer the following questions with at least one paragraph.

1. Why might a Christian understanding of sin lead to a different understanding of social problems, cultural change, or revolution than would a secular worldview?

2. As described in this chapter, what is the difference between a sign and symbol in communication and why is it significant that humans can communicate with symbols?

3. Why does this chapter say that "Christ, the transformer of culture" helps believers live a life of love and avoid a selfish or watered-down Christianity?

4. What does this chapter say about the relationship between beauty and a Christian effort to transform a culture?

Other potential questions:

- How many of the five approaches to culture have you heard, or believed in? Can you think of friends, groups, or cultures influenced by each of them?
- How would you rank the six components of culture in order of importance? Which of the six do you encounter the most in your life, and are they the most influential or important?

UNIT
3

CHRISTIANITY AND CULTURE: A HISTORY

CHAPTER 3 LEARNING OBJECTIVES

Students will be able to:

1. articulate how beliefs, not just actions, enable Christians to change the world. [3.1]
2. tell how Christians acting on biblical beliefs were the first to recognize human rights. [3.2]
3. tell how Christians acting on biblical beliefs were able to curb the practices of slavery and, in many cases, achieve abolition of the institution of slavery. [3.3]
4. tell how Christians acting on biblical beliefs were able to achieve the recognition of basic rights of women and children. [3.4]
5. tell how Christians acting on biblical beliefs promoted education throughout history and established of some of the most important educational institutions in the world. [3.5]
6. tell how Christians acting on biblical beliefs contributed to the development of modern medicine. [3.6]
7. tell how Christians acting on biblical beliefs developed a legacy of charitable practices and established countless modern charity institutions. [3.7]
8. tell how Christians acting on biblical beliefs laid the foundation for modern science. [3.8]
9. tell how Christians acting on biblical beliefs advanced artistic skills and expression in numerous fields. [3.9]
10. explain the responsibility of current generations of Christians to continue the legacy of shaping culture by being used by God to do so. [3.10]

Chapter 3 Discussion Questions

1. **In what ways do academics show their disdain for Christianity? Is this hostility justified?** [3.1]

2. **What's the difference between Christians and Christianity?** [3.2]

3. **How do beliefs influence culture?** [3.2]

4. **Where can the roots of human rights be found in the Bible?** [3.3]

5. **How did the biblical view of human rights shape history? [3.3]**

6. **Do some non-Christian philosophers and historians admit Christianity was a shaping force in the modern understanding of human rights? [3.3]**

7. **Did the Christian view of human rights have an impact beyond the Christianized Western World? [3.3]**

8. **Slavery has been a universal practice throughout history. How were slaves treated in the Bible? [3.4]**

9. **How did the early church deal with slavery? [3.4]**

10. **How did the medieval church deal with slavery? [3.4]**

11. **What role did Christians play in the final abolition of slavery in the West? [3.4]**

12. **What influence has Christianity had in promoting women's rights? [3.5]**

13. What have Christians done to alleviate the suffering of women around the world? [3.5]

14. What influence did Christianity have on the development of public education? [3.6]

15. How did Christianity help shape modern schooling? [3.6]

16. What influence did Christianity have on the development of modern medicine? [3.7]

17. What influence did Christianity have on the development of modern charity? [3.8]

18. Can you name any well-known charities or nonprofits with a huge social impact that were started as Christian organizations? [3.8]

19. How did the Christian worldview lay the foundation for the development of modern science? [3.9]

20. Who were some influential Christians who helped start the Scientific Revolution? [3.9]

21. Did Christian scientists see their work as an extension of their faith? [3.9]

22. What influence did Christians have on the development of the arts? [3.10]

23. What influence did Christians have on the development of music? [3.10]

“J-Shaped Cultures” Video

In this engaging video, Paul Copan asks and answers these important questions: What was it about the early Christians that drew people into their communities? What has the gospel done to transform cultures? What were the core values of the Protestant Reformation and what impact did the Reformation have on Western civilization?

Copan goes on to show how the Christian faith has had far more impact on our modern understanding of democracy and human rights than the ancient Greeks, the Renaissance, or the Enlightenment—a truth affirmed by many atheistic historians and philosophers.

While the historical impact of Christianity in addressing evil and improving culture doesn't prove the Christian faith is true, it does give many good reasons to believe in God as revealed in Jesus Christ. Copan closes with the obvious by saying there is a marked difference between a Shiva-shaped culture and a Jesus-shaped culture, and asking, “Would you rather have your son be like Krishna or Jesus?”

To access this video, go to www.summitu.com/utc and enter the passcode found in the back of your manual.

"J-Shaped Cultures" Video Outline

What about the early Christians drew people into their communities?

- ______________________ was accepted in Christ.
- It was a loving family with one Father and one Messiah.
- They shared all things with others.
- They loved all yet were ______________________ by all.
- They obeyed the law but surpassed the law by their lives.
- They were poor yet they made many rich.

Reforms and advances inspired by the Christian faith in the Middle Ages:

- Copying and preserving manuscripts
- ______________________ endeavors and church planting (e.g., St. Patrick)
- Establishing universities and centers of learning

Transformative core values of the Protestant Reformation:

- The priesthood of every believer before God
- The right of believers to study the ______________________ for themselves in their own language
- The appropriateness of pursuing any honest vocation to the glory of God

Protestant contributions ("killer apps") to Western Civilization:

- Strong work ethic
- Civilized competition
- Modern science
- Modern medicine
- Property rights
- A free market

Christian missionaries were responsible for remarkable gains:

- Religious ______________________
- Mass education
- Mass printing
- Major colonial reforms (e.g., abolishing slavery, widow burning, foot binding)
- Codification of legal protection for nonwhites

The basis for democracy and human rights:

Our modern notions of democracy and human rights did not arise from the ancient Greeks, the Renaissance or Enlightenment influences. Many leading atheists acknowledge that Christianity provided the basis for modern democracy and human rights.

Historical impact of Christianity:

The historical impact of Christianity in addressing evil and improving culture doesn't prove the Christian faith is true, but it does give many compelling reasons for accepting the Christian worldview.

The positive fruits of Christianity can be seen in the transformation it has brought to individuals and societies. There is a marked difference between a Shiva-shaped culture and a Jesus-shaped culture.

"J-Shaped Cultures" Discussion Questions

1. **What about the early Christians drew people into their communities?**

2. **Upon what transformative values was Protestant Reformation based?**

3. According to historian Naill Ferguson, what were some "killer apps" developed by Protestantism that greatly advanced Western Civilization?

4. Where do our modern ideas of democracy and human rights come from?

5. Does the historical impact of Christianity in addressing evil and improving culture prove that Christianity is true?

"How to Move Ideas"

Jesus was a storyteller, and Warren Smith shows how we can follow the Lord's example in promoting ideas. Stories help us to remember abstract ideas by providing meaning and context. Stories invite immersion and teach in ways that mere proclamation cannot.

Smith defines the various elements of a good story and outlines how to become better storytellers. He explains the difference between narrative and metanarrative, contrasts the secular and Christian metanarratives, and offers wisdom on how to tell the Christian story in a postmodern world.

To access this video, go to www.summitu.com/utc and enter the passcode found in the back of your manual.

"How to Move Ideas" Video Outline

Stories Matter

We learn best through stories. It's how the Bible teaches; it's how________________ taught.

- Stories invite immersion: is the story real? Declarations of the truth invite testing and resistance: is the declaration true?
- Stories help us remember abstract ideas.
- Stories provide meaning and context.
- Stories allow us to engage in the willing suspension of ______________________.

If you want people to know the truth, tell them the truth. If you want people to love the truth, tell them a story.

What Is a Story?

A story is a narrative that tells "what happened next."

Aristotle said a story has to have a beginning, a middle, and an end. The story has an arc and has to reach a conclusion.

Great stories accomplish the following:

- Communicate ______________________
- Elicit emotions
- Lead to conclusions—what is real and not real
- Have lessons that are embedded and not explicit

What Is a Metanarrative?

A metanarrative is the story of the stories. It is the grand story. Our minds seek order, so we reconcile stories into a grand metanarrative.

Secular culture and Christianity have different metanarratives:

1. Secular culture:
    - Mankind is essentially ______________________.
    - The church is inconsequential.
    - The material world is all there is.
2. Christianity:
    - Mankind is ______________________.
    - The church will prevail.
    - The spiritual world is real and consequential.

We can influence the metanarratives of our culture by actively engaging in telling good stories and by recovering biblical storytelling.

▶ "How to Move Ideas" Discussion Questions

1. **Why are stories more powerful than simply declaring the truth?**

2. **What is a metanarrative? What is the metanarrative of the Bible?**

3. **What are some important differences between the metanarratives of Christianity and the secular culture?**

4. **How can Christians influence the metanarratives of our time?**

5. **How does storytelling fit into a postmodern world?**

Chapter 3 Key Points

Key Questions:

1. How have the beliefs of Christians over the course of history motivated them to shape their culture?
2. What positive cultural changes have Christians been uniquely responsible for over the centuries?

Key Terms:

1. Religion
2. Orthodoxy
3. Orthopraxy
4. Human Rights
5. Theory of Forms
6. Suttee
7. Society for Effecting Abolition of Slave Trade
8. Patronage
9. Platonic Humanism
10. Postmodernism

Key Players:

1. William of Ockham
2. John Locke
3. Krishna Mohan Bannerjee
4. St. Eligius
5. Josiah Wedgewood
6. Shi Meiyu
7. Tsuda Umeko
8. Alcuin of York
9. Geert Groote
10. Benjamin Rush
11. Thomas Perceval
12. Francis Bacon
13. Robert Boyle
14. Francis Collins
15. Sir Isaac Newton
16. William Carey

Key Works:

1. *City of God* by Augustine
2. *The Soul of Science* by Nancy Pearcey and Charles Thaxton*
3. *The Language of God: A Scientist Provides Evidence for Belief* by Francis Collins

**Short answer or essay question on the exam*

Chapter 3 Assignment

Answer the following questions with at least one paragraph.

1. **Describe the connection between Christianity and the movement to end slavery, both in the ancient world and in the eighteenth and nineteenth centuries, as outlined in the chapter?**

2. **What role did Christians play in restoring and promoting education from the medieval era to the modern age?**

3. **Why might we attribute the development of charity and charitable institutions to early Christianity rather than paganism?**

4. **How did biblical Christianity contribute to the Scientific Revolution?**

Other potential questions:

- Consider some instances throughout history in which people have used Christianity to justify sinful or selfish things (including slavery, mistreatment of women, etc.). How would you respond to people who criticize Christianity for these things? How do you think about both the good and bad things that are attributed to Christians?
- Do you think other worldviews have less to contribute to the realm of arts and creativity than Christianity does, or is that largely true only of modern and postmodern Secularism?

UNIT
4

Christianity and Culture: A Plan

Chapter 4 Learning Objectives

Students will be able to:

1. identify how shaping culture involves a strategy of developing a posture of engagement as well as establishing a direction of engagement. [4.1]
2. describe a culture-shaping posture which involves contemplation about current culture, cultivation of new culture, and community within culture. [4.2]
3. explain how the creation/fall/redemption metanarrative of the Christian worldview guides the direction of the Christian's cultural engagement. [4.3]
4. examine the challenges that come with engaging culture and recognize ways to avoid such pitfalls. [4.4]
5. articulate the necessity of cultivating virtuous habits of engagement. [4.5]

Chapter 4 Discussion Questions

1. What two things are necessary to shape culture? [4.1]

2. How do we develop a posture of cultural engagement? [4.2]

3. What is cultural literacy and why is it important? [4.2]

4. How can we learn to contemplate (read) the culture around us and orient ourselves to what is happening? [4.2]

5. **How can we learn to cultivate culture?** [4.2]

6. **What would you list as the most influential songs and TV shows of the last decade?** [4.2]

7. **What does it take to "write" culture?** [4.2]

8. **What role does virtue play in writing culture?** [4.2]

9. **What role does awareness play in writing culture?** [4.2]

10. **What role does community play in writing culture?** [4.2]

11. **What insights does sociologist Randall Collins offer on developing culture-changing communities?** [4.2]

12. **Have you been in the kind of group described above?** [4.2]

13. How would a biblical worldview affect our ability to change culture? [4.3]

14. What can we learn from the biblical story of creation that should affect our interaction with culture? [4.4]

15. How does the story of the fall define the idea of sin? [4.3]

16. How does the biblical view of sin differ from what non-Christians believe? [4.3]

17. How does redemption affect our ability to change culture? [4.3]

18. What are some things that could stop us from being culture changers? [4.4]

19. Is it possible to get too close to culture in our attempt to change it? Is there ever a time to pull away? [4.4]

20. Does lasting cultural change come from the bottom up or the top down? [4.5]

"Cultural Issues in the Coming Years" Reading

The attempt by evangelicals to change American culture through political power peaked during the 1980s and 90s with the Moral Majority. Since then, Stetzer notes, "evangelicals appear to be on the losing side for those who considered it a war." Today's Christians generally focus on three approaches to interacting with the world around them. They are cultural engagers, cultural defenders, and cultural creators.

Stetzer briefly shares what characterizes each approach and points out that, while they are different, all are important if Christians are going to share Jesus today while loving and living with those who think differently. Ultimately, our good works in action are what glorify God (1 Peter 2:12) and win a hearing for the gospel.

Cultural Issues in the Coming Years

by Ed Stetzer

At some point during the 1980s and 90s, a desire birthed among politically conservative Christians to begin to stand for things that mattered to them culturally in more active ways than before.

What followed was a ground swell of support for what would become known as the "Moral Majority." Their understanding was that those who held the beliefs they championed were actually the majority in the country. Some believed that through the right flavor of political activism, they would win the "culture war."

Fast forward a few decades and, despite these efforts, evangelicals appear to be on the losing side for those who considered it a war.

That's not a matter of preference or desire; it's a matter of numbers. Simple math shows that most of the core issues on which the religious right was focused are trending the wrong direction from evangelical belief and practice.

It didn't work.

When I said that a few years ago, it ended up being quoted in the *Washington Post* and was listed as a key quote of 2012. It seemed news then.

Now, that idea just seems like common sense and most people would agree. Actually, recent surveys show that the vast majority of pastors tend to agree. (I should add that I don't use the term "culture war" except in references where others use it—I don't think you can war against a people in culture and reach them at the same time.)

So the question is, what do we do now? How do we find our way out of a rather awkward cultural moment?

I believe Christians can and will generally focus on three approaches in the years to come.

Cultural Engagers

First, I think there will be some who will be culture engagers. This is where I fit in, but I am aware enough to know I'm not the only one who thinks about engaging culture and that my way is not the only way to do so.

That being said, those who are culture engagers are those who believe we must understand the people around us in order to meaningfully engage them for the cause of Christ. We think about planting churches that are culturally appropriate for the setting, equipping our people with the tools they need for wise and appropriate cultural engagement, and how we can be biblically faithful and culturally engaged at the same time.

This issue still remains. And, as the culture is shifting, most churches (yes, most) are still living as if they lived in a different era, not engaging the people around them.

I teach and write about this topic often because it is so widely misunderstood. Christians need to engage culture for the cause of Christ, not run from it because people are worldly. Paul explained that he did not call us to "leave the world" (1 Corinthians 5:10) but rather to "become all things to all men" so as to engage them with the gospel (1 Corinthians 9:22).

Christians need to recognize that holiness is separation from sin, not separation from sinners. Put another way, holiness does not mean separation from people in the culture around us, but separation for the sin in culture around us.

For Christians to identify with and be identified with Christ, we need to do more of what He did. We need to be accused of the things he was accused of. We need to spend more time, not less, with the people he did.

Our churches need to better understand when we need to reflect and when we need to reject the culture in which God has placed us. As one who cares about discerning culture engagement, I will spend more of my time helping churches understand and engage the cultures around them.

We need more culture engagers and more churches engaging culture.

Cultural Defenders

I do not think, however, that we only need the particular emphasis about which I am enthusiastic.

Other approaches to culture will be essential. For this too-simple article, the second approach would be that of *culture defenders*. These people are the ones who will take a stand in both the political and social arenas on issues that have to do with human flourishing.

They will, hopefully in a winsome and gracious manner, stand in the public square to speak on issues of life, family, and morality. They will be the evangelical voice on important issues where Christians are concerned.

They will defend certain positions, arguing that it is better for human flourishing to value certain things in any culture. These people will participate in important work and start organizations that carry it out, as well as supporting those who are already involved.

Though the work or organizations may not be inherently "Christian," culture defenders will engage with them for the sake of the gospel. I imagine this may be the most difficult work, but people's religious liberty will have to be defended, the greater good will need to be advanced, and truth will need to be said.

I imagine that some culture engagers and culture creators will roll their eyes, thinking that the culture defenders are not helpful or as discerning as they are. And, some, indeed, won't be helpful—fighting in ways that are unhelpful and counterproductive. However, culture defenders will be an important part of our future engagement with culture as we move to the new cultural reality of our time.

We need more culture defenders and churches that will stand winsomely for the truth.

Cultural Creators

A third way Christians will approach culture is as creators. Now, I need to distinguish here between culture creation and evangelical culture creation.

Two-thousand-and-fourteen was the year of the Christian film. Evangelicals released all kinds of different films last year. The unimaginable success of *God's Not Dead* caught people completely off-guard, both Christian and not.

Many of these films were made by Christians for either Christian consumption or evangelistic purposes. Their messages are overt and clear, and they are meant to challenge those who do not share the evangelical worldview.

There is nothing wrong with these types of films. There are probably some in this vein I could do without (and some my family enjoyed together), but they help and encourage many.

However, other films written and developed by Christians do not have an overt Christian message. This type of movie seeks to shape culture in a completely different way than the others—they are creating culture that engages the broader culture.

They are not evangelistic, but they are creating and presenting a picture of a different—and better—reality to a culture that needs a picture of the vision they present.

The purpose is to create art that crosses religious boundaries, yet communicates particular constructs that reflect those of the Christian artist.

These types of projects are being produced in several genres of art, including music, theater, and film. The idea is that Christians, having been changed by the power of the gospel, espouse a worldview that creates culture. As believers, they engage in activities that shape the culture around them.

Andy Crouch has written about this in his book *Culture Making*. I would encourage you to read what he has written about the creation of culture. We need a lot more culture creators. For two examples, and there are many others, see the music of Lecrae and the movie *The Blind Side*. Neither see Christian as a genre, but rather hold up Christian values and a better way.

We need more Christians in culture creation and we need more churches encouraging them that way.

Culture Matters

When we assess our current situation, I believe that we find the need for all three types of respondents: culture engagers, defenders, and creators.

Many Christians will go about this in different ways—and it won't fit in three nice little categories. Regardless, it does matter that we think well about culture: how we engage it, defend things within it, and create it. And, we need to do so "Christianly."

The challenge will be developing ways that honor Christ, while loving and living with those who think differently. And that's our new and great challenge.

These three different types of people interacting with culture—engagers, defenders, and creators—need to stop shouting at each other and start acknowledging the value that each brings to this new culture moment. All three types of cultural interaction are important.

In this new and shifting context, we need all hands on deck, and even though we're working in different ways, we need to work together.

If we are not a moral majority, how do we show and share Jesus in the cultural moment where we find ourselves?

Somehow, as God's people, that's how we should engage culture—that because of our good works they might glorify God (1 Peter 2:12) and, ultimately, might consider the truth claims and gospel and the Christian worldview that undergirds it.

This essay originally appeared as an article on *Christianity Today's* website on March 6, 2015. Reproduction rights were granted by Ed Stetzer.

"Cultural Issues in the Coming Years" Discussion Questions

1. **What comes to mind when you hear the term "Moral Majority"? Do you think Christians should be more involved or less involved in politics?**

2. **What are the main characteristics of cultural engagers?**

3. **What marks a person as a cultural defender?**

4. **What makes someone a cultural creator?**

5. **What is your opinion of "Christian" movies? Do you think they are a positive or negative witness to the culture in general?**

"Engaging the Culture" Video

Americans have more of everything than anyone else in history, but all this abundance has created apathy. It's time for Christians to wake up, acquire a sense of urgency, and expect our efforts to actually make a difference. We have to focus on what God cares about: God cares about his glory (Revelation 21:23); God cares that we bear his image (Genesis 1:26–28); and God cares that we love our neighbor (Matthew 22:37–40).

Dr. Meyers turns God's concerns into three questions that should guide our culture-shaping activities: What brings glory to God? What helps people better bear his image? How do we love our neighbor? He shares some encouraging examples of businesses started by Christians that are making a difference in millions of lives. He concludes by showing how the concept of justice in America has changed for the worse and suggests ways Christians are working to bring about needed reforms.

To access this video, go to www.summitu.com/utc and enter the passcode found in the back of your manual.

"Engaging the Culture" Video Outline

Americans have more of everything than anyone else in history, but all this abundance has created ______________________. It's time for Christians to wake up, to reclaim a sense of urgency, and to believe that we can actually make a difference.

In his book *To End All Wars*, Ernest Gordon shows how a culture of death in a POW camp in Thailand was transformed into a culture of life. If the prisoners could change a killing culture without resources, how much more should Christians be able to change the culture around us, given all the resources we possess?

What God Cares About:

- God cares about his ______________________ (Revelation 21:23).
- God cares that we bear his image (Genesis 1:26–28).
- God cares that we love our ______________________ (Matthew 22:37–40).

Key questions to guide the focus on changing culture:

- What brings glory to God?
- What helps people better bear his image?
- How do we love our neighbor?

Inspiring Examples:

Two outstanding examples of practical programs started by Christians bring glory to God, help people better bear his image, and help people love their neighbors.

1. **M-pesa:** Using cell phone minutes as a medium of exchange, this innovative bartering system removes barriers that keep people from succeeding and more fully displays God's image.
2. **Paradigm Project:** This personal cookstove needs 70 percent less fuel, saves lives, leads to less deforestation, improves the environment, and gives people more time to better themselves.

Justice in America:

The Justice system in America is broken, as evidenced by our having the second highest prison population in the world behind North Korea.

The ______________________ believed that rights were given by God and were to be secured and protected by government, a view known as *inherent rights*. But the current justice system has switched to the view that the goal of justice is the *right ordering of society*, which is nothing more than a redistribution of wealth.

Attempts by Christians to bring glory to God, help people better bear his image, and help people love their neighbors in the judicial arena focus on restoring rights to both victims and criminals, not just incarcerating criminals.

"ENGAGING IN CULTURE" DISCUSSION QUESTIONS

1. **What does it take for Christians to become culture shapers?**

2. **What are some things Ernest Gordon and his fellow POWs did to change Chungkai from a culture of death to a culture of life?**

3. **What does God care about and how should these things guide our focus in interacting with culture?**

4. **What are some examples of initiatives guided by these questions?**

5. **How has the idea of justice changed for the worse in America?**

Chapter 4 Key Points

Key Questions:

1. How can Christians develop a posture for cultural engagement?
2. How can Christians maintain a direction for cultural engagement?
3. What are the dangers of cultural engagement and how should they be dealt with?

Key Terms:

1. Cultural Literacy
2. Cultural Texts*
3. Cultural Capital
4. Cynicism
5. Discernment
6. Groupthink
7. The Inklings
8. Mere Christianity*

**Short answer or essay question on the exam*

Key Verses:

1. Genesis 1:28
2. Genesis 3:22
3. Revelation 21:1

Key Players:

1. C. S. Lewis
2. J. R. R. Tolkien
3. Dietrich Bonhoeffer

Key Works:

1. The Burned-Over District

Chapter 4 Assignment

Answer the following questions with at least one paragraph.

1. **How is contemplating and understanding a culture a part of love?**

2. **What makes a community so important to shaping culture?**

3. **How does sin hinder the development of culture and how can the gospel correct this?**

4. **How might a community help overcome the three challenges described in this chapter (fear, friendly fire, and getting too close)?**

Other potential questions:

- Samuel Johnson said, "The supreme end of education is expert discernment in all things—the power to tell the good from the bad, the genuine from the counterfeit, and to prefer the good and the genuine to the bad and the counterfeit." What do you think of Samuel Johnson's description of education's purpose? How does it compare or differ from what you typically think of education, or how your culture typically represents education?
- How does redemption play a role in creativity if non-Christians can also be innovative and creative, as seen with people like Steve Jobs, or in business ventures that are not related to religion, like Uber or Airbnb?

UNIT 5

THINKING AND SPEAKING CLEARLY

CHAPTER 5 LEARNING OBJECTIVES

Students will be able to:

1. articulate the necessity of well-informed arguments for engaging a hostile culture. [5.1]
2. examine the role of logic and its dependence on clearly defined words and critical thinking. [5.2]
3. analyze the structure of logical arguments, examine what constitutes a good argument, and analyze logical fallacies and how to avoid them. [5.3]
4. examine the process of persuasion and how to build the trust and credibility it requires, while avoiding fear of a hostile audience and the temptation to use propaganda. [5.4]
5. articulate the role dialogue plays in our efforts to persuade, and how to dialogue effectively. [5.5]
6. explain the qualities of effective persuasion. [5.6]

Chapter 5 Discussion Questions

1. **Can you think of some recent movies that show how our view of politics and politicians has changed since *Mr. Smith Goes to Washington*?** [5.1]

2. **How can truth be understood and tested?** [5.2]

3. **What is logic and how does it pertain to clear thinking?** [5.2]

4. **Why does logical reasoning require the clear definition of words?** [5.2]

5. **How can language be used to manipulate others?** [5.2]

6. **Why does good reasoning require critical thinking?** [5.2]

7. **What are the key characteristics of clear thinking and effective communication?** [5.2]

8. **What are the components of a good argument?** [5.3]

9. What are "deductive arguments" and "categorical syllogisms"? [5.3]

10. What are "inductive arguments?" [5.3]

11. Upon what fallacies are bad arguments based? [5.3]

12. Can you come up with an argument based upon one of the above fallacies that might fool listeners into thinking it's a sound argument? [5.3]

13. Why are trust and credibility important in persuading others? [5.4]

14. What are the keys to forming a persuasive message? [5.4]

15. How can hostility and opposition be turned into agreement? [5.4]

16. What is the difference between propaganda and persuasion? [5.4]

17. What is the difference between persuasion and manipulation? [5.4]

18. Why is it important to dialogue well? [5.4]

19. What is the Columbo tactic as outlined by Greg Koukl? [5.5]

20. How can you recognize and refute faulty argument? [5.5]

21. Which characteristics displayed by Jefferson Smith in *Mr. Smith Goes To Washington* can help us gain credibility in our culture? [5.6]

"The Christian Mind" Reading

This first chapter of the book *Discipleship of the Mind* by James W. Sire gives a broad overview of the Christian mind. The foundational assumption of the Christian mind is that God is God and we are not. Our proper response to this truth is to *fear* the Lord, which is the path to wisdom (Proverbs 1:7) and to clothe ourselves with *humility*, which is the way to avoid spiritual pride and ultimately to be exalted.

The Christian mind constantly needs to be formed and reformed. This requires regular Bible study and reading good books from a Christian perspective. It also involves examining our past beliefs and accepting new insights. When it comes to acquiring specific content, the tools of sociology and philosophy are most helpful. Sociology involves our collective behavior as human beings (external) and philosophy has to do with our intellectual assumptions (internal). The goal in acquiring the mind of Christ is to be transformed into his image.

The Christian Mind

by James Sire

I came alive on a ranch on the rim of the Nebraska Sand Hills. I grew up like Wordsworth who,

> ...bounded o'er the mountains, by the sides
> Of the deep rivers, and the lonely streams,
> Wherever nature led.[1]

I loved riding horses and hiking in the hills. I loved the little stream that flowed past our house. I began to learn the cattle business, for my father and grandfather who lived with us raised purebred Herefords. I was sensuously awake, immersed in experience. But my mind was a blank. I never had a philosophic thought in my life.

Annie Dillard in *An American Childhood* puts it this way:

> Living you stand under a waterfall. ...The hard water pelts your skull, bangs in bits on your shoulders and arms. The strong water dashes down beside you and you feel it along your calves and thighs rising roughly back up, up to the rolling surface, full of bubbles that slide up your skin and break on you at full speed.[2]

Indeed life begins like that. Sheer experience. Then sometime during childhood, usually not all at once, we wake up. We don't just take in sensations. We wake up to ourselves and others. We become conscious that we are separate from the rest of the cosmos. You become aware that you are you. I found out I am I.

For me this occurred sometime just before the seventh grade. We had moved from the country to a small town in northern Nebraska. I had begun attending the village church just across the street from our house. And I had become a Christian. My best friend was the son of a missionary on furlough from Africa. We spent a lot of time together discussing all kinds of things, some of them religious.

One day the same question occurred to both of us, and we couldn't puzzle out an answer: If God is all powerful, why would he ask people to believe in him? Why didn't he make them believe in him?

Predestination and free will—there it was, one of the all-time philosophic stumpers. Our minds were turned on. Counsel was sought from my friend's father. The answer was, as I recall, a rather good one. But the damage—some would say—was done. My mind would never turn off again. Experience alone—standing thoughtless under the waterfall—was no longer enough. I would have to know why—why the waterfall, why me, why anybody, why anything at all. And, since I was a Christian and knew that God was always involved in some way, the answers would have to be Christian.

Now, nearly fifty years later, my mind on that point has not changed. God has got to be involved in every thought—the conscious or unconscious backdrop, to all consciousness, all nonconsciousness. But how? What does it mean to have a Christian mind? On that my mind has changed over the years.

I have long wanted to put down in orderly fashion my best thoughts on just what a Christian mind is, how it comes into formation, how it can be shaped and honed and made to reflect more and more the mind of Christ. And I have begun to do this over the past twenty years, often lecturing on what I labeled the Christian world view. It has only been recently, however, that I have taken seriously what many others have known all along.

The Christian mind does not begin with a world view, not even the Christian world view. It begins with an attitude. Granted that attitude is rooted in the Christian world view, it is nonetheless first of all an attitude. As an adolescent I would never have asked about predestination and free will if I had not already been impressed by God's awesome power. My question came from a primitive recognition that God is God and I am not.

The Christian Mind as an Attitude toward God

God is God and I am not. Put in its simplest form that is the basic orientation of every Christian mind—child, adolescent or adult, simple of profound. The Bible puts it much more elegantly, of course.

> The fear of the Lord is the beginning of knowledge,
> But fools despise wisdom and discipline. (Prov. 1:7)

Variations on this text appear twice more in Proverbs and once in the Psalms (Prov. 9:10; 15:33; Ps. 111:10). But perhaps Job, when he quotes this proverb, says it best.

Struggling to understand his undeserved suffering, Job asks his friends who have come to comfort him:

> Where then does wisdom come from?
> Where does understanding dwell?
> It is hidden from the eyes of every living thing,
> Concealed even from the birds of the air.
> Destruction and Death say,
> "Only a rumor of it has reached our ears."
> God understands the way to it
> And he alone knows where it dwells,
> For he views the ends of the earth
> And sees everything under the heavens...
> And he said to man,
> "The fear of the Lord—that is wisdom,
> and to shun evil is understanding." (Job 28:20–24, 28)

Each of these proverbial sayings begins with the same phrase: *the fear of the Lord*. If one is to be wise or have knowledge or good understanding, then the fear of the Lord must come first.

What is this fear? Our English word is inadequate for the concept, for it suggests being scared of the dark or some imagined denizen of the night or of an armed robber who holds us at gunpoint. These are intense but passing emotions. The *fear of the Lord* is more sustained, more like *awe*. Yet *awe* doesn't suggest for most of us the strange numinous quality that should at least be the background of our attitude.

We can get a better sense from Wordsworth's boyhood experience when one evening he stole a boat and rowed out on a mountain lake.[3]

> It was an act of stealth
> And troubled pleasure, nor without the voice
> Of mountain echoes did my boat move on.

Facing the shore, as one does when rowing out, he used as his reference point a craggy peak in front of him. As he rowed, suddenly from behind that first peak appeared a much higher peak hidden from view from the shore. With each stroke of the oars, the mountain rose higher, till it seemed to stride after him. Wordsworth quickly turned back to shore, remoored the boat,

> And through the meadows homeward went, in grave
> And serious mood; but after I had seen
> That spectacle, for many days my brain
> Worked with a dim and undetermined sense
> Of unknown modes of being; o'er my thoughts
> There hung a darkness, call it solitude
> Or blank desertion.

That "serious mood," that "dim and undetermined sense of unknown modes of being," that "darkness," that sense that something is going on here, and I don't know what it is, those moods when they persist over days, over our lives—that is what the *fear of the Lord* is like. It is predicated on a lot more than a mountain rising up on the horizon. It is predicated on God as God—Yahweh, the great I AM, HE WHO IS (Ex. 3:14). We are all his creatures—finite, fallen. He is the infinite, the perfect. When we see where we stand in relation to him, we can only stand in awe.

Like Moses we are faced with the God who spoke out of the burning bush: "Do not come any closer. Take off your sandals, for the place where you are standing is holy ground." As God identified himself as "the God of your father, the God of Abraham, the God of Isaac and the God of Jacob," Moses "hid his face, because he was afraid to looks at God" (Ex. 3:5–6). Moses indeed knew his proper place: he stood in "a worshipping submission (*fear*) to the God of the covenant who has revealed Himself by name."[4]

Two of the basic texts mentioning the *fear of the Lord* as the beginning of wisdom also add a further dimension. The psalmist says, "all who follow his precepts have good understanding" (Ps. 111:10); and Job says, "to shun evil is understanding" (Job 28:28). This brings out what is already implicit in the Hebrew concept of *wisdom*. Wisdom is more than intellectual knowledge. True, knowledge is involved (Prov. 9:10), but the main matter is wisdom—the practical outworking of genuine knowledge. In Hebrew thought, "wisdom is the art of being successful, of forming the correct plan to gain the desired results."[5] That means that a truly Christian mind is not going to be the useless appendage that is often thought, a mind that engages in theological debate but never enters the realm of life as lived. Genuine Christian thought will result in obedience to God Knowledge must lead to action. We will see more of how this works out in chapter six.

The main point here is that the Christian mind has a spiritual base. It begins with an attitude toward God. He is the source of all wisdom, all knowledge. What a contrast to René Descartes who founded his whole method on the one thing he took as indubitable, his own ego: "I think; therefore I am"! Quite the opposite is true. We are dependent on God as I AM and hence as our creator. We are *not* because we think; we think because we are—in fact, because we are like God.

The Christian Mind as an Attitude toward Ourselves

The flip side of the Christian mind is our attitude toward ourselves. This can be stated in one word: *humility*.

But what a word! We founder at every attempt to make it characteristic of our lives. But Jesus was humble, and in this as in many other things he is both our model and our pioneer.

> Have this mind among yourselves, which is yours in Christ Jesus, who, though he was in the form of God, did not count equality with God a thing to be grasped, but emptied himself, taking the form of a servant, being born in the likeness of men. And being found in human form he humbled himself and became obedient unto death, even the death on a cross. Therefore God has highly exalted him and bestowed on him a name which is above every name, that at the name of Jesus every knee should bow, in heaven and on earth and under the earth, and every tongue confess that Jesus Christ is Lord, to the glory of God the Father. (Phil. 2:5–11 RSV)

Jesus left what was rightfully his—his place in glory. He became everything we are as human beings, even bearing in our place the burden of our sins. Jesus is humble. And—dare we say it? Of course, we do. God is humble. Jesus is the kind of God God is.[6] In his infinite knowledge and wisdom, in his absolute moral perfection, in the total awesomeness of his power, he has the character of humility. "God so loved the world," we so often say. But only if he were also humble could his love be expressed as it was in sending himself in his Son to take on the form of his own creation and to pay the just penalty for our sin.

It is indeed Jesus' humility that led to his exaltation. As Paul says, "Therefore God has highly exalted him." There is a fragment from the Greek philosopher Heraclitus which has always fascinated me as a commentary on this notion: "The way up and down is one and the same."[7] The way to glory for Jesus was by the cross. The way to glory for us is by following Jesus in a similar humility. John Howard Yoder writes, "Only at one point, only on one subject—but then consistently, universally—is Jesus our example: in his cross."[8]

"We have the mind of Christ," says Paul (I Cor. 2:16) as he concludes another long passage about the central message of the Christian faith. What he means is not that we somehow have the physical mind of Christ or even his supernatural mind in some in mystic form, but that we have the mentality of Jesus as he lived a life that led to the cross. In the much misunderstood second chapter of I Corinthians, Paul is not putting down intelligence or true wisdom, as so many have thought. He is instead saying that God's foolishness, the foolishness of the cross, is wiser than the wisdom of the world. And we who are Christians have that mind. We live in the shadow of the cross of Christ, shouldering our own cross, bearing the burdens of one another, standing counter to the world and suffering for it. To have the mind of Christ is no mystical experience granted to those Christians who are especially holy. It is simply the attitude of humility toward oneself and service to God and others.[9]

A Recipe for Humility?

But how can we be humble? We fail so miserably when we consciously try. When we examine ourselves to see just how humble we are, we become proud of our humility and undercut our efforts. Are we forever trapped in a paradox? Well, I'm no expert in humility, but I don't think so. Humility turns out to be not a product of direct effort but a byproduct of the fear of the Lord. If I keep my eyes on God and keep my mind off myself, humility will follow. Humility is then a byproduct of our spiritual orientation—how we understand our relationship with God.

> The apostle Peter puts it this way:
> Clothe yourselves with humility toward one another, because,
> "God opposes the proud
> but gives grace to the humble."
> Humble yourselves, therefore, under God's mighty hand, that he may lift you up
> in due time. (I Pet. 5:5–6)

The apostle James agrees: "Humble yourselves before the Lord, and he will lift you up" (Jas. 4:10). For both Peter and James humility is not produced by comparing oneself to others or by self-abasement, saying to oneself, "Poor me! I'm just worm." Humility is produced by seeing oneself in the light of who God is. Then, too, both Peter and James see Christian humility producing the same results for Jesus' followers as it did for Jesus. God raised Jesus from the dead and brought him into glory. We too will be raised and brought to glory. Glory and humility are not so far apart after all!

Humility also applies to our theology. We believe as Christians that God omniscient and that we, as much as we know, as much as God has told us in his word, are finite and fallible in our knowledge. We should, therefore, keep our developing views of everything—God, human beings, nature, ourselves—in perspective. On any of these we could be wrong.

There is an old proverb worth our reflection:

> When someone is honestly 55% right, that's very good and there's no use wrangling. And if someone is 60% right, it's wonderful, it's great luck, and let him thank God. But what's to be said about 75% right? Wise people say this is suspicious. Well, and what about 100% right? Whoever says he's 100% right is a fanatic, a thug, and the worst kind of rascal.[10]

In our more lucid moments we all acknowledge this. But when we come to our most cherished beliefs, those we hold most dearly and tenaciously, we forget we are prone to error. We strike out against anyone who questions our fundamental beliefs or wishes to state his or hers somewhat differently. We suddenly become proud that we know what our critic does not. We lose whatever humility we had and lock ourselves in a tidy room where we become bishop and king of our own point land.

Or we become locked in the tidy confines of our social enclave. This is what happened to the religious leader of Jesus' day. The Shema was indelibly engraved on their psyche: "Hear, O Israel: The Lord our God, the Lord is one" (Deut. 6:4). They thought they knew what it meant. So when Jesus said, "I know him [God] because I am from him and he sent me" (Jn. 7:28–29), they refused to believe him. After all, they reasoned, God is one. There could not be a person so intimately attached to God that he could practically proclaim divinity. For the unity of God must be preserved. Here before them was one who was challenging their most fundamental conviction about the nature of God. If they are right about God, then Jesus can't be. What were they to do?

We know what they did. John tells us that "they picked up stones to stone him, but Jesus hid himself, slipping away from the temple grounds" (Jn. 8:59).

How can we prevent the same sort of intellectual pride in ourselves? I think it can best be countered by recognizing just what it is we are often claiming. We are claiming to know God perfectly. How can we do that? He is infinite. We are finite. He can reveal anything he wants to anyone he chooses. But we can still misunderstand his revelation. When I become so sure that I have it right that I stand against all comers, I come close to standing against God himself, making him conform to the box in which my contempt of him has put him. But God is bigger than my box or anyone's box. "I am who I am," said God to Moses. This difficult-to-translate phrase may well include the idea "I will be what I will be" or "I will be whoever I show myself to be." In any case, it is the death of any perfect human theology of God.

I like the lines of Alfred, Lord Tennyson:

> Our little systems have their day;
> They have their day and cease to be;
> They are but broken lights of thee,
> And thou O Lord, art more than they.[11]

Lesslie Newbigin echoes this in prose:

> We can never claim that either our understanding or our action is absolutely right. We have no way of proving that we are right. That kind of proof belongs only at the end.[12]

And John Stott comments,

> Systematic theology is certainly a legitimate and even necessary academic discipline, but God did not choose to reveal himself in systematic form, and all systems are exposed to the same temptation, namely to trim God's revelation to fit our system instead of adapting our system to accommodate his revelation.[13]

There is, of course, a balance. We need to be confident enough in our beliefs to act but not so dogmatic about them that we do not allow them to come under scrutiny. We should recognize the inadequacy of our own understanding and the sinfulness of many of our actions and yet commit ourselves to kingdom actions with a vision of the city of God always in our sights. Jesus has gone before us through death.

We should, then, put these twin attitudes of fear and humility into the perspective of the end times. What is worth preserving in our lives will be like the wealth of the nations that Isaiah envisions the kings of the surrounding nations bringing into Zion, the city of David (Isa. 60:1–14), and that the book of Revelation sees being brought into the heavenly city at the end of time (20:24–27). But there will be much dross that will be left behind.

The Christian Mind in Motion

The Christian mind is always in both formation and reformation. For any given person or community of believers it is never a finished product. On the one hand, it is being hewed from a Christian's growing grasp of Scripture in the context of a recalcitrant culture. On the other hand, it is being reformed through experience with God and his people and a growing understanding of what Scripture really teaches.

In *formation* it seeks to operate under the values of the kingdom of God. This requires persistent Bible study, not just as we engage in private devotions each day, but also as we intentionally address Scripture with the tough questions of life. What is God really like? How can we know him and know that we know him? How should we then live? We shall see how those questions are answered in the ensuing chapters.

Moreover, in formation the Christian mind requires reading of books written from a Christian perspective. Others have been down these paths before us; their trailblazing can make the way easier for us.

Finally, in formation the Christian mind requires persistent obedience to God, practicing what we learn from studying Scripture and reading Christian books. This is what Os Guinness calls "the responsibility of knowledge."[14] If we think we know yet do not do, then from a purely biblical sense we do not really know. We will look at this theme in chapter six.

In *reformation* the Christian mind is self-critical. Regardless of how long we have been Christians, we must be critical of our past understanding. Doubt itself can be the midpoint between error and truth. Most of all, a Christian mind is always open to new understanding from Scripture. Each time we read the Bible we should take the attitude that the last time we read the passages we are reading today we might have misunderstood them, at least in part. There might be much more for us this time. This will keep us open to the possibility of growth in knowledge.

In reformation the Christian mind is always being informed by our experience. We act on the truth by obeying it, that is, by conforming our lives to the way we think things are. When the results are what we expect (or better, which is often the case), our beliefs are confirmed. When the results in our lives belie our understanding we have to rethink our views. This becomes an endless process this side of glory.

Finally, in both formation and reformation the Christian mind is other-critical: It constantly seeks to understand and weigh the value of its environment. This requires various methods of observation and analysis, including: reading widely in books written from all major world-view perspectives, and paying attention to what is going on in the society and the world around us.

Two Basic Methods

The Christian mind begins with an attitude. But attitude is only the beginning. There must be some content, and some method toward getting content. What are the first steps toward the specific formation of the Christian mind?

Two basic methods of analysis are involved, one using the tools of sociology, the other the tools of philosophy. The first involves reflecting on our actions as human beings. What we do and what our society does affects who we are and what we think. So we look at the cultural forces that mold us from the outside.

The second method of analysis involves reflecting on our basis intellectual commitments, the assumptions we make before we think. We look, in other words, at the inner workings of our minds. Both kinds of analysis are necessary to the development of a fully conscious Christian mind.

Using the tools of sociology—especially the sociology of knowledge—we can begin to see how such social forces as *individualism* or *pluralism* or *privatization* affect, not only the way we act and think about ourselves and society, but even the ways we understand Scripture. We can discover that our very grasp of God's revelation is qualified by the social and cultural context in which we live. For example, so much are we influenced by the pervasiveness of individualism, especially in North America, that we see Paul's instructions to the churches as a community as advice only to us as individuals. When Paul in Ephesians writes, "Put on the full armor of God so that you can take your stand against the devil's schemes" (Eph. 6:11), we see ourselves as individuals putting on the armor. But the *you* here is plural in Greek. It is first of all the church that is to put on the armor, not the individual. But John Wayne, the Lone Ranger, Lee Iacocca, Humphrey Bogart, Horatio Alger—all the heroes of our culture—lie in the background of our thought and affect our hermeneutic, our way of reading the Bible.

Using the tools of intellectual analysis, on the other hand, helps us see just what we are actually assuming before we do any thinking at all. Then we ask Scripture those tough questions whose answers should be at the root of our mindset. What is God really like? Who am I? Who are we all? How should we then live? When we use the tools of intellectual analysis well, we can deliberately shape our minds. Or better, through such reflection, God will shape our minds more and more into the image of his Son.

[1] William Wordsworth, "Lines Composed a Few Miles above Tinturn Abbey," lines 68–70, frequently anthologized.

[2] Annie Dillard, *An American Childhood* (New York: Harper and Row, 1987), p. 125.

[3] William Wordsworth, *The Prelude*, I ll. 356–400.

[4] Derek Kidner, *Proverbs* (Downers Grove, Ill.: InterVarsity Press,1964), p. 59.

[5] D. A. Hubbard, "Wisdom," *The New Bible Dictionary* (Grand Rapids: Eerdmans, 1962), p. 1333. Ronald E Murphy in "Wisdom," *Harper's Dictionary* (San Francisco, 1985), p. 1135, says Hebrew wisdom involved the practical skill of coping with life (Prov 1:5; 11:14), and the pursuit of a life of proper ethical conduct (Prov 2:9–11 and throughout)."

[6] William Barclay puts it this way: "Jesus is the exact demonstration of what God is like, of the mind of God, of the attitude of God to man. In Jesus we see one who fed the hungry, healed the sick, comforted the sorrowing, was the friend of outcasts and sinners. And, because Jesus is one with God, he is the guarantee that God is like that." See *Jesus as They Saw Him* (Grand Rapids: Eerdmans, 1978) p. 333.

[7] Heraclitus, Fragment 60, in Kathleen Freeman, *Ancilla to the Pre-Socratic Philosophers* (Cambridge, Mass.: Harvard University Press, 1957), p. 29.

[8] John Howard Yoder, *The Politics of Jesus* (Grand Rapids: Eerdmans, 1972), pp. 97–98.

[9] For a careful explanation of this passage see Gordon D. Fee, *The First Epistle to the Corinthians*, The New International Commentary on the New Testament (Grand Rapids: Eerdmans, 1987) pp. 27–120, esp. p. 120. For a refutation of the anti-intellectual interpretations of the passage, see Ranald Macaulay and Jerram Barrs, *Being Human* (Downers Grove, Ill.: InterVarsity Press, 1978), pp. 148–53.

[10] Czeslaw Milosz, *The Captive Mind* (New York: Vintage, 1953), p. 3.

[11] Alfred, Lord Tennyson, "Prologue" to *In Memoriam A. H. H.*, ll. 17–20.

[12] Lesslie Newbigin, *Foolishness to the Greeks* (Grand Rapids: Eerdmans, 1986), p. 60.

[13] David Edwards and John Stott, *Evangelical Essentials* (Downers Grove, Ill.: InterVarsity Press, 1989) p. 37.

[14] Os Guinness, "Knowing Means Doing: A Challenge to Think Christianly," *Radix* 18, no. 1 (1987).

"The Christian Mind" Discussion Questions

1. **What is the attitude of the Christian mind toward God?**

2. **What is the attitude of the Christian mind toward ourselves?**

3. **How can we avoid the sin of spiritual pride?**

4. Why does the Christian mind need both "formation" and "reformation"?

5. What are two helpful methods of informing the Christian mind?

"Critical Thinking" Video

Christians can recognize errors in reasoning by learning to ask questions, analyze what they hear, and engage in basic logic. Mary Jo Sharp offers four questions to start with: What do you mean by that? How do you know that? Why do you believe that? What is your source? She challenges Christians to analyze what we see and hear and not just be passive receptors. She goes on to give several examples of logical fallacies using commercials and TV shows and explains how to avoid being tripped up by them.

To access this video, go to www.summitu.com/utc and enter the passcode found in the back of your manual.

▶ "Critical Thinking" Video Outline

"What is thinking? It is the activity of searching out what must be true, or cannot be true, in the light of given facts or assumptions" (Dallas Willard).

Why should we engage in critical thinking?

1. The world doesn't do it anymore, so we have to emphasize it.
2. Belief in God is not magic; it should be based on discernment.
3. God created humans in his image with ____________________ minds.
4. We are to love God with all of our minds.
5. We shouldn't conform to the world.

Recognizing and dealing with errors in reasoning

____________________ what you see and hear:

- Don't be a passive receptor.
- Don't allow your feelings to get in the way of good reasoning.
- Break down what's being said rather than reacting to what's being said.
- Listen to see if you can find an argument.

Ask ____________________ for further clarification:

- What do you mean by that?
- How do you know that?
- Why do you believe that?
- What is your source?

Recognize material ____________________, errors in reasoning, and don't fall for them:

- *Ad hominem*
- Appeal to pity
- Appeal to shame
- Straw man
- Red herring
- Appeal to the popular
- Either/Or
- False analogy
- Loaded questions
- Hasty generalization
- Genetic fallacy

Poor reasoning will lead you away from truth; ____________________ will lead you toward truth.

"Critical Thinking" Discussion Questions

1. **What is critical thinking and why is it important?**

2. **What are some keys to analyzing what you see and hear?**

3. **Why are good questions essential for further clarification?**

4. **Can you come up with examples of these common material fallacies, errors in reasoning, from social media or advertising?**

5. **What does the Bible have to say about critical thinking based on truth and accurate information?**

Chapter 5 Key Points

Key Questions:

1. What roles do thinking logically and communicating effectively play in influencing our culture for Christ?
2. What are the basic principles of logic?
3. What fallacies should be avoided?

Key Players:

1. Aristotle
2. Philo

Key Terms:

1. *Ad Hominem*
2. Appeal to Authority
3. Appeal to Ignorance
4. Appeal to Pity
5. Attacking the Motive
6. Bandwagon
7. Begging the Question*
8. Cogent
9. Critical Thinking
10. Deductive Argument
11. Equivocation
12. *Ethos, Pathos*, and *Logos**
13. Fallacy
14. Fallacy of Division
15. False Cause
16. False Dilemma*
17. Hasty Generalization
18. Inductive Argument
19. Loaded Question
20. Logic*
21. Premise
22. Propaganda
23. Pygmalion Effect
24. Red Herring
25. Slippery Slope
26. Sound
27. Straw Man*
28. *Tu Quoque*
29. Valid
30. Weak Analogy

**Short answer or essay question on the exam*

Chapter 5 Assignment

Answer the following questions with at least one paragraph.

1. **Why does the Christian worldview lead us to trust that logic is a reliable tool for thinking well about earthly and spiritual truths?**

2. **Why is careful use of words so important to the Christian worldview in connection to the doctrine of *imago Dei*?**

3. **What's the difference between persuasion and propaganda?**

4. **Describe the idea behind the Columbo Tactic and how it works.**

Other potential questions:

- Can an argument be logically consistent and still be wrong? Can it be logically inconsistent/incorrect but still be correct? If so, why care about logic?
- Think about arguments you hear in various media forms and everyday conversations. What fallacies do you encounter most frequently?
- Does the increasing use of social media make argumentation, persuasion, and logic more or less common, or is there little or no connection?

UNIT 6

TECHNOLOGY

CHAPTER 6 LEARNING OBJECTIVES

Students will be able to:

1. identify whether technology is neutral. [6.1]
2. differentiate between the good and the not-so-good side of technology. [6.2]
3. explain reasons why Christians should be leading the way in calling for deeper thinking about technology's potential and pitfalls. [6.3]
4. articulate ideas that Christians could embrace to wisely interact with technology. [6.4]
5. describe why there is tension for Christians in embracing technology. [6.5]

Chapter 6 Discussion Questions

1. **What are some ways in which technology impacts our lives? [6.1]**

2. **What is technology? [6.2]**

3. **What are some good aspects of information technology? [6.2]**

4. **What are some negative aspects of information technology? [6.2]**

5. **What do you think are the three most important information technology advances of the recent past? List the greatest benefit and downside of each. [6.5]**

6. **How is information technology a double-edged sword? [6.2]**

7. **How does information technology tempt us to lose focus? [6.2]**

8. **How does information technology tempt us to isolate ourselves? [6.2]**

9. **How does information technology tempt us to be superficial? [6.2]**

10. **How does information technology tempt us to give in to evil? [6.2]**

11. **What are the most frustrating and negative aspects of technology to you? [6.5]**

12. **How does Christianity debunk the idea that technology is neutral? [6.3]**

13. How does Christianity balance technology's orientation to creation? [6.3]

14. How does Christianity help redeem technology? [6.3]

15. What is a "technolopy" and how can Christianity save us from it? [6.3]

16. How can Christianity counter technology's negative effect on communication? [6.3]

17. How can Christians address the problems of technology by bearing God's image as a "restorer"? [6.4]

18. How can Christians address the problems of technology by bearing God's image as a "renewer"? [6.4]

19. How can Christians address the problems of technology by bearing God's image as a "relator"? [6.4]

20. How can Christians address the problems of technology by bearing God's image as a "repairer"? [6.4]

21. How can we keep our balance when it comes to technology? [6.5]

"Connectivity and Its Disconnects" Reading

In the introduction to her book, Sherry Turkle notes that being as "connected" as we are makes it easy to "disconnect" from the real world. Even in public places people are often tuned into their own private networks. "Technology makes it easy to communicate when we wish and to disengage at will. … The new technologies allow us to 'dial down' human contact."

With constant connections come new anxieties and insecurities, especially for young people. They are connected all day but confused about companionship. Friendships are nurtured on social networking sites but less time is spent in face to face interaction. Virtual reality replaces the real world. Turkle goes on to predict that, "Their digitized friendships … may prepare them … for relationships that could bring superficiality to a higher power, that is for relationships with the inanimate (robots)."

"Technology reshapes the landscape of our emotional lives, but is it offering us the lives we want to lead?"

Connectivity and Its Disconnects

by Sherry Turkle

Online connections were first conceived as a substitute for face-to-face contact, when the latter was for some reason impractical: Don't have time to make a phone call? Shoot off a text message. But very quickly, the text message became the connection of choice. We discovered the network—the world of connectivity—to be uniquely suited to the overworked and overscheduled life it makes possible. And now we look to the network to defend us against loneliness even as we use it to control the intensity of our connections. Technology makes it easy to communicate when we wish and to disengage at will.

A few years ago at a dinner party in Paris, I met Ellen, an ambitious, elegant young woman in her early thirties, thrilled to be working at her dream job in advertising. Once a week, she would call her grandmother in Philadelphia using Skype, an Internet service that functions as a telephone with a Web camera. Before Skype, Ellen's calls to her grandmother were costly and brief. With Skype, the calls are free and give the compelling sense that the other person is present—Skype is an almost real-time video link. Ellen could now call more frequently: "Twice a week and I stay on the call for an hour," she told me. It should have been rewarding; instead, when I met her, Ellen was unhappy. She knew that her grandmother was unaware that Skype allows surreptitious multitasking. Her grandmother could see Ellen's face on the screen but not her hands. Ellen admitted to me, "I do my e-mail during the calls. I'm not really paying attention to our conversation."

Ellen's multitasking removed her to another place. She felt her grandmother was talking to someone who was not really there. During their Skype conversations, Ellen and her grandmother were more connected than they had ever been before, but at the same time, each was alone. Ellen felt guilty and confused: she knew that her grandmother was happy, even if their intimacy was now, for Ellen, another task among multitasks.

I have often observed this distinctive confusion: these days, whether you are online or not, it is easy for people to end up unsure if they are closer together or further apart. I remember my own sense of disorientation the first time I realized that I was "alone together; I had traveled an exhausting thirty-six hours to attend a conference on advanced robotic technology held in central Japan. The packed grand ballroom was Wi-Fi enabled: the speaker was using the Web for his presentation, laptops were open throughout the audience, fingers were flying, and there was a sense of great concentration and intensity. But not many in the audience were attending to the speaker. Most people seemed to be doing their email, downloading files, and surfing the Net. The man next to me was searching for a *New Yorker* cartoon to illustrate his upcoming presentation. Every once in a while, audience members gave the speaker some attention, lowering their laptop screens in a kind of curtsy, a gesture of courtesy.

Outside, in the hallways, the people milling around me were looking past me to virtual others. They were on their laptops and their phones, connecting to colleagues at the conference going on around them and to others around the globe. There but not there. Of course, clusters of people chatted with each other, making dinner plans, "networking" in that old sense of the word, the one that implies having a coffee or sharing a meal. But at this conference, it was clear that what people mostly want from public space is to be alone with their personal networks. It is good to come together physically, but it is more important to stay tethered to our devices. I thought of how Sigmund Freud considered the power of communities both to shape and to subvert us, and a psychoanalytic pun came to mind: "connectivity and its discontents."

The phrase comes back to me months later as I interview management consultants who seem to have lost touch with their best instincts for what makes them competitive. They complain about the BlackBerry revolution, yet accept it as inevitable while decrying it as corrosive. They say they used to talk to each other as they waited to give presentations or took taxis to the airport; now they spend that time doing e-mail. Some tell me they are making better use of their "downtime; but they argue without conviction. The time that they once used to talk as they waited for appointments or drove to the airport was never downtime. It was the time when far-flung global teams solidified relationships and refined ideas.

In corporations, among friends, and within academic departments, people readily admit that they would rather leave a voicemail or send an e-mail than talk face-to-face. Some who say "I live my life on my BlackBerry" are forthright about avoiding the "real-time" commitment of a phone call. The new technologies allow us to "dial down" human contact, to titrate its nature and extent. I recently overheard a conversation in a restaurant between two women. "No one answers the phone in our house anymore," the first woman proclaimed with some consternation. "It used to be that the kids would race to pick up the phone. Now they are up in their rooms, knowing no one is going to call them, and texting and going on Facebook or whatever instead." Parents with teenage children will be nodding at this very familiar story in recognition and perhaps a sense of wonderment that this has happened, and so quickly. And teenagers will simply be saying, "Well, what's your point?"

A thirteen-year-old tells me she "hates the phone and never listens to voice-mail." Texting offers just the right amount of access, just the right amount of control. She is a modern Goldilocks: for her, texting puts people not too close, not too far, but at just the right distance. The world is now full of modern Goldilockses, people who take comfort in being in touch with a lot of people whom they also keep at bay. A twenty-one-year-old college student reflects on the new balance: "I don't use my phone for calls any more. I don't have the time to just go on and on. I like texting, Twitter, looking at someone's Facebook wall. I learn what I need to know."

Randy, twenty-seven, has a younger sister—a Goldilocks who got her distances wrong. Randy is an American lawyer now working in California. His family lives in New York, and he flies to the East Coast to see them three or four times a year. When I [met] Randy, his sister Nora, twenty-four, had just announced her engagement and wedding date via e-mail to a list of friends and family. "That," Randy says to me bitterly, "is how I got the news." He doesn't know if he is more angry or hurt. "It doesn't feel right that she didn't call," he says. "I was getting ready for a trip home. Couldn't she have told me then? She's my sister, but I didn't have a private moment when she told me in person. Or at least a call, just the two of us. When I told her I was upset, she sort of understood, but laughed and said that she and her fiancé just wanted to do things simply, as simply as possible. I feel very far away from her."

Nora did not mean to offend her brother. She saw e-mail as efficient and did not see beyond. We have long turned to technology to make us more efficient in work; now Nora illustrates how we want it to make us more efficient in our private lives. But when technology engineers intimacy, relationships can be reduced to mere connections. And then, easy connection becomes redefined as intimacy. Put otherwise, cyberintimacies slide into cybersolitudes.

And with constant connection comes new anxieties of disconnection, a kind of panic. Even Randy, who longs for a phone call from Nora on such an important matter as her wedding, is never without his BlackBerry. He holds it in his hands during our entire conversation. Once, he puts it in his pocket. A few moments later, it comes out, fingered like a talisman. In interviews with young and old, I find people genuinely terrified of being cut off from the "grid." People say that the loss of a cell phone can "feel like a death." One television producer in her mid-forties tells me that without her smartphone, "I felt like I had lost my mind." Whether or not our devices are in use, without them we feel disconnected, adrift. A danger even to ourselves, we insist on our right to send text messages while driving our cars and object to rules that would limit the practice.[1]

Only a decade ago, I would have been mystified that fifteen-year-olds in my urban neighborhood, a neighborhood of parks and shopping malls, of front stoops and coffee shops, would feel the need to send and receive close to six thousand messages a month via portable digital devices or that best friends would assume that when they visited, it would usually be on the virtual real estate of Facebook.[2] It might have seemed intrusive, if not illegal, that my mobile phone would tell me the location of all my acquaintances within a ten-mile radius.[3] But these days we are accustomed to all this. Life in a media bubble has come to seem natural. So has the end of a certain public etiquette: on the street, we speak into the invisible microphones on our mobile phones and appear to be talking to ourselves. We share intimacies with the air as though unconcerned about who can hear us or the details of our physical surroundings.

I once described the computer as a second self, a mirror of mind. Now the metaphor no longer goes far enough. Our new devices provide space for the emergence of a new state of the self, itself, split between the screen and the physical real, wired into existence through technology.

Teenagers tell me they sleep with their cell phone, and even when it isn't on their person, when it has been banished to the school locker, for instance, they know when their phone is vibrating. The technology has become like a phantom limb, it is so much a part of them. These young people are among the first to grow up with an expectation of continuous connection: always on, and always on them. And they are among the first to grow up not necessarily thinking of simulation as second best. All of this makes them fluent with technology but brings a set of new insecurities. They nurture friendships on social-networking sites and then wonder if they are among friends. They are connected all day but are not sure if they have communicated. They become confused about companionship. Can they find it in their lives on the screen? Could they find it with a robot? Their digitized friendships—played out with emoticon emotions, so often predicated on rapid response rather than reflection—may prepare them, at times through nothing more than their superficiality, for relationships that could bring superficiality to a higher power, that is, for relationships with the inanimate. They come to accept lower expectations for connection and, finally, the idea that robot friendships could be sufficient unto the day.

Overwhelmed by the volume and velocity of our lives, we turn to technology to help us find time. But technology makes us busier than ever and ever more in search of retreat. Gradually, we come to see our online life as life itself. We come to see what robots offer as relationship. The simplification of relationship is no longer a source of complaint. It becomes what we want. These seem the gathering clouds of a perfect storm.

Technology reshapes the landscape of our emotional lives, but is it offering us the lives we want to lead? Many roboticists are enthusiastic about having robots tend to our children and our aging parents, for instance. Are these psychologically, socially, and ethically acceptable propositions? What are our responsibilities here? And are we comfortable with virtual environments that propose themselves not as places for recreation but as new worlds to live in? What do we have, now that we have what we say we want—now that we have what technology makes easy?[4] This is the time to begin these conversations, together. It is too late to leave the future to the futurists.

This essay originally appeared as a section in Sherry Turkle, *Alone Together: Why We Expect More from Technology and Less from Each Other* (New York: Basic Book, 2011), 13–17. It is reproduced here with the permission of the publisher.

[1] See, for example, Matt Richtel, "In Study, Texting Lifts Crash Risk by Large Margin," *New York Times*, July 27, 2009, www.nytimes.com/2009/09/09/technology/09distracted.html (accessed September 9, 2009). As I complete this book, Oprah Winfrey has made texting while driving a personal crusade, encouraging people across America to sign an online pledge to not text and drive. See "Oprah's No Phone Zone," Oprah.com, www.oprah.com/packages/no-phone-zone.html (accessed May 30, 2010).

[2] The teenage national average as of January 2010 is closer to thirty-five hundred; my affluent, urban neighborhood has a far higher number. Roger Entner, "Under-aged Texting: Usage and Actual Cost," Nielsen.com, January 27, 2010, http://blog.nielsen.com/nielsenwire/online_mobile/under-aged-texting-usage-andactual-cost (accessed May 30, 2010). On texting's impact on teenage life, see Katie Hafner, "Texting May Be Taking Its Toll," *New York Times*, May 25, 2009, www.nytimes.com/2009/05/25/health/26teen.html?_r=2&8dpc (accessed July 21, 2009).

[3] To find friends in the neighborhood, Loopt for the iPhone is a popular "app."

[4] A witty experiment suggests that Facebook "friends" won't even show up when you invite them to a party. Hal Niedzviecki, "Facebook in a Crowd," *New York Times*, October 24, 2008, www.nytimes.com/2008/10/26/magazine/26lives-t.html (accessed July 27, 2010).

"Connectivity and Its Disconnects" Discussion Questions

1. **What does the term "alone together" mean?**

2. **Do you prefer to communicate by text, email, or instant message rather than by phone or in person? If so, explain why.**

3. **What are some differences between how you use your phone and how your parents used phones when they were your age? Do you think the changes are for the better?**

4. **How would a typical week be different for you if you didn't have a smartphone?**

5. **Do you think we will one day have meaningful relationships with robots? How will it start?**

"Bioethics" Video

This lecture defines bioethics and what it has to say about the beginning of human life, the end of human life, and the very nature of human beings. Are we free to transcend our natural limits and become better? Klusendorf demonstrates how worldviews inform bioethics and outlines the five areas every worldview must address: metaphysics, epistemology, anthropology, cosmology, and ethics. He then contrasts the two main worldviews that shape current thinking: scientific materialism and Christian theism. He delves into topics like cloning and embryonic research, using case studies to illustrate and clarify complex issues.

To access this video, go to www.summitu.com/utc and enter the passcode found in the back of your manual.

"Bioethics" Video Outline

Bioethics is more than the study of medical ethics. It also deals with profound world-view questions like these:

1. What is the proper end of medicine? Is it to heal people or enhance them?
2. What is the ______________________ of human beings? Are we endowed with value or do we earn our value through performance?
3. What is the nature of right and wrong? Is it based on consensus?
4. What should public policy look like when there is no consensus?

Key areas of debate in bioethics

1. Beginning of life issues:
    - What is the moral and legal status of ______________________?
    - How far should we go with infertility treatments?
    - What rules should apply to surrogacy?
2. End of life issues:
    - Should we allow ______________________ suicide?
    - Should we allow people to die by withholding treatment?
3. Nature of human beings:
    - What makes us persons of ______________________? Are we endowed with value or do we earn our value through performance?
    - Are we free to transcend our natural limits and become better through genetics?

Worldviews in conflict in bioethics: Christianity and scientific materialism

There are five questions every worldview must answer. Christianity and scientific materialism answer them differently.

1. **______________________:** What is the nature of reality?
2. **Epistemology:** How do we know about the world around us?
3. **Anthropology:** How did we get here and what is our nature as human beings?
4. **Cosmology:** Where did we come from and where are we going?
5. **______________________:** What is right and what is wrong?

Case Studies:

- End of life treatment: Should we hasten death by withholding treatment?
- Infertility: Should we abort extra embryos—selective reduction?
- Human enhancement: Should we simply repair or enhance the human body?

"Bioethics" Discussion Questions

1. **What gives us value as human beings?**

2. **What is the proper goal of medicine? Is it to heal people or enhance them?**

3. **What are the five questions every worldview must answer?**

4. How are these questions answered by Christian theism?

5. How are these questions answered by scientific materialism?

6. How would you resolve some of the dilemmas being debated today in bioethics?

Chapter 6 Key Points

Key Questions:

1. What is technology?
2. What are the negative effects of technology?
3. How can Christians utilize technology to positively change culture?

Key Players:

1. Neil Postman
2. Sherry Turkle

Key Terms:

1. Cyberculture
2. Idol
3. Information Technology*
4. Sin of Commission
5. Sin of Omission
6. Technology
7. Terasem
8. Wisdom*

Key Works:

1. *Alone Together* by Sherry Turkle
2. *Amusing Ourselves to Death* by Neil Postman
3. *The Technological Society* by Jacques Ellul
4. *Technopoly* by Neil Postman

**Short answer or essay question on the exam*

Chapter 6 Assignment

Answer the following questions with at least one paragraph.

1. **Think about technology as it is broadly defined in this chapter. How is technology as much a way of thinking and acting as it is pieces of hardware and software?**

2. **In what ways does modern technology encourage superficial relationships and discourage close friendship or meaningful connections?**

3. **How can modern attitudes toward technology change our orientation to creation or even threaten our humanity?**

4. **This chapter describes different perspectives of time encouraged by the impulses of modern life and technology and by Christian practices. How do they differ?**

Other potential questions:

- Think about the tradeoffs of the technologies that you commonly use. What do you gain from them and at what cost? Have you ever considered that technology might come with drawbacks as well as advantages?
- How prominent or dominant is technology in your life? Consider making a list of what people, relationships, habits, and practices are most important in your life. Compare it to a list of how you spend your time each day. What do you do first in the morning and how much time do you spend on various activities? How closely do your lists match?

UNIT 7

7

The Arts and Entertainment

Chapter 7 Learning Objectives

Students will be able to:

1. chronicle the story of a prospective screenwriter and actor. [7.1]
2. analyze how the arts became amusement and assess what amusement does to the spiritual life of Christians. [7.2]
3. identify the battle of worldviews and distinguish how Marxism, Postmodernism, Islam, and New Spirituality process the entertainment culture. [7.3]
4. explain why Christians should care enough to engage and transform the entertainment culture for the glory of Christ. [7.4]
5. explain why Christians should not settle for bit parts in other stories, but live their God-given story. [7.5]
6. conclude God wants Christians to go deeper, to wait patiently through the silence, and to work hard while fully trusting him. [7.6]

Chapter 7 Discussion Questions

1. **What is the difference between "entertainment" and "amusement"?** [7.2]

2. **"Soul-sickness" and "shallowness" are symptoms of what deeper malady?** [7.2]

3. **How has our entertainment culture twisted the arts?** [7.2]

4. **What role did art play in ancient cultures?** [7.2]

5. **What impact did the Enlightenment have on art?** [7.2]

6. **How has the sacred-secular split affected how we view art today?** [7.2]

7. **How does the amusement culture enslave our affections?** [7.2]

8. **Do you think violent video games and pornography lead to violence and sexual crimes? Can you cite any proof to support your opinion?** [7.2]

9. How does the amusement culture make us restless? [7.2]

10. How does the amusement culture destroy contentment? [7.2]

11. How does the amusement culture make us angry? [7.2]

12. Does the entertainment culture affect our worldview? [7.3]

13. Just how influential is today's entertainment culture? [7.3]

14. How do Marxism and Postmodernism approach today's entertainment culture? [7.3]

15. How do Islam and New Spirituality approach today's entertainment culture? [7.3]

16. Why should Christians care about the arts and entertainment? [7.4]

17. **Why do we need discernment when it comes to the arts and entertainment?** [7.5]

18. **What movies and books have had the most profound impact on you?** [7.5]

19. **How can we get away from mindless entertainment and find a meaningful purpose in life?** [7.5]

20. **How does adversity help us to live God's bigger story?** [7.6]

"The Impact of the Net" Reading

The Internet has changed our world forever in ways that can't be undone. The ability to upload and download at near the speed of light makes the Net a thoroughfare for business and commerce. Bidirectional communication and seamless interconnectivity make it the world's meetinghouse where people gather to chat, gossip, argue, and flirt on vast social networks.

The medium (paper, ink, film, videotape, vinyl, plastic) is no longer important now that information is digitized and can be created and shared across platforms. The Net has enabled all-purpose tools to replace special-purpose tools like the camera, tape recorder, video recorder, boom box, and so on. And the quality of digital products is so much better while the cost of creating and transmitting them through the Net is so much less.

The four main qualities that are seamlessly combined in the Net and accessible to any Net-connected device almost anywhere in the world are

- interactivity
- hyperlinking
- searchability
- multimedia

These features give us instant access to an almost infinite amount of information. We can switch between reading and listening and watching with a touch of the finger. We can also be in contact with friends and family 24/7. We are hyper-connected to a hyper world.

The Impact of the Net

by Nicholas Carr

The way the Web has progressed as a medium replays, with the velocity of a time-lapse film, the entire history of modern media. Hundreds of years have been compressed into a couple of decades. The first information-processing machine that the Net replicated was Gutenberg's press. Because text is fairly simple to translate into software code and to share over networks—it doesn't require a lot of memory to store, a lot of bandwidth to transmit, or a lot of processing power to render on a screen—early Web sites were usually constructed entirely of typographical symbols. The very term we came to use to describe what we look at online—*pages*—emphasized the connection with printed documents. Publishers of magazines and newspapers, realizing that large quantities of text could, for the first time in history, be broadcast the way radio and TV programs had always been, were among the first businesses to open online outlets, posting articles, excerpts, and other pieces of writing on their sites. The ease with which words could be transmitted led, as well, to the widespread and extraordinarily rapid adoption of e-mail, rendering the personal letter obsolete.

As the cost of memory and bandwidth fell, it became possible to incorporate photographs and drawings into Web pages. At first, the images, like the text they often accompanied, were in black and white, and their low resolution made them blurry. They looked like the first photos printed in newspapers a hundred years ago. But the capacity of the Net expanded to handle color pictures, and the size and quality of the images increased enormously. Soon, simple animations began to play online, mimicking the herky-jerky motions of the flip books, or kineographs, that were popular at the end of the nineteenth century.

Next, the Web began to take over the work of our traditional sound-processing equipment—radios and phonographs and tape decks. The earliest sounds to be heard online were spoken words, but soon snippets of music, and then entire songs and even symphonies, were streaming through sites, at ever-higher levels of fidelity. The network's ability to handle audio streams was aided by the development of software algorithms, such as the one used to produce MP3 files, that erase from music and other recordings sounds that are hard for the human ear to hear. The algorithms allowed sound files to be compressed to much smaller sizes with only slight sacrifices in quality. Telephone calls also began to be routed over the fiber-optic cables of the Internet, bypassing traditional phone lines.

Finally, video came online, as the Net subsumed the technologies of cinema and television. Because the transmission and display of moving pictures place great demands on computers and networks, the first online videos played in tiny windows inside browsers. The pictures would often stutter or drop out, and they were usually out of sync with their soundtracks. But here, too, gains came swiftly. Within just a few years, elaborate three-dimensional games were being played online, and companies like Netflix and Apple were sending high-definition movies and TV shows over the network and onto screens in customers' homes. Even the long-promised "picture phone" is finally becoming a reality, as webcams become a regular feature of computers and Net-connected televisions, and popular Internet telephone services like Skype incorporate video transmissions.

The Net differs from most of the mass media it replaces in an obvious and very important way: it's bidirectional. We can send messages through the network as well as receive them. That's made the system all the more useful. The ability to exchange information online, to upload as well as download, has turned the Net into a thoroughfare for business and commerce. With a few clicks, people can search virtual catalogues, place orders, track shipments, and update information in corporate databases. But the Net doesn't just connect us with businesses; it connects us with one another. It's a personal broadcasting medium as well as a commercial one. Millions of people use it to distribute their own digital creations, in the form of blogs, videos, photos, songs, and podcasts, as well as to critique, edit, or otherwise modify the creations of others. The vast, volunteer-written encyclopedia Wikipedia, the largely amateur-produced YouTube video service, the massive Flickr photo repository, the sprawling Huffington Post blog compendium—all of these popular media services were unimaginable before the Web came along. The interactivity of the medium has also turned it into the world's meetinghouse, where people gather to chat, gossip, argue, show off, and flirt on Facebook, Twitter, MySpace, and all sorts of other social (and sometimes antisocial) networks.

As the uses of the Internet have proliferated, the time we devote to the medium has grown apace, even as speedier connections have allowed us to do more during every minute we're logged on. By 2009, adults in North America were spending an average of twelve hours online a week, double the average in 2005.[1] If you consider only those adults with Internet access, online hours jump considerably, to more than seventeen a week. For younger adults, the figure is higher still, with people in their twenties spending more than nineteen hours a week online.[2] American children between the ages of two and eleven were using the Net about eleven hours a week in 2009, an increase of more than sixty percent since 2004.[3] The typical European adult was online nearly eight hours a week in 2009, up about thirty percent since 2005. Europeans in their twenties were online about twelve hours a week on average.[4] A 2008 international survey of 27,500 adults between the ages of eighteen and fifty-five found that people are spending thirty percent of their leisure time online, with the Chinese being the most intensive surfers, devoting forty-four percent of their off-work hours to the Net.[5]

These figures don't include the time people spend using their mobile phones and other handheld computers to exchange text messages, which also continues to increase rapidly. Text messaging now represents one of the most common uses of computers, particularly for the young. By the beginning of 2009, the average American cell phone user was sending or receiving nearly 400 texts a month, more than a fourfold increase from 2006. The average American teen was sending or receiving a mind-boggling 2,272 texts a month.[6] Worldwide, well over two trillion text messages zip between mobile phones every year, far outstripping the number of voice calls.[7] Thanks to our ever-present messaging systems and devices, we "never really have to disconnect," says Danah Boyd, a social scientist who works for Microsoft.[8]

It's often assumed that the time we devote to the Net comes out of the time we would otherwise spend watching TV. But statistics suggest otherwise. Most studies of media activity indicate that as Net use has gone up, television viewing has either held steady or increased. The Nielsen Company's long-running media-tracking survey reveals that the time Americans devote to TV viewing has been going up throughout the Web era. The hours we spend in front of the tube rose another two percent between 2008 and 2009, reaching 153 hours a month, the highest level since Nielsen began collecting data in the 1950s (and that doesn't include the time people spend watching TV shows on their computers).[9] In Europe as well, people continue to watch television as much as they ever have. The average European viewed more than a dozen hours of TV a week in 2009, nearly an hour more than in 2004.[10]

A 2006 study by Jupiter Research revealed "a huge overlap" between TV viewing and Web surfing, with forty-two percent of the most avid TV fans (those watching thirty-five or more hours of programming a week) also being among the most intensive users of the Net (those spending thirty or more hours online a week).[11] The growth in our online time has, in other words, expanded the total amount of time we spend in front of screens. According to an extensive 2009 study conducted by Ball State University's Center for Media Design, most Americans, no matter what their age, spend at least eight and a half hours a day looking at a television, a computer monitor, or the screen of their mobile phone. Frequently, they use two or even all three of the devices simultaneously.[12]

What does seem to be decreasing as Net use grows is the time we spend reading print publications—particularly newspapers and magazines, but also books. Of the four major categories of personal media, print is now the least used, lagging well behind television, computers, and radio. By 2008, according to the U.S. Bureau of Labor Statistics, the time that the average American over the age of fourteen devoted to reading printed works had fallen to 143 minutes a week, a drop of eleven percent since 2004. Young adults between the ages of twenty-five and thirty-four, who are among the most avid Net users, were reading printed works for a total of just forty-nine minutes a week in 2008, down a precipitous twenty-nine percent from 2004.[13] In a small but telling 2008 study conducted for Adweek magazine, four typical Americans—a barber, a chemist, an elementary school principal, and a real estate agent—were shadowed during the course of a day to document their media usage. The people displayed very different habits, but they shared one thing in common, according to the magazine: "None of the four cracked open any print media during their observed hours."[14] Because of the ubiquity of text on the Net and our phones, we're almost certainly reading more words today than we did twenty years ago, but we're devoting much less time to reading words printed on paper.

The Internet, like the personal computer before it, has proven to be so useful in so many ways that we've welcomed every expansion of its scope. Rarely have we paused to ponder, much less question, the media revolution that has been playing out all around us, in our homes, our workplaces, our schools. Until the Net arrived, the history of media had been a tale of fragmentation. Different technologies progressed down different paths, leading to a proliferation of special-purpose tools. Books and newspapers could present text and images, but they couldn't handle sounds or moving pictures. Visual media like cinema and TV were unsuited to the display of text, except in the smallest of quantities. Radios, telephones, phonographs, and tape players were limited to transmitting sounds. If you wanted to add up numbers, you used a calculator. If you wanted to look up facts, you consulted a set of encyclopedias or a *World Almanac*. The production end of the business was every bit as fragmented as the consumption end. If a company wanted to sell words, it printed them on paper. If it wanted to sell movies, it wound them onto spools of film. If it wanted to sell songs, it pressed them onto vinyl records or recorded them onto magnetic tape. If it wanted to distribute TV shows and commercials, it shot them through the air from a big antenna or sent them down thick black coaxial cables.

Once information is digitized, the boundaries between media dissolve. We replace our special-purpose tools with an all-purpose tool. And because the economics of digital production and distribution are almost always superior to what came before—the cost of creating electronic products and transmitting them through the Net is a small fraction of the cost of manufacturing physical goods and shipping them through warehouses and into stores—the shift happens very quickly, following capitalism's inexorable logic. Today, nearly all media companies distribute digital versions of their products through the Net, and the growth in the consumption of media goods is taking place almost entirely online.

That doesn't mean that traditional forms of media have disappeared. We still buy books and subscribe to magazines. We still go to the movies and listen to the radio. Some of us still buy music on CDs and movies on DVDs. A few of us will even pick up a newspaper now and then. When old technologies are supplanted by new ones, the old technologies often continue to be used for a long time, sometimes indefinitely. Decades after the invention of movable type, many books were still being handwritten by scribes or printed from woodblocks and some of the most beautiful books continue to be produced in those ways today. Quite a few people still listen to vinyl records, use film cameras to take photographs, and look up phone numbers in the printed Yellow Pages. But the old technologies lose their economic and cultural force. They become progress's dead ends. It's the new technologies that govern production and consumption, that guide people's behavior and shape their perceptions. That's why the future of knowledge and culture no longer lies in books or newspapers or TV shows or radio programs or records or CDs. It lies in digital files shot through our universal medium at the speed of light.

A new medium is never an addition to an old one," wrote McLuhan in *Understanding Media*, "nor does it leave the old one in peace. It never ceases to oppress the older media until it finds new shapes and positions for them."[15] His observation rings particularly true today. Traditional media, even electronic ones, are being refashioned and repositioned as they go through the shift to online distribution.

When the Net absorbs a medium, it re-creates that medium in its own image. It not only dissolves the medium's physical form; it injects the medium's content with hyperlinks, breaks up the content into searchable chunks, and surrounds the content with the content of all the other media it has absorbed. All these changes in the form of the content also change the way we use, experience, and even understand the content.

A page of online text viewed through a computer screen may seem similar to a page of printed text. But scrolling or clicking through a Web document involves physical actions and sensory stimuli very different from those involved in holding and turning the pages of a book or a magazine. Research has shown that the cognitive act of reading draws not just on our sense of sight but also on our sense of touch. It's tactile as well as visual. "All reading," writes Anne Mangen, a Norwegian literary studies professor, is "multi-sensory." There's "a crucial link" between "the sensory-motor experience of the materiality" of a written work and "the cognitive processing of the text content."[16] The shift from paper to screen doesn't just change the way we navigate a piece of writing. It also influences the degree of attention we devote to it and the depth of our immersion in it.

Hyperlinks also alter our experience of media. Links are in one sense a variation on the textual allusions, citations, and footnotes that have long been common elements of documents. But their effect on us as we read is not at all the same. Links don't just point us to related or supplemental works; they propel us toward them. They encourage us to dip in and out of a series of texts rather than devote sustained attention to any one of them. Hyperlinks are designed to grab our attention. Their value as navigational tools is inextricable from the distraction they cause.

The searchability of online works also represents a variation on older navigational aids such as tables of contents, indexes, and concordances. But here, too, the effects are different. As with links, the ease and ready availability of searching make it much simpler to jump between digital documents than it ever was to jump between printed ones. Our attachment to any one text becomes more tenuous, more provisional. Searches also lead to the fragmentation of online works. A search engine often draws our attention to a particular snippet of text, a few words or sentences that have strong relevance to whatever we're searching for at the moment, while providing little incentive for taking in the work as a whole. We don't see the forest when we search the Web. We don't even see the trees. We see twigs and leaves. As companies like Google and Microsoft perfect search engines for video and audio content, more products are undergoing the fragmentation that already characterizes written works.

By combining many different kinds of information on a single screen, the multimedia Net further fragments content and disrupts our concentration. A single Web page may contain a few chunks of text, a video or audio stream, a set of navigational tools, various advertisements, and several small software applications, or "widgets," running in their own windows. We all know how distracting this cacophony of stimuli can be. We joke about it all the time. A new e-mail message announces its arrival as we're glancing over the latest headlines at a newspaper's site. A few seconds later, our RSS reader tells us that one of our favorite bloggers has uploaded a new post. A moment after that, our mobile phone plays the ringtone that signals an incoming text message. Simultaneously, a Facebook or Twitter alert blinks on-screen. In addition to everything flowing through the network, we also have immediate access to all the other software programs running on our computers—they, too, compete for a piece of our mind. Whenever we turn on our computer, we are plunged into an "ecosystem of interruption technologies," as the blogger and science fiction writer Cory Doctorow terms it.[17]

Interactivity, hyperlinking, searchability, multimedia—all these qualities of the Net bring attractive benefits. Along with the unprecedented volume of information available online, they're the main reasons that most of us are drawn to using the Net so much. We like to be able to switch between reading and listening and watching without having to get up and turn on another appliance or dig through a pile of magazines or disks. We like to be able to find and be transported instantly to relevant data—without having to sort through lots of extraneous stuff. We like to be in touch with friends, family members, and colleagues. We like to feel connected—and we hate to feel disconnected. The Internet doesn't change our intellectual habits against our will. But change them it does.

Our use of the Net will only grow, and its impact on us will only strengthen, as it becomes ever more present in our lives. Like the clock and the book before it, the computer continues to get smaller and cheaper as technology advances. Inexpensive laptops gave us the ability to take the Internet with us when we left our office or our home. But the laptop was itself a cumbersome device, and connecting one to the Internet was not always easy. The introduction of the tiny netbook and the even tinier smartphone solves those problems. Powerful pocket-sized computers like the Apple iPhone, the Motorola Droid, and the Google Nexus One come bundled with Internet access. Along with the incorporation of Internet services into everything from car dashboards to televisions to the cabins of airplanes, these small devices promise to more deeply integrate the Web into our everyday activities, making our universal medium all the more universal.

As the Net expands, other media contract. By changing the economics of production and distribution, the Net has cut into the profitability of many news, information, and entertainment businesses, particularly those that have traditionally sold physical products. Sales of music CDs have fallen steadily over the last decade, dropping twenty percent in 2008 alone.[18] Sales of movie DVDs, a major recent source of profits for Hollywood studios, are also now in decline, falling six percent during 2008 and then plunging another fourteen percent during the first half of 2009.[19] Unit sales of greeting cards and postcards are dropping.[20] The volume of mail sent through the U.S. Postal Service declined at its fastest pace ever during 2009.[21] Universities are discontinuing the printed editions of scholarly monographs and journals and moving to strictly electronic distribution.[22] Public schools are pushing students to use online reference materials in place of what California Governor Arnold Schwarzenegger refers to as "antiquated, heavy, expensive textbooks."[23] Everywhere you look, you see signs of the Net's growing hegemony over the packaging and flow of information.

Nowhere have the effects been so unsettling as in the newspaper industry, which faces particularly severe financial challenges as readers and advertisers embrace the Net as their medium of choice. The decline in Americans' newspaper reading began decades ago, when radio and TV began consuming more of peoples' leisure time, but the Internet has accelerated the trend. Between 2008 and 2009, newspaper circulation dropped more than seven percent, while visits to newspaper Web sites grew by more than ten percent.[24] One of America's oldest dailies, *the Christian Science Monitor*, announced in early 2009 that after a hundred years it was stopping its presses. The Web would become its main channel for distributing news. The move, said the paper's publisher, Jonathan Wells, was a harbinger of what lay in store for other newspapers. "Changes in the industry—changes in the concept of news and the economics underlying the industry—hit the *Monitor* first," he explained.[25]

He was soon proved correct. Within months, Colorado's oldest newspaper, *the Rocky Mountain News*, had gone out of business; *the Seattle Post-Intelligencer* had abandoned its print edition and fired most of its staff; *the Washington Post* had shut down all its U.S. bureaus and let more than a hundred journalists go; and the owners of more than thirty other U.S. newspapers, including the *Los Angeles Times, Chicago Tribune,*

Philadelphia Inquirer, and *Minneapolis Star Tribune*, had filed for bankruptcy. Tim Brooks, the managing director of Guardian News and Media, which publishes *The Guardian* and *The Independent* in Britain, announced that all his company's future investments would go into multimedia digital products, mainly delivered through its Web sites. "The days when you can trade in just words are gone," he told an industry conference.[26]

[1] Forrester Research, "Consumers' Behavior Online: A 2007 Deep Dive," April 18, 2008, www.forrester.com/Research/Document/0,72111,45266,00.html.

[2] Forrester Research, "Consumer Behavior Online: A 2009 Deep Dive: July 27, 2009, www.forrester.com/Research/Document/0,7211,54327,00.html.

[3] Nielsen Company, "Time Spent Online among Kids Increases 63 Percent in the Last Five Years, According to Nielsen," media alert, July 6, 2009, www.nielsen-online.com/pr/pr_090706.pdf.

[4] Forrester Research, "A Deep Dive into European Consumers' Online Behavior, 2009," August 13, 2009, www.forrester.com/Research/Document/0,7211,54524,00.html.

[5] TNS Global, "Digital World, Digital Life," December 2008, www.tnsglobal.com/_assets/files/TNS_Market_Research_Digital_World_Digital_Life.pdf.

[6] Nielsen Company, "Texting Now More Popular than Calling," news release, September 22, 2008, www.nielsenmobile.com/html/press%20releases/TextsVersusCalls.html; Eric Zeman, "U.S. Teens Sent 2,272 Text Messages per Month in 4Q08," Over the Air Blog (Information Week), May 26, 2009, www.informationweek.com/blog/main/archives/2009/05/us_ teens_sent_2.html.

[7] Steven Cherry, "thx 4 the revnu," IEEE Spectrum, October 2008.

[8] Sara Rimer, "Play with Your Food, Just Don't Textl" New York Times, May 26, 2009.

[9] Nielsen Company, "A2/M2 Three Screen Report: 1st Quarter 2009," May 20, 2009, http://blog.nielsen.com/nielsenwire/wp-content/uploads/2009/05/nielsen_threescreenreport_Q109.pdf.

[10] Forrester Research, "How European Teens Consume Media," December 4, 2009, www.forrester.com/rb/Research/how_european_teens_consume _media/q/id/53763/t/2.

[11] Heidi Dawley, "Time-wise, Internet Is Now TV's Equal," Media Life, February 1, 2006.

[12] Council for Research Excellence, "The Video Consumer Mapping Study," March 26, 2009, www.researchexcellence.com/vcm_overview.pdf.

[13] Bureau of Labor Statistics, "American Time Use Survey," 2004-2008, www .bls.gov/tus/.

[14] Noreen O'Leary, "Welcome to My World," Adweek, November 17, 2008.

[15] Marshall McLuhan, Understanding Media: The Extensions of Man, critical ed., ed. W. Terrence Gordon (Corte Madera, CA: Gingko, 2003), 237.

[16] Anne Mangen, "Hypertext Fiction Reading: Haptics and Immersion," Journal of Research in Reading, 31, no. 4 (2008): 404-19

[17] Cory Doctorow, "Writing in the Age of Distraction," Locus, January 2009.

[18] Ben Sisario, "Music Sales Fell in 2008, but Climbed on the Web," New York Times, December 31, 2008.

[19] Ronald Grover, "Hollywood Is Worried as DVD Sales Slow," BusinessWeek, February 19, 2009; Richard Corliss, "Why Netflix Stinks," Time, August 10, 2009.

[20] Chrystal Szeto, "U.S. Greeting Cards and Postcards," Pitney Bowes Background Paper No. 20, November 21, 2005, www.postinsight.com/files/ Nov21_GreetingCards_Final.pdf.

[21] Brigid Schulte, "So Long, Snail Shells," Washington Post, July 25, 2009.

[22] Scott Jaschik, "Farewell to the Printed Monograph," Inside Higher Ed, March 23, 2009, www.insidehighered.com/news/2009/03/23/Michigan.

[23] Arnold Schwarzenegger, "Digital Textbooks Can Save Money, Improve Learning," Mercury News, June 7, 2009.

[24] Tim Arango, "Fall in Newspaper Sales Accelerates to Pass 7%," New York Times, April 27, 2009.

[25] David Cook, "Monitor Shifts from Print to Web-Based Strategy," Christian Science Monitor, October 28, 2008.

[26] Tom Hall, "'We Will Never Launch Another Paper,'" PrintWeek, February 20, 2009, www.printweek.com/news/881913/We-will-launch-paper.

The "Impact of the Net" Discussion Questions

1. **What are some important innovations that result from the Internet being bidirectional?**

2. **How has the Net and the web impacted the use of printed material?**

3. **What are some things the internet—and internet-connected devices—have largely replaced or made obsolete?**

4. **How have hyperlinks changed the way we learn?**

5. **What are the main features that cause us to be so dependent—addicted even—to the internet?**

"AMUSING OURSELVES TO DEATH" VIDEO

John Stonestreet explains why, when it comes to entertainment, it no longer works to draw a line and say, "Everything on this side is good and everything on that side is bad." We have to "exegete entertainment," which means understanding how entertainment

- powerfully shapes cultures worldwide;
- is loaded with ideas; and
- changes how we experience the world.

Stonestreet warns about five ways entertainment can negatively change us:

- Ideas and images come at us so fast we don't pause to think.
- We are fooled into caring about meaningless things and distracted from caring about important things.
- Celebrity-ism: Psalm 135:15–18 warns that we become what we worship.
- Escapism: We use devices to avoid relationships.
- Addiction: The cure is to read good books and develop good habits of conversation.

To access this video, go to www.summitu.com/utc and enter the passcode found in the back of your manual.

"Amusing Ourselves to Death" Video Outline

When it comes to entertainment, it no longer works to draw a line and say, "Everything on this side is good and everything on that side is bad." We have to "exegete entertainment." This mean recognizing three truths about entertainment:

1.____________________ powerfully shapes cultures worldwide:

We schedule our lives around entertainment choices. Even when it's quiet we focus on our e-devices.

The value of art is reduced to personal taste. Entertainment dumbs us down. It's all about what we like, not what has value.

Music has more shaping influence than laws or politics.

2. Entertainment is loaded with ____________________:

Entertainment doesn't argue ideas; it assumes them. It appeals to the imagination, not reasoned argument. This is certainly true with issues like the traditional family. A succession of popular TV shows changed the American idea of family:

- *The Cosby Show*: family is the ____________________.
- *Will & Grace*: family can be nontraditional (i.e., gay).
- *Friends*: family is insignificant.
- *Seinfeld*: family is the ____________________.
- *Modern Family*: family is anything you want it to be.

Never watch or listen to anything without asking yourself: What's being said? What are the ideas behind the words and actions?

3. Entertainment changes how we experience the world:

Ideas and images come at us so fast; we don't pause to think, which results in our ____________________ leading our thinking.

We are fooled into caring about meaningless things and distracted from caring about important things.

Celebrity-ism: Psalm 135:15–18 warns that we become what we ______________. A culture that worships "celebrity" has chosen style over substance.

Escapism: Entertainment has grown from public events to include the personal and private. We use devices to avoid ____________________.

Addiction: Addiction to entertainment can be overcome by facing and admitting your addiction, reading good books, and developing good habits of conversation.

"Amusing Ourselves to Death" Discussion Questions

1. **When it comes to entertainment, why does it no longer works to draw a line and say, "Everything on this side is good and everything on that side is bad"?**

2. **What are some signs that entertainment has taken over our culture?**

3. **How has entertainment changed our idea of the traditional family?**

4. **What are some ways to deal with the dangers posed by modern entertainment?**

5. **What are the steps to overcoming an entertainment addiction?**

Chapter 7 Key Points

Key Questions:

1. What effect do entertainment and amusement have on us as individuals and as a society?
2. How does the Christian worldview offer a unique perspective on the entertainment culture?
3. What are Christians able to do as image bearers in order to have a positive effect on the entertainment culture?

Key Passages:

1. Galatians 5:16–18*

Key Works:

1. 1984 by George Orwell*
2. *Amusing Ourselves to Death* by Neil Postman
3. *Brave New World* by Aldous Huxley*

Key Terms:

1. Age of Enlightenment*
2. Amusement
3. Art
4. Cultural Anorexics
5. Cultural Gluttons
6. Discernment
7. Entertainment
8. Equilibrium-Tension-Resolution
9. Flow
10. Formalism
11. Gratitude
12. Kinnor
13. Lower-Story Worldview
14. Molech
15. Motivated Abilities
16. Myelination
17. Romanticism
18. Realism
19. Upper-Story Worldview

**Short answer or essay question on the exam*

CHAPTER 7 ASSIGNMENT

Answer the following questions with at least one paragraph.

1. **Explain the metaphor of truth as a building divided into an upper floor and a lower floor.**

2. **How can an obsession with amusement lead to warped or enslaved emotions and desires?**

3. **Describe a Postmodern approach to art and entertainment.**

4. **What is the role of a community or companions for a Christian's engagement with a culture of amusement?**

Other potential questions:

- Which worldview's understanding of truth and beauty is most prominent in the art and entertainment that you see most often?
- Do you see technology and entertainment as having increased restlessness in modern culture or in your own life? If so, how and what can you do to address either?

UNIT 8

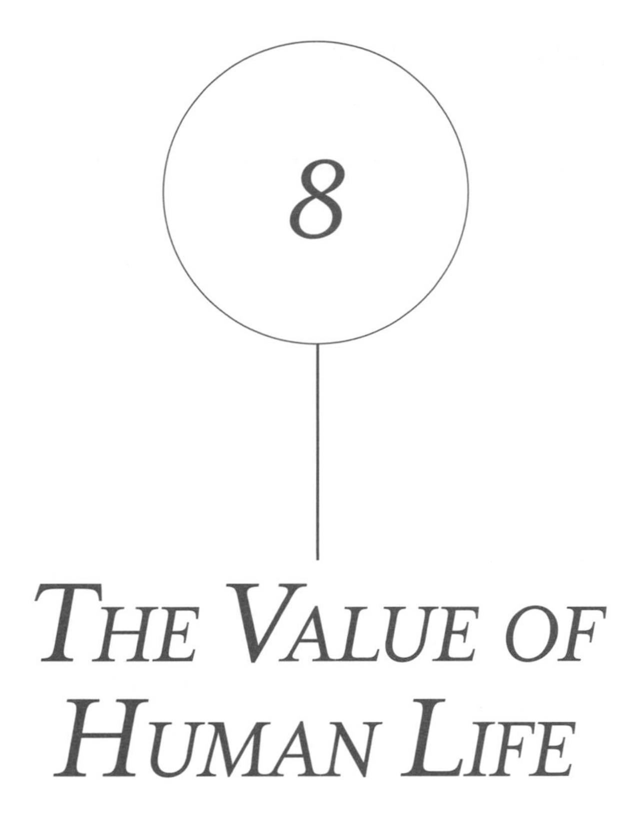

The Value of Human Life

Chapter 8 Learning Objectives

Students will be able to:

1. discuss why people do not value life and desire to profit from ending the life of an unborn human being. [8.1]
2. analyze how the value of life has been treated in America and why it is a worldview issue drawing on philosophy, science, and theology. [8.2]
3. inspect the root of the problem of devaluing human life and the current ways life is devalued through abortion, euthanasia, and other biotechnologies. [8.3]
4. explain three implications of how the *imago Dei*, or the image of God, affects the value of human life. [8.4]
5. describe ways to defend a pro-life stance against common objections from Secularist arguments and ways to respond to fallacious attacks. [8.5]
6. conclude that human life is special. [8.6]

CHAPTER 8 DISCUSSION QUESTIONS

1. What impact did the Roe v. Wade decision have on abortion in the U.S.? [8.1]

2. What is the *Humanist Manifesto* and how has it affected American society? [8.2]

3. What influence did Secular Humanists have on the sexual revolution? [8.2]

4. What was the most serious consequence of the sexual revolution? [8.2]

5. How has ultrasound technology impacted elective abortions? [8.3]

6. If there is no God or absolute moral laws, upon what is human value based? [8.3]

7. What do the performance and utilitarian views of human value have in common? [8.3]

8. How has technology further diminished the value of human life? [8.4]

9. What's wrong with harvesting stem cells from unwanted embryos to help save lives? [8.4]

10. If your mother had Parkinson's disease, would you want her treated with stem cells from human embryos? What if those embryos were going to be disposed of anyway? [8.4]

11. What is euthanasia? [8.5]

12. What is the Christian view of euthanasia? [8.5]

13. How is the *imago Dei* the foundation for understanding when human life begins? [8.6]

14. How is the *imago Dei* the foundation for human dignity? [8.6]

15. What arguments would you use to try to convince an atheist that he or she bears God's image? [8.7]

16. How can Christians answer the argument, "Abortion should be allowed in order to protect women from bad consequences"? [8.7]

17. **How can Christians answer the argument, "If you can't trust me with a choice, how can you trust me with a child"?** [8.7]

18. **How can Christians answer the argument, "Making abortion illegal will force women into back-alley abortions and lead to their deaths"?** [8.7]

19. **How can Christians answer the argument, "It's my body and my choice"?** [8.7]

20. **How can Christians answer the argument, "Abortion should be allowed in the case of rape"?** [8.7]

21. How can Christians awaken the conscience of America? [8.7]

22. How can Christians answer fallacious attacks such as, "You're biased" or "It's complicated"? [8.7]

23. How should Christians respond to the "culture of death" all around us? [8.8]

“The Case for the Pro-Life Position” Part 1

Many Christians feel underprepared to handle the tough, unavoidable issue of abortion. In the first of this two-part lecture, Scott Klusendorf endeavors to prepare Christians for the defense of unborn children. Using simple techniques and nonthreatening questions, He shows how to keep the main question the main question: what are the unborn? He also defeats several common pro-choice arguments, using a powerful technique aptly labeled “trot out the toddler.”

To access this video, go to www.summitu.com/utc and enter the passcode found in the back of your manual.

"The Case for the Pro-Life Position" Part 1 Video Outline

The central question in the abortion debate is: **What is the ________________ ?**

Pro-choice proponents insist on the following:

- Abortion is a fundamental liberty that the state shouldn't infringe upon.
- Pro-lifers are free to believe what they want but not free to impose their beliefs on others.
- For equality across society, the government should fund ________________ programs, including abortion.
- We should trust women to make the best personal decisions about their bodies.
- We don't know when life begins so we can't know if the unborn are human.

Because people disagree on whether the unborn are human doesn't mean the question has no answer. The absence of consensus doesn't mean the absence of ________________ . In either case, the unborn should be given the benefit of the doubt.

"Trot out the toddler" tactic. Substitute "toddler" for "unborn" and see what it does to the argument.

- A mother has the constitutional right to terminate her "toddler."
- Parents should be able to get rid of an unwanted "toddler" without government interference.
- A woman's choice to surgically kill her "toddler" is her private business.
- Women who find their "toddlers" inconvenient or unaffordable are free to dispose of them.

What people are assuming about the toddler they aren't assuming about the embryo—that it's a human being.

________________ shows that from the earliest stages of development we are unique, distinct, and whole human beings. We are not constructed piece by piece but developed from within.

Pro-choice arguments against the pro-life position:

- The majority of pregnancies are spontaneously aborted, meaning it's natural. But how does it follow that the embryos aren't human or that we can kill them?
- Poor countries have high infant mortality rates. But does it follow that these children aren't human or aren't valuable?

People don't want to hear the ________________ because they have a vested interest in abortion, either personal, political, or financial.

"The Case for the Pro-Life Position"
Part 1 Discussion Questions

1. **What are the key questions in the debate over abortion?**

2. **How would you answer these pro-choice assertions?**

3. **What is the 'trot out the toddler" tactic?**

4. What does the science of embryology have to say about unborn babies?

5. Do you think it's appropriate to show the graphic violence of abortion in making the case for pro-life?

"The Case for the Pro-Life Position" Part 2

In the second of this two-part lecture, Scott Klusendorf distinguishes between what science and philosophy have to say about the unborn. He examines four differences between the unborn and adults (size, level of development, environment, and degree of dependence) and explains why these are not grounds for killing unborn children.

Klusendorf gives examples of five faulty arguments used by pro-choice proponents and shows how they really don't address the main issue—whether those who are unborn are human—but try to change the subject. He concludes by presenting a compelling pro-life argument in less than a minute.

To access this video, go to www.summitu.com/utc and enter the passcode found in the back of your manual.

"The Case for the Pro-Life Position" Part 2 Video Outline

What do science and philosophy have to say about the unborn?

____________________: From the earliest stage of development, unborn babies are distinct, living, and whole human beings.

__________________: There is no radical or relevant difference between unborn children and adults that justifies killing at an earlier age.

Science tells us what those who are unborn are—human. Philosophy tells us how to treat them—as having intrinsic value.

Four differences between the unborn and adults: SLED

- ________________
- Level of development
- ________________
- Degree of dependence

The differences in these areas are not good reasons to say an embryo can be killed but not an adult.

Five faulty ways pro-choice proponents argue

1. Assume rather than argue (e.g., "When did you stop beating your brother?")
2. Assert rather than argue (e.g., "Women have the right to choose.")
3. ________________ the person rather than refute the argument (such as "If you are a man, you have no say.")
4. Advance a radical theory of bodily rights (e.g., "A mother's autonomy trumps the unborn child's right to life.")
5. Hide behind the ________________ (e.g., "Rape victims shouldn't be forced to have an unwanted child.")

These objections don't address the issue—whether those who are unborn are human beings—but try to change the subject.

Pro-life argument in a nutshell: From the earliest stage, unborn children are distinct, living, and whole human beings as established by the science of embryology. Philosophy teaches that there is no radical or relevant difference between unborn children and adults. Differences of size, level of development, environment, or dependence are not good reasons to say unborn children can be killed but not adults.

"The Case for the Pro-Life Position" Part 2

Discussion Questions

1. **Can you explain the roles science and philosophy play in unborn human beings?**

2. **What are some differences between unborn babies and adults and why don't the differences justify abortion?**

3. **What are some examples of faulty arguments used by pro-choice proponents?**

4. **How would you answer the argument that those who are unborn have no right to life until they have self-awareness and a desire to be alive?**

5. **Can you give the pro-life argument in less than a minute?**

Chapter 8 Key Points

Key Questions:

1. How is life devalued in today's culture?
2. What are the philosophical foundations of the culture of death?
3. How can Christians defend the sanctity of life?
4. What are the consequences of a culture that accepts abortion, embryonic stem-cell research, and euthanasia?

Key Verses:

1. James 1:27

Key Works:

1. *Humanist Manifesto*

Key Persons:

1. Margaret Sanger
2. John Stuart Mill
3. Peter Singer
4. Judith Jarvis Thomson

Key Events:

1. *Roe v. Wade*

Key Terms:

1. Abortion
2. Active Euthanasia
3. Contraception
4. Embryo
5. Embryonic Stem Cell
6. Endowment View of Human Life
7. Fetus
8. Hippocratic Oath*
9. Infanticide
10. Late-Term Abortion
11. Partial-Birth Abortion
12. Passive Euthanasia
13. Performance View of Human Life
14. Physician Assisted Suicide
15. SLED*
16. Stem Cell
17. Utilitarian View of Human Life

Key Organizations:

1. Live Action
2. Planned Parenthood
3. Save the Storks

**Short answer or essay question on the exam*

Chapter 8 Assignment

Answer the following questions with at least one paragraph.

1. **Describe the utilitarian and performance views of human value. What do they have in common?**

2. **How might the three views of human value (utilitarian, performance, and intrinsic) approach the issue of embryonic stem-cell research? What reasons would each view have for justifying or condemning it?**

3. **Why is the Christian worldview essential for a healthy understanding of the dignity of human life and why should the treatment of embryos and unborn children be especially relevant to Christians?**

4. **What is the SLED argument and how does it assert the sanctity of unborn humans?**

Other potential questions:

- Is the attempt to end particularly gruesome kinds of abortion (such as partial-birth abortions) a sign that people are becoming more pro-life, or that abortion is actually becoming more palatable?
- Does fighting to end a particular kind of abortion ultimately weaken or strengthen the legality of abortion as a whole?
- Francis Shaeffer said, "Every abortion clinic should have a sign in front of it saying, "Open by the permission of the church." In what ways is the church complicit in abortion? What does your church do to end abortion? What will you do?

UNIT 9

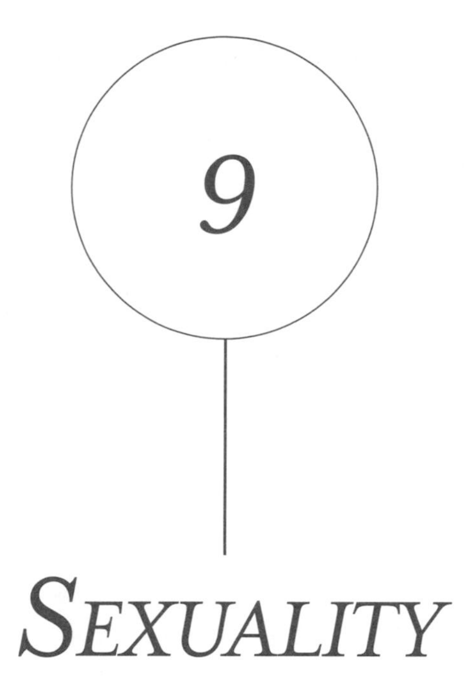

SEXUALITY

CHAPTER 9 LEARNING OBJECTIVES

Students will be able to:

1. describe why sexual orientation is the central aspect of identity and why there is a cost to sexual freedom. [9.1]

2. identify where the revolt against the biblical view of sexuality came from and speculate where it is headed. [9.2]

3. identify how God's view of sexuality is addressed in the Old and New Testaments and describe why sexual brokenness destroys the flourishing of humans and redefines gender relationships. [9.3]

4. explain several alternatives to counteract common approaches to sexual brokenness. [9.4]

5. describe how sexuality can be viewed as a battle and why Christians should be running toward good and not running away from evil. [9.5]

Chapter 9 Discussion Questions

1. **How important is sexual identity in American culture?** [9.1]

2. **Does God hate sex and demand its suppression?** [9.1]

3. **What are the roots of the sexual revolution?** [9.2]

4. **What are the consequences of the sexual revolution?** [9.2]

5. **How has the sexual revolution legitimized same-sex attraction? [9.2]**

6. **What are the consequences of the rise in pornography fueled by the sexual revolution? [9.2]**

7. **How has the sexual revolution led to sexual confusion? [9.2]**

8. **How has the sexual revolution led to desperation and despair? [9.2]**

9. Is the idea of being chaste until marriage even viable in today's world? [9.2]

10. What impact has the church had on the sexual revolution? [9.2]

11. What does the Old Testament teach about sexuality? [9.3]

12. What does the New Testament teach about sexuality? [9.3]

13. How has the sexual revolution affected health and wellness? [9.3]

14. How has the sexual revolution redefined gender relationships? [9.3]

15. Why must the Christian response to the sexual revolution include elevating intimacy? [9.4]

16. Why must the Christian response to the sexual revolution include realizing our true identity? [9.4]

17. Why must the Christian response to the sexual revolution include pursuing purity? [9.4]

18. Why must the Christian response to the sexual revolution include repentance and reconciliation? [9.4]

19. Why must the Christian response to the sexual revolution include living chastely? [9.4]

20. Why must the Christian response to the sexual revolution include selfless grace? [9.4]

21. Why must the Christian response to the sexual revolution include true friendship? [9.4]

22. Do you have any friends in the LBGT community? If so, is the friendship different from your other friendships? [9.4]

"The Hermeneutics of Sexuality" Video

Moody Bible Institute professor Christopher Yuan contrasts two different views of homosexuality: The traditional view and the revisionist view. The traditional view says God has reserved sexuality for a man and woman in the context of marriage. Anything outside of that is unacceptable to God. The revisionist view contends that biblical passages condemn "something," but it's not monogamous gay relationships.

Using hermeneutics—the science and art of biblical interpretation—Yuan examines the traditional and revisionist views of key Old and New Testaments texts: Genesis 19, Leviticus 18 and 20, Romans 1, 1 Corinthians 6 and 1 Timothy 1. He also discusses the relationship between David and Jonathan and deals with Jesus's silence on the subject.

To access this video, go to www.summitu.com/utc and enter the passcode found in the back of your manual.

“The Hermeneutics of Sexuality” Video Outline

______________________ : God has reserved sexuality for a man and woman in the context of marriage. Anything outside of that is unacceptable to God.

__________________ : Biblical passages condemn “something,” but it’s not monogamous gay relationships.

__________________ : The science and art of biblical interpretation. Hermeneutics applied to key texts:

Genesis 19

- Revisionist view: The sins were gang rape and inhospitality (Ezekiel 16:48).
- Traditional view: The sins were gang rape, inhospitality, and homosexuality.

Leviticus 18:22; 20:13

- Revisionist view: *To'evah*, “abomination,” refers to uncleanness, not immorality.
- Traditional view: *To'evah* refers to immortality. The action is an abomination, not the people.

David and Jonathan

- Revisionist view: David and Jonathan were lovers.
- Traditional view: Love doesn’t have to be sexual. David and Jonathan were one spirit, not one __________________ .

Slavery

- Revisionist view: The Bible gets it __________________ sometimes. It condones slavery and is wrong; it condemns homosexuality and is wrong.
- Traditional view: The Bible never condones modern slavery, e.g., slavery of one race of people for a lifetime.

Jesus’s testimony

- Revisionist view: Jesus was __________________ about homosexuality; it wasn’t an important issue to him.
- Traditional view: Jesus was silent about a lot of things, such as bestiality and incest, because there was universal consensus.

Romans 1:26–27

- Revisionist view: "Unnatural" means acting opposite to one's natural orientation.
- Traditional view: "Unnatural" means not normal or right. Other writers use the word to refer to homosexuality.

1 Corinthians 6:9–10; 1 Timothy 1:9–10

- Revisionist view: These passages deal with sexual and economic exploitation, for instance, pedophilia.
- Traditional view: These passages affirm what the Old Testament teaches, that homosexuality is a ________________ .

"And that is what some of you were. But you were washed, you were sanctified, you were justified in the name of the Lord Jesus Christ and by the Spirit of our God" (1 Corinthians 6:11).

"THE HERMENEUTICS OF SEXUALITY" DISCUSSION QUESTIONS

1. **What is hermeneutics?**

2. **What are some key differences between the traditional and revisionist views of homosexuality?**

3. **Why did God destroy Sodom?**

4. **What is the revisionist view of Leviticus 18:22 and 20:13 and the traditional rebuttal?**

5. **How would you answer the claim that David and Jonathan had a homosexual relationship?**

"The Worldview behind Porn" Video

Author and speaker Sean McDowell takes a hard look at the worldview behind pornography, examining in depth its prevalence in society, its damage to God's design, and its underlying script. He exposes the three biggest myths about porn: (1) It doesn't affect me; (2) I will quit later; (3) I'm not hurting anybody.

McDowell shows how pornography affects the brain, especially in young adults. In conclusion, he offers hope for those entangled in the seemingly inescapable web of pornographic addiction.

To access this video, go to www.summitu.com/utc and enter the passcode found in the back of your manual.

"The Worldview behind Porn" Video Outline

__________________, Greek for "writing about prostitutes," is a 100 billion-dollars-a-year business. Most men and 30 percent of women watch porn.

Three biggest myths about porn

1. **Porn doesn't __________________ me.**

   Porn affects how men look at women. It portrays women as objects to be used for pleasure. It promotes voyeurism instead of involvement in healthy relationships.

   The script of porn:

   - Sex is best outside a loving, committed relationship.
   - All women want sex from men.
   - When women say "no" they really mean "yes."

2. **I will __________________ porn later.**

   If we can't control our sexual urges before marriage, we won't be able to control them after. Marriage doesn't change our self-discipline.

   Unrealistic porn images impact the brain's pleasure mechanism and can keep us from bonding to our spouses the way we should.

   Porn impacts neurochemicals such as dopamine, which short-circuit the pleasure process, and oxytocin, the bonding hormone, which creates in a woman the desire to bond with a man.

3. **I'm not __________________ anybody.**

   Porn hurts those who use it and others, even if they don't know it. Science has shown that porn stimulates dominant behavior in men and creates poor self-image in women.

How to get free from porn

Porn addiction is a __________________ battle. Satan uses it to create shame, which leads to discouragement and questioning God's power.

Porn is the hardest addiction to break; God alone can set a person free. It requires:

- True desire for God's healing.
- __________________ one is an addict.
- Depending on God's grace poured through other people.

▶ "The Worldview behind Porn" Discussion Questions

1. **How would you debunk the myth "Porn doesn't affect me"?**

2. **How would you debunk the myth "I will quit porn later"?**

3. **How would you debunk the myth "Watching porn doesn't hurt anybody"?**

4. **How does porn affect the brain?**

5. **What are the steps to getting free from porn?**

Chapter 9 Key Points

Key Questions:

1. What are the philosophical and historical roots of the sexual revolution?
2. What are the consequences of the sexual revolution?
3. How should Christians respond to the sexual revolution and the brokenness it has caused?

Key Verses:

1. Genesis 1:27
2. Leviticus 18:6–23
3. Matthew 19:4–6
4. 1 Corinthians 6:13–18*
5. Hebrews 13:4

Key Persons:

1. Sigmund Freud
2. Alfred Kinsey
3. Matthew Vines
4. Elisabeth Elliot
5. Andy Stanley

Key Works:

1. *Sexual Behavior in the Human Female* by Alfred Kinsey
2. *Sexual Behavior in the Human Male* by Alfred Kinsey
3. *Three Essays on the Theory of Sexuality* by Sigmund Freud

Key Terms:

1. Accountability
2. Age of Enlightenment
3. Cohabitation
4. Chastity
5. Hypocrisy
6. Pedophilia
7. Personal Autonomy
8. Political Correctness
9. *Porneia*
10. Pornography
11. Revolution
12. Repentance
13. Sexual Brokenness*
14. Sexual Purity
15. Sexual Revolution
16. "tWorld," "iWorld," and "rWorld"*

Key Events:

1. *Obergefell v. Hodges*

**Short answer or essay question on the exam*

Chapter 9 Assignment

Answer the following questions with at least one paragraph.

1. **What are the physical or biological consequences of viewing or reading pornographic material?**

2. **In what ways has the church either contributed to the sexual revolution or hampered its own ability to respond to it?**

3. **If sexual morality is so important to the Christian worldview, why did Jesus never condemn homosexuality?**

4. **From the Christian worldview, what is the problem with perceiving people's identities in terms of their sexual behavior, whether heterosexual, homosexual, or otherwise?**

Other potential questions:

- As popular ideas about sexual morality continue to change, biblical principles will become increasingly unpopular. How do you think the church ought to uphold unpopular principles? Do you think this will become more difficult in coming years?
- Bruce Marshall's *Father Smith* describes sex as "a substitute for religion." Used in a different context, do you see any parallels between the secular culture's veneration of sexual "liberty" and traditional religious practices?

UNIT 10

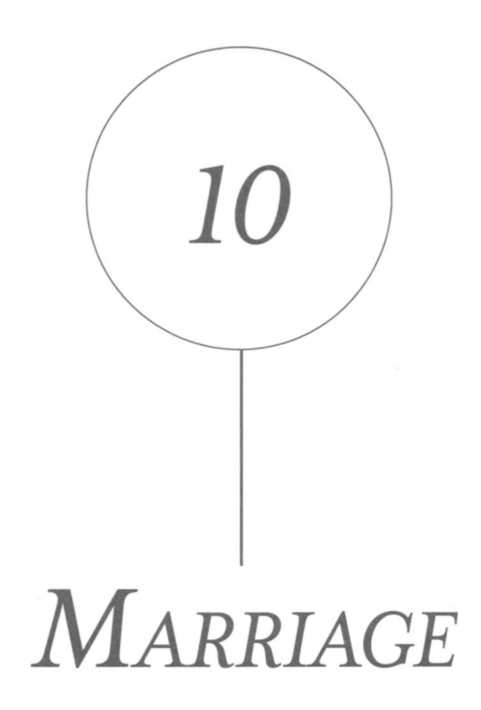

Marriage

Chapter 10 Learning Objectives

Students will be able to:

1. express why marriage is good. [10.1]
2. define marriage and survey what other worldviews say about marriage. [10.2]
3. identify four truths that the Bible teaches about marriage. [10.3]
4. explain several actions Christians could take to make the case for God's view of marriage and a path toward a better society. [10.4]
5. conclude that the family was God's idea and it is a good idea. [10.5]

Chapter 10 Discussion Questions

1. **What is the relationship between marriage and society? [10.1]**

2. **Why is traditional marriage good? [10.1]**

3. **How has the decline in traditional marriage affected children? [10.2]**

4. **What has been the historical definition of traditional marriage? [10.2]**

5. **How is this definition of marriage being changed in the U.S. today? [10.2]**

6. **What does Secularism say about marriage? [10.2]**

7. **What does Marxism say about marriage? [10.2]**

8. **What does Postmodernism say about marriage? [10.2]**

9. What does New Spirituality say about marriage? [10.2]

10. What does Islam say about marriage? [10.2]

11. What does Genesis teach about marriage? [10.3]

12. How did the sin in the garden of Eden affect marriage? [10.4]

13. In what ways does Satan wage war on traditional marriages and families? [10.4]

14. What aspects of marriage make it a social good? [10.4]

15. How is traditional marriage in the state's interest? [10.4]

16. How does marriage enable limited government? [10.4]

17. Are the arguments for traditional marriage really just arguments against same-sex marriage? [10.4]

18. What is the harm in expanding the meaning and purpose of marriage? [10.4]

19. Marriage isn't the only or necessarily ideal state for adults. What does it mean to "redeem singleness"? [10.4]

20. One of the main purposes for marriage is having and raising responsible children for the good of society. If you plan to marry, do you plan to have children? [10.4]

21. Why is reconciliation important for families? [10.4]

▶ "SAME-SEX MARRIAGE" VIDEO

John Stonestreet defines traditional marriage and gives three reasons why it is good for society: (1) sex makes babies; (2) society needs babies; and (3) babies do better with a mom and a dad. This traditional view of marriage is being challenged today by a revisionist view of marriage.

Stonestreet explains where this idea started, explores why it's not healthy for society, and addresses the dilemma faced by Christians who feel the tension between holding to what the church has always taught about marriage and obeying the command to love your neighbor.

To access this video, go to www.summitu.com/utc and enter the passcode found in the back of your manual.

▶ "Same-Sex Marriage" Video Outline

What is marriage?

____________________ **or conjugal view:** One man, one woman in a monogamous relationship. Marriage, sex, and babies always go together. Only in the twentieth century has there been an attempt to separate them.

The traditional view is best for society for three reasons:

1. Sex makes babies.
2. Society needs babies.
3. Babies do better with a mom and dad.

Our culture has replaced the traditional view with the ________________, that marriage is no longer about oneness and babies; it's about strong feelings.

But ____________________ relationships shouldn't be considered marriages because they can't produce babies. Marriage laws already discriminate against certain unions:

- Those who are too young
- Those who are currently married
- Incestuous relationships

The revisionist view holds that there are no grounds to limit marriage from *any* loving couple (or more than two people). This view doesn't expand marriage; it redefines it.

How should Christians respond to same-sex marriage?

The cultural battle has already been lost. What will Christians do about it? How will we stand for truth in a time when there's a price to pay, e.g., social stigma, loss of job, or criminal charges?

1. Maintain a balance between standing up for the truth and loving our neighbor.
2. Treat all people as being made in the image of God.
3. Remember that our sexual preference isn't our __________________.
4. All Christians have to be chaste—properly sexual. God can give us the strength and maturity to deal with our drives.
5. ________________ isn't for everyone; some people remain single. Our highest purpose isn't to be married; it's to glorify God.

"SAME-SEX MARRIAGE" DISCUSSION QUESTIONS

1. **What is the traditional or conjugal view of marriage?**

2. **What is the revisionist view of marriage?**

3. **How would you counter the revisionist view and its support of same-sex marriage without using the Bible?**

4. **How should Christians respond to same-sex marriage?**

5. **Do you have any gay friends with whom you have talked about these issues? Without breaking a confidence, can you share how they view this issue?**

"Why Marriage Matters" Video

John Stonestreet begins with three reasons why the traditional marriage-family unit of man, woman, and children has always existed in all societies throughout history: 1) Sex makes babies; 2) Society needs babies; and 3) Children do best with a mom and dad. He outlines what research has shown about how traditional marriage enriches culture and benefits society in various ways.

Stonestreet also shows how marriage benefits individuals. When it comes to children, they do better if their parents are married, even if their parents aren't happy. When it comes to adults, married people live longer, have better sex, are financially better off, and have more physical security than singles or cohabitating couples.

To access this video, go to www.summitu.com/utc and enter the passcode found in the back of your manual.

 "Why Marriage Matters" Video Outline

Something like traditional marriage (man, woman, children) has always existed in all societies throughout history. This natural relationship has only been challenged in the last few decades.

Three reasons for traditional marriage

1. Sex makes babies.
2. Society needs babies.
3. Children do best with a mom and dad.

What research shows about the natural, traditional family

1. Marriage ________________ society.

   British anthropologist Joseph Unwin found:

   - Cultures with a strong sexual ethic tied to marriage were more productive and prosperous.
   - Cultures without a strong sexual ethic lacked creative cultural energy.
   - Cultures which began with but lost strong sexual ethics for three generations inevitably experienced cultural demise.
   - There are no exceptions to these findings. "It can be demonstrated from history that no society has ever survived after its family life deteriorated" (David Popenoe).

   Social benefits of marriage:

   - Best situation for ________________
   - Produces wealth
   - Encourages pro-social behavior (protects women and children)
   - Generates social capital, e.g., in the networks of relationships enabling a society to function effectively

2. Marriage benefits ________________.

   For children:

   - Myth repeated as though it was true: "Kids will do better if their parents are happy than if their parents are married." This is not true by any measure. Kids do better if their parents are married, even if their parents aren't happy.
   - Kids from no-fault divorce homes have similar trauma to the kids who went through the Holocaust.

For adults:

- ____________________ benefits: married people live longer.
- Sexual satisfaction: married people have better sex than singles or cohabitating couples.
- Financial benefits: retired married people are generally better off than retired singles.
- ____________________ security: more domestic violence occurs in households with cohabiting couples than with traditionally married couples.

"Why Marriage Matters" Discussion Questions

1. **What are the three main reasons why traditional marriage has been the norm in all societies throughout history?**

2. **Historically speaking, what's the relationship between a society's view of marriage and its well-being?**

3. **What are some of the ways traditional marriage benefits a society?**

4. **Does the correlation between traditional marriage and the well-being of society still hold true?**

5. **How does traditional marriage enrich children and adults?**

Chapter 10 Key Points

Key Questions:

1. What is marriage?
2. How is marriage good for society?
3. How can Christians support the traditional view of marriage?
4. What cultural trends and worldviews have led to the recent decline of marriage?

Key Passages:

1. Genesis 1:26–30
2. Genesis 2:18–24
3. Genesis 3:15–16
4. Ephesians 5:31–33*

Key Events:

1. *Obergefell v. Hodges**

Key Persons:

1. Michel Foucault
2. Marquis de Sade

Key Terms:

1. Capitalism
2. Dominion
3. Human Flourishing
4. Idolatry
5. Libertarianism
6. Marriage
7. Natural Law
8. Polygamy
9. Polyamory
10. Polygamy
11. Postmodernism
12. Proletariat
13. *Meod Tôwb*
14. Traditional Marriage*

Key Works:

1. *The Communist Manifesto*
2. Quran
3. Hadith

Short answer or essay question on the exam

Chapter 10 Assignment

Answer the following questions with at least one paragraph.

1. **How can the Christian worldview criticize Islam's approval of polygamy when so many prominent figures in the Bible also practiced it?**

2. **Some people who support same-sex marriage say that passages like Ephesians 5:31–32 are concerned with a couple's commitment to each other, not the sexes of those involved. How does a deeper understanding of marriage, from Genesis through the New Testament, contradict that view?**

3. **How is it possible to make the case for marriage from nature or what is sometimes called general revelation?**

4. **One argument against same-sex marriage is that it is contradicts God's design for families to procreate, producing the next generation. Does that also invalidate traditional marriages that do not or cannot produce children?**

UNIT 11

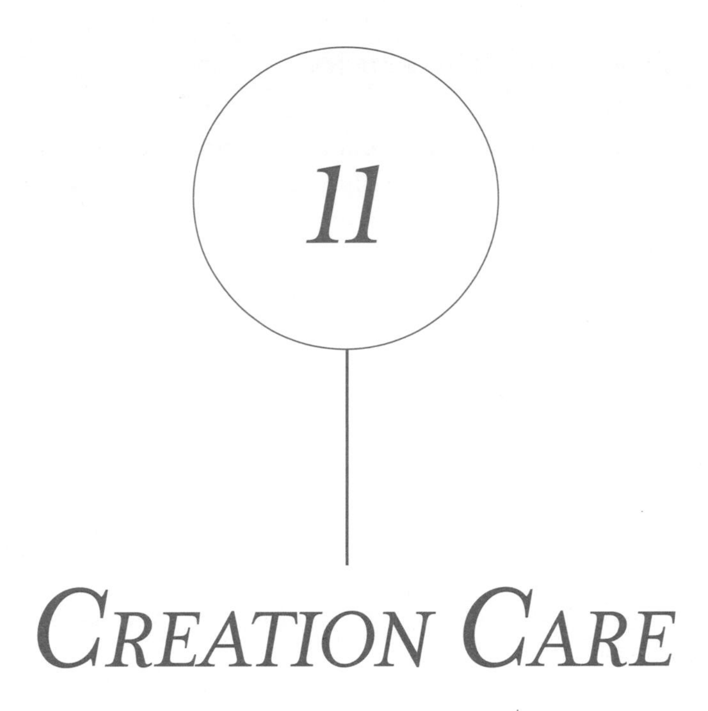

Creation Care

Chapter 11 Learning Objectives

Students will be able to:

1. retell the tragedy of preventable death from environmental issues. [11.1]
2. explain the two myths that keep Christians sidelined from addressing the environmental movement. [11.2]
3. identify truths that the Bible teaches about creation and caring for the environment. [11.3]
4. explain the perspective of showing stewardship through six loving actions Christians could take. [11.4]
5. conclude that if Christians want to help nature we have to help people. [11.5]

CHAPTER 11 DISCUSSION QUESTIONS

1. **Chemicals like DDT often have positive and negative effects. Some pesticides increase crop yield but cause cancer. How would you decide which chemicals or processes should be legal and which should be banned? [11.1]**

2. **God commanded humans to be stewards of his creation (Genesis 1:28). How have we done as stewards so far? [11.1]**

3. **What's the difference between conservationism and environmentalism? [11.2]**

4. **What are some myths behind environmentalism? [11.2]**

5. **What is deep ecology? [11.2]**

6. **Why should Christians care about the environment? [11.3]**

7. **What does the Bible teach about creation? [11.3]**

8. **What did other ancient religions and worldviews say about creation? [11.3]**

9. How did God intend humans to relate to creation? [11.3]

10. What effect did sin have on creation and our stewardship of it? [11.3]

11. How did the early church address the subject of creation stewardship? [11.3]

12. Does environmentalism pose a threat to people? [11.4]

13. Is the world on the brink of environmental disaster? [11.4]

14. Is our current level of population growth sustainable? [11.4]

15. Does climate change represent a looming disaster? [11.4]

16. Will resource depletion bring about the end of humanity? [11.4]

17. **How do you feel about the need for change when it comes to the following: internal combustion engines, carbon emissions, wind and solar power, fossil fuels, meat consumption, and deforestation? [11.4]**

18. **What responsibility do humans have for the care of animals? [11.4]**

19. **How can we care for creation and enjoy it more? [11.4]**

20. **How can we get away from a consumptive mindset? [11.4]**

21. What is the greatest threat to the environment? [11.4]

22. Why not just let the government take care of the environment? [11.4]

23. What role do incentives and information have in changing human behavior? [11.4]

"A Christian Environmental Ethic" Reading

This essay discusses three general principles of a Christian environmental ethic and stewardship:

1. The Principle of Creation Value: God created, sustains and values all his creation.
2. The Principle of Sustained Order and Purpose: God created and sustains creation in a certain order to meet specific purposes.
3. The Principle of Universal Corruption and Redemption: Everything in the created universe is subject to corruption by sin and ultimate redemption through Jesus Christ.

God has made a covenant with creation, promising to redeem, restore, and renew the physical world in the new heaven and earth (2 Peter 3:13; Revelation 21:1). In the meantime, he has made human beings in his image and set them as stewards over his creation (Genesis 1:26–28). Bergstrom defines biblical stewardship and briefly examines what it means in relation to each of these principles.

A Christian Environmental Ethic

by John C. Bergstrom

The system of values and beliefs that influence how a person thinks and acts is known as that person's ethical system or ethics. The purpose of this paper is to discuss three general principles of a Christian environmental ethic and applications of this ethic to natural resource and environmental stewardship. The three general principles of a Christian environmental ethic are: 1) God created and therefore values all of His works of creation (Principle of Creation Value); 2) God created and sustains all elements and systems in His creation within particular orders to meet certain ongoing purposes (Principle of Sustained Order and Purpose); and 3) Everything in the created world and universe is subject to corruption by sin and ultimate redemption through Jesus Christ (Principle of Universal Corruption and Redemption).

Principle of Creation Value

The Principle of Creation Value first recognizes that God created the heavens and earth and all things found therein (Genesis 1; Psalm 146:6; Acts 14:15; Revelation 4:11). For example, Revelation 4:11 states: "You are worthy, our Lord and God, to receive glory and honor and power, for you created all things, and by your will they were created and have their being." (Revelation 4:11 NIV).[1] The Bible also teaches that although God allows people to utilize elements of nature, God retains ownership of all His creation (Psalm 24:1; Psalm 89:11; Leviticus 25:23; Colossians 1:15–16). For example, Psalm 24:1 states; "The earth is the Lord's, and everything in it, the world, and all who live in it" (Psalm 24:1 NIV).

The Bible teaches that God loves and enjoys all that He has created. Psalm 145:16–17, for example, states: "You open your hand and satisfy the desires of every living thing. The Lord is righteous in all his ways and loving toward all he has made" (Psalm 145:16–17 NIV). Thus, an important implication of the Principle of Creation Value from an ethical standpoint is that God places value on elements of nature independent of human use and human-centered values (Genesis 1:25; Psalm 104:31; Psalm 148:9–13). This God-centered inherent value of nature is termed theistic intrinsic value.[2]

Plato's philosophy influenced the Gnostic view of the physical world that arose within the first-century Christian church. Followers of Gnosticism taught that the spiritual world contains all that is good, and that everything in the physical or material world is bad.[3] Thus, under Gnosticism, nature would have a negative value and is something that should be disregarded in a person's life.

Christians in the modern church who say that "nature really doesn't matter because it's part of the physical world" are carrying on the heritage of Plato and the Gnostics. This position, which has a very low view of nature's value, is not supported by the Scriptures. As pointed out by Schaeffer,[4] the greatest testimony to the lasting value and importance of the physical world is that Jesus Christ's physical body was resurrected from the dead and exists today in the unseen spiritual world. In the new heaven and earth that God will someday create, Scripture teaches that in addition to Christians being given new, resurrected bodies, nature will also be renewed. As discussed in more detail later in the paper, both people and nature will therefore have existence and value in eternity.

The other extreme position on the value and importance of the physical world and nature that Christians should not fall into is one that improperly elevates the status of nature to being equal to or even above people. The "equality between people and nature" viewpoint in considered first. In modern times, certain secular environmental ethics or philosophies such as "deep ecology" teach that people and nature have equal status and value in the world.[5] Such viewpoints on the parity between people and nature can enter into the church as erroneous teaching.[6,7] Scripture teaches although God values nature, He places a special higher value on people who He "crowned with glory and honor" as the climax of His creation (Genesis 1:26–30; Psalm 8:5–8). The "nature above people" viewpoint is considered next.

Romans 1:20–23 states: "For since the creation of the world God's invisible qualities—his eternal power and divine nature—have been clearly seen, being understood from what has been made, so that men are without excuse. For although they knew God, they neither glorified him as God nor gave thanks to him, but their thinking became futile and foolish hearts were darkened. Although they claimed to be wise, they became fools and exchanged the glory of the immortal God for images made to look like mortal man and birds and animals and reptiles" (Romans

1:20–23 NIV). This passage refers to people who knew or at least knew of God but elevated nature to be objects or idols of worship. The worship of anything in nature violates the Second Commandment in which God states: "You shall not make for yourself an idol in the form of anything in heaven above or on the earth beneath or in the waters below. You shall not bow down to them or worship them" (Exodus 20:4–5 NIV).

Principle of Sustained Order and Purpose

The Principle of Sustained Order and Purpose implies that God originally created all elements of nature to fit and function together in an orderly fashion within interrelated systems to meet certain ongoing purposes. God's direct involvement in natural systems did not end after the original creation period described in Genesis 1. The triune God continues to hold together or sustain the functioning of nature, accomplishing His intended order and purpose of all nonliving and living elements of nature and natural systems.

What are the various purposes of nature according to the Bible? One of the reasons God created and continues to sustain nature, as discussed above under the Principle of Creation Value, is for God himself to love and enjoy. Another purpose is to help meet people's needs such as food and shelter (Genesis 2:15; Genesis 9:3). A third major purpose of nature is to glorify and reveal God to people everywhere (Psalm 19:1–4; Romans 1:18–20). For example, Psalm 19:14 states: "The heavens declare the glory of God; the skies proclaim the work of his hands. Day after day they pour forth speech; night after night they display knowledge. There is no speech or language where their voice is not heard. Their voice goes out into all the earth, their words to the ends of the world." (Psalm 19:14 NIV).

To meet their intended purposes, God created and sustains all of creation within particular orders. The first large-scale Creation ordering of interest is the Biblical hierarchy between God, people and nature. Understanding and applying a Christian environmental ethic requires a proper interpretation of Biblical verses establishing and describing this basic hierarchy. A key verse is Genesis 1:28 which states: "So God created man in his own image, in the image of God he created him, male and female he created them. God blessed them and said to them, 'Be fruitful and increase in number; fill the earth and subdue it. Rule over the fish of the sea and the birds of the air and over every living creature that moves on the ground'" (Genesis 1:28 NIV).

Genesis 1:28 establishes that in God's basic ordering of Creation, people have dominion over nature. However, Genesis 1:28 also clearly states the people are creations of God. As creations of God, people are under the authority or dominion of God. Thus, from the perspective of God's authority and control, people and nature are in the same class or order—all of Creation including people must submit to God's plans and ways. The basic Biblical relationships and ordering between God, people and nature are illustrated in Figure 1. A similar illustration is provided and discussed by Schaeffer.[8]

Figure1. Principle of Sustained Order and Purpose General Biblical Hierarchy

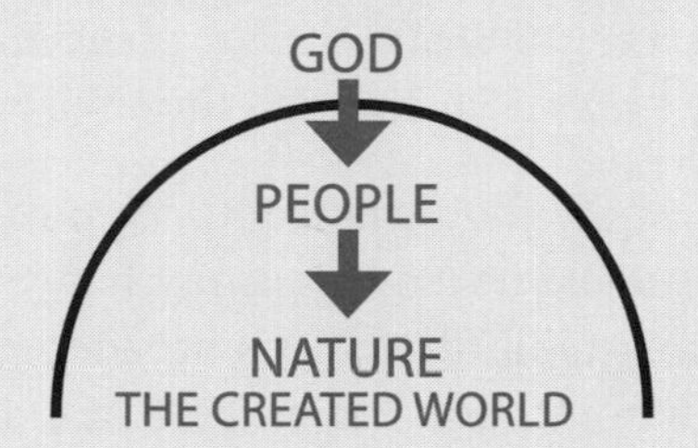

In Figure 1, it is first shown that there is a fundamental separation between God and his creation including people. God is above people and nature and both people and elements of nature such as plants and animals must interact and live together within the same created world governed by God's ways and plans. Thus, people share a common heritage and bond with plants, animals, and other elements of nature as fellow creations of God. People, like plants and animals, must also cope with living in a physical world and universe created and controlled by God.

The diagram also illustrates that within the physical world and universe, people are above nature. People are above nature by the grace and will of God only—not by our own power and ingenuity. God created people in His image to exercise Godly dominion over nature. Godly dominion over nature, as discussed in more detail later in the paper, means that people act as stewards or caretakers of nature who are ultimately responsible to God for their use and management of nature.

In addition to the major large-scale relationships or orders between God, people and nature illustrated in Figure 1, God created and sustains elements of nature within particular orders to meet deliberate purposes. The food chain system shown in Figure 2 illustrate how living and nonliving elements of nature in an ecosystem fit and function together to provide life-support for each other.

Figure2. God's Order Within Nature: Simple Food Chain or System

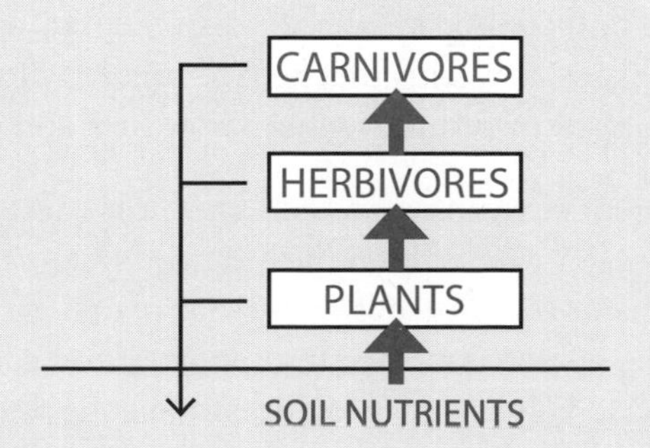

As illustrated in Figure 2, living plants take nutrients from the soil. Herbivores such as rabbits or deer eat plants for food. Carnivores such as mountain lions eat other animals for food. When plants and animals die, microorganisms in the environment decompose the plant and animal body material into basic chemicals that go back into the soil. These chemicals are then taken up by plants for nutrients completing the cycling of life-supporting chemicals through the environment.

People are also dependent on the food chain and chemical cycling systems illustrated in Figure 2. The linkages and interrelationships between people and elements of nature and natural systems are illustrated at a broader scale in Figure 3. Figure 3 illustrates the planet earth home God has provided for all of us, and the global interrelationships between people and nature.

Figure3. Global Interrelationships between People and Nature on God's Earth

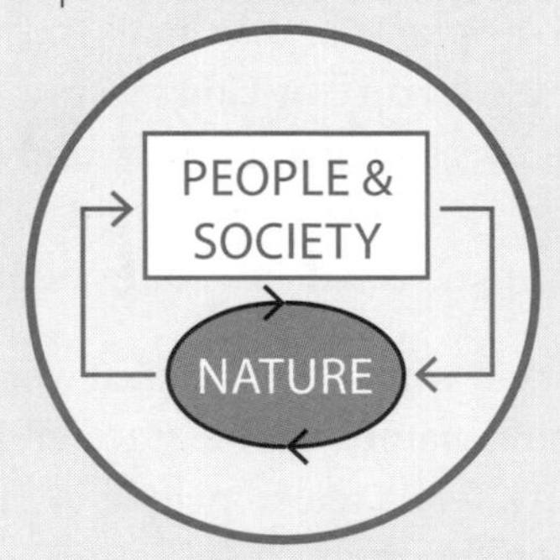

The scientific study of natural life-support systems falls under the realm of ecology. The word ecology is derived from the Greek root words, "eco" meaning "house" and "logy" meaning "study". The word ecology can therefore be literally interpreted to mean "house study" or the "study of the house". The "house" being referred to here is the planet earth and its natural systems. Before describing how the earth's natural systems provide life-support, consider the artificial life-support systems that people build into the various dwellings we call home at a small scale.

The actual physical dwellings in which we live were constructed by people with certain life-support systems in mind. These artificial life-support systems include: air circulation systems to regulate oxygen (O2) and carbon dioxide (CO2) levels so that indoor air is healthy to breathe; water systems to provide safe and secure drinking water supplies; heating and cooling systems to regulate indoor temperatures at healthy levels; and waste disposal systems that help to prevent illness by safely and regularly removing potential germ-producing human wastes and garbage.

The planet earth and different environments such as forests, deserts, oceans, lakes and rivers were created by God with natural life-support systems in his mind and design. God built several major chemical cycles into our planet earth home. Each of these cycles helps to provide all that is needed to support life on earth. For example, the carbon and oxygen cycle helps to provide breathable air and regulate global temperatures at livable levels. The hydrologic cycle helps to provide water to drink and for a multitude of other purposes.

The different chemical cycles also contribute to the provision of mineral resources such as coal, oil and natural gas that we use as fuel for transportation, electricity, and heating. These cycles also support renewable resources such as trees and fish and wildlife. We use trees for consumptive uses such as lumber, and to support nonconsumptive uses such as recreation and aesthetic enjoyment. We use fish and wildlife for consumptive uses such as harvesting ocean fish for food, and hunting of wildlife on public and private lands. We also use fish and wildlife for nonconsumptive recreational uses and aesthetic enjoyment such as wildlife observation and photography.[9]

When people use elements of nature for commercial production and consumption, and even recreational and aesthetic enjoyment, some level of waste-by products enter the environment. Smoke stakes into the air and effluent discharge pipes into rivers are obvious evidence of these waste by-products. When people use a forest or park for recreation, waste by-products are emitted into the air from automobiles, RVs, ATVs, and motorboats. Solid wastes in the form of litter are also often left behind.

God has built waste assimilation and treatment capabilities into natural systems. For example, scientists have documented the natural ability of wetlands to filter chemicals out of water that are potentially harmful to human health. However, excessive use of a particular natural system such as a wetland area by people for waste by-product disposal may threaten the continued ability of that natural system to assimilate and treat wastes.

The God-given role of people as caretakers or managers of elements of nature and natural systems is illustrated through several linkages. People manage nature, for example, by cultivating the land to grow and harvest crops for food through agriculture, and to grow and harvest trees for wood products through forestry. People manage lakes and rivers for producing electricity, providing drinking water and to support many types of recreational activities such as boating and swimming. People may also be involved in managing entire ecosystems to provide fish and wildlife habitat and other broad environmental services such as protection of regional air and water quality, or even regulation of global climate.

Principle of Universal Corruption and Redemption

The Principle of Universal Corruption and Redemption has familiar implications with respect to the relationship between men and women created in God's image by God their Creator. The Scriptures are clear that all men and women have sinned and fall short of God's expectations for a righteous life. Thus, we are all in need of forgiveness and saving faith through a personal relationship with Jesus Christ (1 John 1:8–9). The Scriptures also teach that all of creation has been corrupted by sin (Romans 8:20–22). The effects of this universal corruption include not just separation of people from God, but also separation of people from themselves, each other, and nature.

The separation of people from nature as a result of sin entering the world at the time of the Fall of Mankind taught in the Bible (Genesis, Chapter 3) is of particular interest to the topic of this paper. First, this separation occurs at a physical level. Nature provides beneficial services to people, but since the Fall, nature can also be the source of physical harm to people—the physical harm to people caused by tornadoes and hurricanes are graphic examples. The Fall also has resulted in a spiritual separation between people and nature. Prior to the Fall, God, people and nature had close spiritual fellowship with each other. The introduction of sin into the world and its corrupting effects on all of God's created works broke apart this fellowship.

For people, forgiveness and saving faith through Jesus Christ assures personal redemption of the Believer before God, and restoration of the Believer's relationship and fellowship with God. Scripture teaches that God will also redeem nature and restore the relationship and fellowship between God, people and nature in the eternal world. God's plan for redeeming nature is reflected in the creation covenant.[10,11]

The creation covenant is God's promise to redeem, restore, and renew the physical world including nature in the new heaven and earth he will create when the earth we now call home no longer exists (2 Peter 3:13; Revelation 21:1). In the New Testament of the Bible, Romans 8:19–23 speaks to the creation covenant, saying the following: "For the creation waits in eager expectation for the sons of God to be revealed. For the creation was subjected to frustration, not by its own choice, but by the will of the one who subjected it, in hope that the creation itself will be liberated from its bondage to decay and brought into the glorious freedom of the children of God. We know that the whole creation has been groaning as in the pains of childbirth right up to the present time. Not only so, but we ourselves, who have the firstfruits of the Spirit, groan inwardly as we wait eagerly for our adoption as sons, the redemption of our bodies" (Romans 8:20–23 NIV). This passage teaches that the physical universe including nature is not destined for eternal destruction when the world we now live in ends when Jesus Christ returns. Rather, when God gives Believers new bodies in the new heaven and earth, He will also provide a new beginning for nature and rest of the physical world.

In the new heaven and earth, nature will be restored to its pre-Fall magnificence and perfection. In this new Creation of God, both people and nature will be freed from the sufferings caused by the imperfections of the world we live today, including death and decay. People and nature will also no longer battle against each other as so often in the case in our world today.

In the Old Testament of the Bible, there is precedent for God establishing covenants or promises that incorporate nature. Consider, for example, this passage from Genesis 9: "Then God said to Noah and to his sons with him: 'I now establish my covenant with you and with your descendants after you and with every living creature that was with you—the birds, the livestock and all the wild animals, all those that came out of the ark with you—every living creature on earth. I establish my covenant with you: Never again will all life be cut off by the waters of a flood; never again will there be a flood to destroy the earth'" (Genesis 9:8–11 NIV). The beautiful natural rainbow is God's sign and reminder of His covenant with Noah not to destroy life on earth again with a great flood. This covenant clearly includes plants and animals and every "living creature on earth."

The creation covenant referred to in Romans 8 can be thought of as an extension of God's covenant with Noah that includes a promise to protect and sustain both people and nature. God's concern for protecting and sustaining all living creatures was illustrated by Jesus Christ who when speaking about sparrows said that . . . "not one of them (sparrows) will fall to the ground apart from the will of your Father (God)" (Matthew 10:29 NIV). Providing for the continued and restored existence of nature in the new heaven and earth is consistent with what the Bible teaches about God's love and concern for all of His large and small works of Creation.

Practicing a Christian Environmental Ethic through Stewardship

The three general principles of a Christian environmental ethic have practical implications for the role of people as caretakers or managers of nature. The Bible teaches that as caretakers or managers of nature, people are to practice good stewardship. The word "steward" and "stewardship" is used throughout the Old and New Testaments of the Bible (Genesis 15:2; Genesis 44:1; 1 Chronicles 28:1; Matthew 20:8; 1 Corinthians 4:2; Luke 12:42; Luke 16:1–2). The word used for steward in the Bible can also be interpreted as manager or servant.

When the word for steward (manager, servant) is used in the Bible, it refers to a person who is put in charge of taking care of something that does not belong to him or her. This meaning is consistent with the Webster's Dictionary definition of a steward as "one employed in a large household or estate to manage domestic concerns". As stewards of nature, people have been appointed by God to manage the "domestic environmental concerns" of our planet earth home.

According to the Bible, general characteristics and responsibilities of a steward include being faithful, wise and responsible. The steward should be concerned with meeting daily needs and is not to abuse or waste what he or she has been put in charge of managing. The steward is to maintain self-control (not overindulging), be a "problem-solver," and follow the household or estate owner's wishes and instructions with respect to management (Luke 12:42–46; Luke 16:1–9).

How are stewards held accountable according to the Bible? Proper management actions are rewarded with "true riches" (spiritual riches). Improper actions are punished (something is taken away). Stewards over more are held more accountable, especially if they do wrong when they know better (Luke 12:47–48; Luke 16:10–12).

Stewardship and the Principle of Creation Value

Under the Principle of Creation Value, all of God's creations are important and valuable to God. People hold a special particular value to God as living beings created in His image (Genesis 1:26–30). Part of God's provision for the well-being of people is the use of plants, animals, minerals and other elements of nature for meeting our material needs. These uses, for example, include farming the land to meet food and fiber needs and harvesting trees from forests to meet wood product needs.

When using elements of nature for human benefit, the Christian environmental steward keeps in mind that all of creation ultimately belongs to God and is valuable to God independent of human use. This knowledge, when put into practice, means that the Christian environmental steward respects and even loves elements of nature out of respect and love for their Creator, the triune God—Father, Son, and Holy Spirit.

Godly respect and love for elements of nature leads the Christian environmental steward to be a responsible caretaker of nature who does not abuse or misuse what has been entrusted into his or her care by God. The Christian steward or manager of a farm, forest, park or natural area, for example, would not deliberately kill plants and animals under his or care without good reason. Although the Christian environmental steward demonstrates Godly love and care for nature, he or she does not worship nature, only God who is its Creator.

Stewardship and the Principle of Sustained Order and Purpose

Genesis 1 establishes that although both people and nature are created works of God and under God's authority, God has given people dominion over nature. But, how are people to exercise this dominion? God created people in His own image—as His representatives on earth. Because we are under God's authority in all things, we are to do God's will when exercising our dominion over nature.

In Genesis 1:28, God tells people to subdue nature. The word "subdue" is translated from the Hebrew word "kabash" which means to make to serve, by force if necessary. But "subdue" does not mean "abuse," just as the phrase "rule over" in the Bible does not mean "exercise tyranny over."

Some specific instructions pertaining to managing nature are given in Genesis 2: "The Lord God took the man and put him in the Garden of Eden to work it and take care of it" (Genesis 2:15 NIV). The phrase, "to work it" means "to till it" or "to cultivate it"; the general meaning is to use productively. The phrase to "take care of it" means "to keep", "to guard", "to exercise great care over". The intent of "keeping, guarding, caring over" is to sustain the function for which the element of nature or natural system being cared for was originally designed. Sustaining the original God-designed functions of nature is a very important objective from theological, ethical and practical standpoints.

In sum, the "good steward" according to the Bible will manage nature in a wise, self-controlled, and nonwasteful manner, always taking care to sustain the original functions of elements of nature and natural systems. The "poor steward," in contrast, lacks self-control, is wasteful and irresponsible, and cannot be trusted to take proper care of what he or she has been put in charge of managing. The "poor steward" allows the original functions of elements of nature or natural systems to be degraded or ruined.

In the "natural economy" of God's creation, human use and management of natural environments can have positive or negative consequences. Negative consequences of poor use and management can be illustrated by thinking about the end results of not properly maintaining the life-support systems built into a house or apartment building. The most serious consequence of this poor management is that the health and well-being of the dwelling's occupants would likely suffer. In extreme cases, such as when improper use or management of heating equipment allows CO2 in the indoor air to build up to unhealthy levels, death of the dwelling's occupants may result.

If we misuse and mismanage nature, the ability of nature to support provision of goods and commodities of consumptive or nonconsumptive value to people may be significantly reduced. In extreme cases, essential life-support systems may be degraded to the point that plant, animal and human health and life are seriously threatened.[12] However, if we use and manage nature properly as God expects us to, natural systems can continue to provide essential life-support services and various goods and commodities of consumptive or nonconsumptive value to people.

Unfortunately, the poor management or stewardship model often describes how men and women of the world improperly exercise their dominion over nature. An examples of poor stewardship from agriculture is farming a tract of land until the soil is totally "burned out" and incapable of further production. An example from forestry is over harvesting and mismanaging a forest such that new trees can no longer be grown. Exceeding the capacity of air and water resources to absorb and disperse pollution so that air and water become unsafe to consume is an example of poor stewardship in the environmental pollution management area.

The Christian environmental steward understands that the elements of nature or natural systems that he or she may be involved in using or managing are ultimately controlled by God according to His ways and plans. Whether he or she is involved in the use and management of farmland, forestland, parks, natural areas, or air and water resources at a large-scale, the Christian environmental steward realizes that human use and management of nature which run counter to God's ways and plans are detrimental to nature and ultimately to people. There is also a realization that whenever we go our own way rather than following God, He is grieved by our actions.

To carry out his or her responsibilities, the Christian environmental steward attempts to learn as much as he or she can about the God intended order and purpose of nature. This effort includes learning about individual elements of nature, and how these elements of nature function within natural systems created and sustained by God. The Christian environmental steward puts this knowledge into practice by doing his or her best to use and manage nature within the boundaries of God's ways and plans.

Stewardship and the Principle of Universal Corruption and Redemption

An important, overarching implication of the Principle of Universal Corruption and Redemption for the practice of Christian environmental stewardship is that everyone who is involved in the study, use and management of nature is corrupted by sin. Dealing with the effects of sin in our own lives and the lives of others represents a major challenge to Christians involved in the use and care of nature through education, administration or direct management in the field. To effectively meet this challenge, the Christian manager of nature applies Biblical values and guidance to manage both nature and people in a positive manner.

The Christian environmental steward also acknowledges that God will redeem both people and nature in the new heaven and earth. Knowing that God intends one day to redeem nature rather than completely destroying it as some in the church today may think should motivate Christians to view and act differently towards nature. Christians should also be involved as much as possible in the process of redeeming nature here and now on earth as an expression of our own redemption and salvation and the “living out” of our faith (Philippians 2:12–13; James 2:14–25). In the case of a Christian forester or ecologist, for example, being involved in the restoration of a healthy forest ecosystem is consistent with and honors God’s ultimate plan for redeeming nature. In contrast, being responsible for widespread and complete destruction of a particular forest ecosystem does not seem consistent with nor honors God’s plan for redeeming nature.

Principles and Practice of a Christian Environmental Ethic: Conclusions

We are faced in the world today with many natural resource and environmental issues and problems. There are issues and problems related to managing nature and the natural resources provided by nature to provide food for eating, paper for writing, lumber for construction, and areas for people to participate in outdoor recreation and experience aesthetic enjoyment of nature. There are issues and problems related to protecting nature from many source of degradation or damage by people.[13] If nature is degraded or damaged by people (or even by itself), there are issues and problems related to how to go about repairing or mitigating the environmental damage.

Christians are in a unique position to offer thoughtful solutions to the natural resource and environmental problems and issues we face in the world today. As mentioned at the beginning of this paper, there is growing recognition on the part of people from a variety of professional and personal backgrounds that effective, long-term solutions to natural resource and environmental problems and issues requires an appropriate moral basis for action. God’s word found in the Holy Bible provides this moral basis in the form of a Christian environmental ethic that results in responsible and caring stewardship of all of God’s creation.

This essay originally appeared on the *LeaderU* website: John C. Bergstrom, “Principles of an Christian Environmental Ethic,” [article online] http://www.leaderu.com/science/bergstrom-enviroethics.html. Reproduction rights granted by John C. Bergstrom.

[1] All Scripture references in the article are taken from the New International Version (NIV), *The Study Bible: New International Version*. Grand Rapids, MI: Zondervan Bible Publishers, 1985.

[2] Barrett, Christopher B. and John C. Bergstrom. “The Economics of God’s Creation,” *Bulletin of the Association of Christian Economists*. Issue 31, Spring, 1998:4–23.

[3] Brown, Colin. *Philosophy and the Christian Faith*. Downers Grove, IL: InterVarsity Press, 1968.

[4] Schaeffer, *Pollution and the Death of Man: The Christian View of Ecology*.

[5] VanDeVeer, Donald and Christine Pierce. *The Environmental Ethics and Policy Book*. Belmont, CA: Wadsworth Publishing Company, 1998.

[6] Burrell, Kevin L. “The Ethics of Environmentalism.” *Faith and Practice*, Volume 2, Fall, 1996: 16–24.

[7] Campolo, Tony. *How to Rescue Earth without Worshiping Nature*. Nashville, TN: Thomas Nelson, 1992.

[8] Schaeffer, *Pollution and the Death of Man: The Christian View of Ecology*.

[9] Barrett and Bergstrom. “The Economics of God’s Creation.”

[10] Schaeffer, *Pollution and the Death of Man: The Christian View of Ecology*.

[11] VanDyke, et al, *Redeeming Creation: The Biblical Basis for Environmental Stewardship*.

[12] DeWitt, Calvin B. “Seven Degradations of Creation,” *Perspectives*, February, 1989:4–8.

[13] DeWitt, “Seven Degradations of Creation.”

"A Christian Environmental Ethic" Discussion Questions

1. **What does the Bible say about nature (environment) and our relationship/responsibility to it (ethics)?**

2. **What does Genesis 1:28 teach about the order of creation?**

3. **What is the creation covenant?**

4. **How is the role of a "steward" defined in Scripture, and how will our stewardship be judged?**

5. **Should Christians be involved in the various environmental movements of our day?**

"Energy and the Environment" Video

How and why should Christians care for the environment? This series of videos brings together Biola University professors Craig Hazen, Garry DeWeese, John Bloom, and Brent Ridley, and alumnus David Pelser to discuss important questions surrounding environmental ethics, the Bible and the role that Christians should play in creation care.

To access these videos, go to www.summitu.com/utc and enter the passcode found in the back of your manual.

"Energy and the Environment" Video Outline

How and why should Christians care for the environment? This series of videos brings together Biola University professors Craig Hazen, Garry DeWeese, John Bloom, and Brent Ridley, and alumnus David Pelser to discuss important questions surrounding environmental ethics, the Bible, and the role that Christians should play in creation care.

What viewpoints are out there?

Some conservative Christians say, "Jesus is coming back, so it doesn't matter; let it burn." Many evangelicals believe Christians should focus on ________________ rather than the environment. Other Christians believe that the world should be taken care of now because it will be redeemed and renewed one day (Revelation 21–22).

How should we steward the environment?

Humans are stewards of God's creation and are to take care of the earth (Genesis 1:27–30). The advancement of civilization from an agrarian lifestyle to a post-industrial world is putting a heavy strain on the environment. The current challenges are daunting, but we have to tackle them as part of our ________________.

Do we have a responsibility to the environment?

According to the Bible, we have a responsibility to care for God's creation. We have a duty to God the Creator, we have a duty to our fellow human beings, and we have a duty to the Earth.

What is the global warming controversy?

The global warming controversy is an ongoing dispute about the negative effects of ________________ on the global climate. What if global warming is true? What if global warming is false? And what things that are true, regardless of the answer?

Can 7 billion people be good for the environment?

" ________________ " refers to when the human population is so large that the earth can't sustain it. Is the earth overpopulated? What about God's command to multiply and fill the earth? From the Christian perspective, the problem isn't the number of people, but the presence of sin as it relates to our impact on our environment.

“ENERGY AND THE ENVIRONMENT” DISCUSSION QUESTIONS

1. **What are some of the different approaches to the environment and creation care among Christians?**

2. **What does the Bible teach about humanity’s responsibility to care for the earth?**

3. **What is our duty when it comes to protecting and preserving the environment?**

4. **What is the global warming controversy?**

5. **Is the world heading for an overpopulation crisis and, if so, what should be done about it?**

Chapter 11 Key Points

Key Questions:

1. What does the Bible say about creation care?
2. How is creation care a worldview issue?
3. What is the philosophical and historical background of environmentalism?
4. What role should the government play in caring for the environment?
5. How should Christians steward creation?

Key Passages:

1. Genesis 2:19
2. Psalm 24:1
3. Hosea 4:3

Key Persons:

1. Rachel Carson
2. James E. Lovelock
3. Thomas Malthus
4. Peter Singer

Key Works:

1. *Animal Liberation* by Peter Singer
2. *Gaia* by James E. Lovelock
3. *Silent Spring* by Rachel Carson

Key Terms:

1. Animism
2. Conservationism
3. Contingent*
4. Crony Capitalism
5. Deep Ecology
6. Deism
7. Dominion
8. Ecology
9. Economic Interventionism
10. Environmentalism
11. Free-Market Economy
12. Gnosticism
13. Malthusian Catastrophe
14. Materialism
15. Progressivism
16. Sentience
17. *Shalom**
18. Stewardship
19. Tragedy of the Commons

**Short answer or essay question on the exam*

Chapter 11 Assignment

Answer the following questions with at least one paragraph.

1. **How does this chapter's discussion of the two myths about environmentalism show that this issue is not worldview neutral and that it is something Christians ought to care about?**

2. **How is the ancient heresy of Gnosticism related to the way that some Christians treat environmental concerns? What is the danger of such thinking?**

3. **Caring for the earth is an important part of a biblical worldview, but why does a concern for the environment not necessarily lead to a support for greater governmental involvement?**

4. **How could greater economic development actually help reduce pollution or environmental abuse in impoverished areas?**

UNIT
12

POLITICS

CHAPTER 12 LEARNING OBJECTIVES

Students will be able to:

1. examine the issue of what role Christians ought to have in dealing with politics and political leaders. [12.1]
2. evaluate how other worldviews define politics and oppose Christians' involvement in politics. [12.2]
3. discuss ways the Bible shows God's view of equality, justice, and rights should inform Christians' own political involvement. [12.3]
4. explain why Christians are caretakers of their families, the church, and the government and how to be good citizens. [12.4]
5. conclude that politics is an arena of opportunity and responsibility for Christians. [12.5]

CHAPTER 12 DISCUSSION QUESTIONS

1. **Though many think Dietrich Bonhoeffer was a martyr, he was working to bring down his government and assassinate its duly elected leader. Doesn't that make him a terrorist?** [12.1]

2. **Should the church have anything to do with politics?** [12.1]

3. **What is politics?** [12.2]

4. **How does government work?** [12.2]

5. How does Secularism view government? [12.2]

6. How does Marxism view government? [12.2]

7. How does Postmodernism view government? [12.2]

8. How does New Spirituality view government? [12.2]

9. How does Islam view government? [12.2]

10. What do these worldviews think of Christianity's place in government? [12.2]

11. What does the Bible say about government? [12.3]

12. How does God's nature influence politics through equality? [12.3]

13. How does God's nature influence politics through justice? [12.3]

14. How does God's nature influence politics through law? [12.3]

15. How has sin affected our ability to govern ourselves? [12.3]

16. What is "subsidiarity" and how should it affect our involvement in politics? [12.4]

17. **What is "sphere sovereignty" and what boundaries does it establish? [12.4]**

18. **How do we decide the proper balance between the spheres? [12.4]**

19. **What does it mean to be good citizens? [12.4]**

20. **Are Christians ever justified in breaking laws they are convicnced are unjust? [12.4]**

21. What are the consequences of *not* being involved in politics and government? [12.5]

"The Golden Triangle of Freedom" Reading

The Golden Triangle of Freedom is a metaphor for the relationship among virtue, faith, and freedom: Freedom requires virtue, virtue requires faith, and faith requires freedom. The three are dependent on one another. If any one of the three legs of the triangle is weakened or removed, the whole structure ceases to exist. This is the structure upon which our nation was built.

Although well educated, Eric Metaxas admits he had never heard of the Golden Triangle of Freedom and it concerned him that he had missed such a key American concept. In the second chapter of his book *If You Can Keep It*, he explores the history and explains the relevance of the triangle to a new generation of Americans.

The Golden Triangle of Freedom

by Eric Metaxas

Liberty cannot be established without morality, nor without faith.
—Alexis de Tocqueville

When I first heard my friend Os Guinness talk about the Golden Triangle of Freedom, I was taken aback.[1] In fact, I was deeply embarrassed, because what he was describing was so central to the idea of American freedom and the American experiment that it seemed inconceivable that somehow I hadn't heard it all before. I was shocked that although I'd attended decent American schools and a top American university, the concept somehow had eluded me entirely. It was not like so many other things one half hears and never retains. It was not like nearly all the math I had learned in high school, or the grammatical concept of the preterite, or Avogadro's number, things on which I conceivably might be refreshed. It was something I had never heard a whisper about in the first place. But as I spoke with people about Os Guinness's book and this concept, I realized I wasn't the only one who had missed it completely. As far as I could tell, no one knew of it. Virtually no one seemed to understand what the founders had taken for granted as the secret center of their novel idea of self-government. This initially seemed impossible to me, but as time passed I had no option but to accept it and then to begin to be terrified about it. If several generations of people had never heard what most previous generations understood, whether explicitly or implicitly, and if this thing really was the secret formula at the center of our fragile and unprecedented form of government, how could America continue much longer? And it led me to my second terrifying question: If America was indeed a country created not because of ethnic or tribal boundaries but instead because a people had come to believe—and therefore embody—a set of ideas, how could America be said to exist if almost no one anymore knew what those ideas were? If these ideas had essentially evaporated from our national consciousness for forty or so years, weren't we unwittingly but unavoidably becoming Americans in name only—if we hadn't already? At what point would that gruesome reality become true, and at what point would that truth be fatal to us? I had in my mind the usually comical image of a cartoon character who, having sped off the edge of a cliff, finds himself standing in midair, thinking quietly, before he suddenly realizes he's no longer on solid ground—and then vanishes speedily out of frame. Were we speeding *toward* the cliff, so that we might still be stopped from speeding beyond it into thin air? Or had we already sped past the edge, with no possibility of return? I'd like to think we still might have a chance of being tackled before we reach the point of no return, but that won't be up to me. It will be up to those of you who are reading this book. No pressure.

I still hope that perhaps those of us who call ourselves Americans might come to understand where we have come from and where we are now, to understand these vital ideas, to remember them again, and to know what it means to be an American. I realize that knowing these things was nothing less than a duty, one of which I had simply been unaware, that it was first and foremost my duty as an American to know what it means to be an American. As I have said, we were charged—in part by Franklin in his famous words—to keep the republic by knowing our duty as Americans and by doing that duty. So first we must understand what it means to be an American, to understand the ideas that we have generally agreed upon together; and then we must know what all of that further entails, lest "we the people" cease to exist, and America cease to exist, and the world be infinitely poorer for it.

I explained part of this in the previous chapter, but now let's look at this idea at the heart of the founders' history-changing vision, what Os Guinness in his writings has resurrected for our generation and what he has named the Golden Triangle of Freedom.

As he succinctly explains in his book *A Free People's Suicide,* the Golden Triangle of Freedom is, when reduced to its most basic form, that freedom requires virtue; virtue requires faith; and faith requires freedom. The three go round and round, supporting one another ad infinitum. If any one of the three legs of the triangle is removed, the whole structure ceases to exist. Let's look now at each of these three legs in turn.

Freedom Requires Virtue

In the spring of 1787, before the Constitutional Convention of that summer, Benjamin Franklin wrote a short two-paragraph letter to two friends in France, the Abbes Chalut and Arnaud. It had been four years since the end of the revolution, but already the problems with the government they had set up were beginning to show themselves. The Articles of Confederation, which governed the thirteen former colonies, were simply too limited to be effective for a sovereign nation. The most notable example of its shortcomings was shown in the violent uprising that came to be known as Shays' Rebellion. Approximately four thousand Massachusetts citizens actually took up arms against the new national American government. It was eventually put down, but this and other troubles made it clear that something must be done. The founders gathered in Philadelphia to create a government that was stronger than what the Articles of Confederation made possible—but that was not *too* strong. And what they were doing took the form of that document known to us as the Constitution. It would describe the government of the new nation and it would be its legal foundation.

Franklin alludes to the problems they had been having before that summer in the second paragraph of the letter, but it is in the first paragraph that he says something quite surprising to modern American sensibilities. "Only a virtuous people," he declares, "are capable of freedom." It is a staggering statement, especially from Franklin, who was no blue-nosed moralist, nor even a traditional, orthodox Christian. What does he mean by this, and how can he say it so matter-of-factly and so confidently? He is not merely saying that virtue and freedom are linked. He goes far beyond that to say that without one, the other is impossible. If the point isn't clear enough, he goes on to say more. "As nations become corrupt and vicious," he says, "they have more need of masters." The root of the word "vicious" is "vice"—the word simply means "full of vice." So Franklin, without feeling the need to explain himself much, is bluntly saying that "freedom requires virtue." And that less virtue inevitably begets less freedom.

In his day one hardly needed to be a churchgoer to see this. Franklin had from his earliest days been a proponent of Yankee virtue because it was at the center of the culture in which he had been raised in the Massachusetts Bay Colony. In his *Poor Richard's Almanac*, with its pithy moralistic aphorisms (such as "Early to Bed and Early to Rise Makes a Man Healthy, and Wealthy, and Wise"), and in his *Autobiography* we see countless examples of how Franklin understood the inherent value of virtue in society, apart from what it was that made one virtuous, whether religion or simple cultural habit, or a combination of the two.

Franklin is hardly the only one of the founders who thought this way. Despite their many bitter disagreements on many subjects, the founders were in fact of one mind on this one issue. They all not only agreed on it, but they agreed on it so much as mostly to take it for granted, since it was something that everyone seemed to know. This is, of course, what is so strange to us today. How is it that this thing agreed upon by all the founders as necessary to the form of government they created—and the government we enjoy today—is hardly ever mentioned in our time and is so little known as to be thought forgotten? How can we be Americans if we have mislaid this thing so central to the set of ideas bequeathed to us by the founders?

In June 1776 another of the founders, John Adams—who in contrast to Franklin was a committed and theologically orthodox Christian—made the same point. In a letter to his cousin Zabdiel Adams, he writes: "The only foundation of a free Constitution is pure virtue." Again we must ask ourselves: What world did Adams live in that he could say something like that without the need to explain it or qualify it? And what ideological world do we live in that we are so surprised by it? Adams even went on to warn that if the people of the newly formed United States did not have virtue in "greater measure" in the years ahead than they did when he was writing, they would not have a liberty that would last. "They may change their rulers and the forms of government, but they will not obtain a lasting liberty. They will only exchange tyrants and tyrannies." Adams knew that this was the secret, the thing that would tie it all together.

In the *Federalist Papers*, which serve as a kind of Midrash commentary on the Torah of our founding documents, James Madison too makes the link between virtue and freedom:

> As there is a degree of depravity in mankind that requires a certain degree of circumspection and distrust, so there are other qualities in human nature that justify a certain portion of esteem and confidence. Republican government presupposes the existence of these qualities in a higher degree than any other form. Were the pictures that have been drawn by the political jealousy of some among us faithful likenesses of the human character, the inference would be, that there is not sufficient virtue among men for self-government; and that nothing less than the chains of despotism can restrain them from destroying and devouring one another.

All of the founders understood this. But this idea was not a strange belief limited to the late decades of the eighteenth century. In 1831, some forty years after the Constitution came into being, the French political thinker and historian Alexis de Tocqueville traveled to America with his lifelong friend Gustave de Beaumont. The French government—the so-called July Monarchy—had sent them to examine the prisons and penitentiaries in America, with an eye to bringing what they learned back to France. But his travels and investigations in America would range much farther and wider.

Tocqueville found himself generally marveling at the American people and the democracy they had established that flourished now, over a half century since their revolution. Why had the French Revolution ended in a nightmare of guillotine executions and worse? Why had the French struggled endlessly with political upheavals and violence in the decades since their revolution while America had enjoyed unprecedented success? For America's success to have continued so peacefully for so many decades must have some reason or reasons, and perhaps he could divine them in his time there. When he returned to France, he wrote his now-classic two-volume work, *Democracy in America*. The gist of what Tocqueville concludes may ironically best be summed up in a famous quote misattributed to him since at least 1941.[2] It's such an apt summation of his classic book that no less than Eisenhower, Reagan, and Clinton have used it to illustrate what they too saw as the secret at the heart of American success:

> Not until I went into the churches of America and heard her pulpits aflame with righteousness did I understand the secret of her genius and power. America is great because she is good, and if America ever ceases to be good, she will cease to be great.

Though we now know these were someone else's brilliant summation of Tocqueville, we know from the rest of his book that he saw clearly that it was the "goodness" of America's people that made America work. Fifty years after Adams had said it and forty-some years after Franklin had said it, Tocqueville with his own eyes saw the evidence of this wherever he went. For him it was inescapable: *The secret to American freedom was American virtue*. Of course, he didn't mean that Americans were somehow inherently good. No one could or should believe that a disparate group of people on one continent would be somehow inherently better than another group on another continent. That would be akin to racism. This was something about the culture of America, about Americans' shared values. The difference was not in their genetic makeup, nor in their drinking water, nor even in their beliefs. It was in their behavior. That behavior was informed by their beliefs, but if the beliefs hadn't been manifested in their behavior, those beliefs would have made no difference. The word Tocqueville used was "mores"—meaning those habits "of central importance accepted without question and embodying the fundamental moral views of a group." He wrote: "I considered mores to be one of the great general causes responsible for the maintenance of a democratic republic." And then he said that by the term "mores" he meant "habits of the heart." In the same book Tocqueville put it as bluntly as Franklin or Adams had, writing: "Liberty cannot be established without morality."

This idea that freedom of the kind described by the founders requires virtue was central to the thinking of the founding generation and obvious to Tocqueville a half century later. It was the secret at the heart of America.

Virtue Requires Faith

What, then, of the next leg in the Golden Triangle of Freedom? If our modern sensibilities can weather the stormy idea that virtue is inextricably linked to freedom, and that American freedom cannot long be sustained without it, must we also accept the idea that virtue is linked to faith and religion?

Before we consider this idea separately, we should see that for many of the founders the idea of virtue and morality divorced from religion and faith was unthinkable. The link between them was assumed. Perhaps the most famous quotation on this subject comes to us from John Adams from a letter he wrote to the officers in the Massachusetts militia while he was our second president. That he wrote these words in his official capacity as U.S. president is itself remarkable to our modern sensibilities:

> We have no government armed with power capable of contending with human passions unbridled by morality and religion. Avarice, ambition, revenge, or gallantry, would break the strongest cords of our Constitution as a whale goes through a net. Our Constitution was made only for a moral and religious people. It is wholly inadequate to the government of any other.

Adams understood that the secret to self-government is that the people must themselves be self-governing, which is to say they must be motivated by something beyond the law. Each individual must govern himself, and for this morality was plainly necessary. But in the penultimate sentence Adams conflates these ideas of morality and religion, because for him—as for most others of that era—religion was necessary to the success of the American experiment. It could not and should not be forced, but it was nonetheless necessary and should certainly be encouraged, however possible. Adams seems to have had no idea that future generations might not only miss this, but would loudly argue against it. He seems unable to imagine a world that thinks religion beside the point in this conversation about freedom and self-government, or not just beside the point but somehow antithetical to them. Again, how can we have strayed so far from the founders on these most central points?

But we should ask ourselves: Other than one's religion or faith, what could motivate someone to be virtuous and "self-governing"? Once we understand, as the founders did, that self-government and virtue go hand in hand, we must ask: *What would make someone behave virtuously?* Even if the question is merely pragmatic, we must wonder: Why would someone do the right thing? To be sure, the cultural and societal pressure to conform plays a significant role. But if those things are not enough, what is left to motivate someone in that way? And of course we must ask what motivates that cultural and societal pressure in the first place. For the founders there was little to discuss on this subject. The answer—both practically speaking and theoretically—must be religion. (In our day everyone seems to know that helping the poor is important, for example, or that slavery is wrong, or that being good stewards of the environment is important, but what we have completely forgotten is that these ideas all stemmed from the Judeo-Christian tradition in the West. We seem to think that whatever virtues we do possess arose by themselves. History guffaws at the very idea.)

The founders staked their lives and reputations on these fundamental ideas, but five decades later their bet had been proved safe, because when Tocqueville came to visit, he quickly saw that it was indeed religion that worked hand in hand with American freedom. France had long before fallen far from the high ideals of its revolution, but five decades on, America's freedom shone much as it had in its bright beginning. For Tocqueville religion was clearly the reason.

> Upon my arrival in the United States the religious aspect of the country was the first thing that struck my attention; and the longer I stayed there, the more I perceived the great political consequences resulting from this new state of things. In France I had almost always seen the spirit of religion and the spirit of freedom marching in opposite directions. But in America I found they were intimately united and that they reigned in common over the same country.

Tocqueville also said that there was "no country in the world where the Christian religion retains a greater influence over the souls of men than in America." In other words, there is an authority, but it stems from a voluntary—which is to say a free obedience to God, rather than from forced obedience to any man or government of men.

But he not only observed these things; like the founders, he understood how they worked:

> Despotism may govern without faith, but liberty cannot. Religion is much more necessary in the republic which they set forth in glowing colors than in the monarchy which they attack; it is more needed in democratic republics than in any others. How is it possible that society should escape destruction if the moral tie is not strengthened in proportion as the political tie is relaxed? And what can be done with a people who are their own masters if they are not submissive to the Deity?

He understood that the law could not force people to do what was right. In fact, the laws of America didn't try to do this. They provided freedom, and what the citizens did with that freedom was something else altogether. "Thus," Tocqueville writes, "while the law permits the Americans to do what they please, religion prevents them from conceiving, and forbids them to commit, what is rash or unjust."

He also observed that Americans seemed to understand the importance of religion to their way of life and as not less than "indispensable to the maintenance of republican institutions." Tocqueville even goes so far as to say that in the United States, the "sovereign authority is religious." In other words, where there is no human sovereign there must be another sovereign, and for Americans that sovereign was God himself, to whom they would voluntarily submit themselves. Tocqueville writes,

> There is no country in the world where the Christian religion retains a greater influence over the souls of men than in America, and there can be no greater proof of its utility and of its conformity to human nature than that its influence is powerfully felt over the most enlightened and free nation of the earth.

George Washington, often wrongly cited as a mere Deist more beholden to the ideas of the French Enlightenment than to Christian faith, concurred on all of the above. In his farewell address at the end of his second term in 1796, he said:

> Let us with caution indulge the supposition that morality can be maintained without religion. Whatever may be conceded to the influence of refined education on minds of peculiar structure, reason and experience both forbid us to expect that national morality can prevail in exclusion of religious principles.

According to Washington too the Constitution and the laws of the land were insufficient. Virtue and character were vital; and for these to exist, "religious principles" and "religion" must be present.

But if Franklin and Washington are often mischaracterized as irreligious, none is so mischaracterized as Jefferson himself. He may well have been the least religious of all the founding fathers, but if he was the least religious, he was nonetheless tremendously religious when compared with the secularism of most of our cultural leaders today. He's wrongly described as the one pure French Enlightenment Deist in the founding scrum, but this can hardly be true, because the principles that motivated the French Revolution were not only secular but also violently anticlerical, and Jefferson nowhere comes close to this characterization. It can only be that the zeal of modern secularists has caused Jefferson's irreligiosity to be exaggerated and that intellectual sloppiness has allowed many of us to accept that blurred view. Who but a man who believed in God and who took God seriously as an agent in history could write what Jefferson wrote in his *Notes on the State of Virginia* in 1785:

> Can the liberties of a nation be thought secure when we have removed their only firm basis, a conviction in the minds of the people, that those liberties are the gift of God? That they are violated but with his wrath? I tremble for my country when I reflect that God is just, and that His justice cannot sleep forever.

If we suppose he is talking about a clockmaker God of Deist imagination and not the Yahweh of the Hebrew Scriptures, we should consider his letter to Daniel Webster in which he says: "I have always said, and always will say, that the studious perusal of the [Bible] will make better citizens, better fathers, and better husbands."[3]

But once we have seen that the founders unanimously thought virtue necessary to freedom and religion necessary to virtue, we must ask: What allowed religion itself to thrive as it did? And now we have come full circle—or full triangle, if you will—because Guinness says that it is freedom itself that makes religion and faith thrive in America.

True Faith Requires Freedom

The idea that freedom requires virtue, which requires faith—which in turn requires freedom—is at once simple and elegant, but to our modern and often secularly inclined minds it can be a bit disturbing. For many the idea of faith and freedom working together to bolster each other brings about cognitive dissonance. That's because in America today we have stepped backward to a cultural situation less like the earlier times in our own country than like the France of Tocqueville day, in which religion and freedom were thought to be bitterest enemies.

"In France," Tocqueville wrote, "I had almost always seen the spirit of religion and the spirit of freedom marching in opposite directions. But in America I found they were intimately united and that they reigned in common over the same country."

America in the twenty-first century has generally returned to the worldview of the eighteenth-century French Enlightenment rationalists, who were so appalled at the religious wars of the previous century that they recoiled from all religion, unable to fathom a world in which religion and freedom could be mutually supporting. England too, had become generally skeptical of the orthodox Christian faith, especially among its cultural elites, and many Church of England pastors were themselves preaching a kind of French Enlightenment rationalism from their state-sanctioned pulpits. But Tocqueville saw the error in such thinking and saw that the truth of the matter was borne out in American society.

> The philosophers of the eighteenth century explained in a very simple manner the gradual decay of religious faith. Religious zeal, said they, must necessarily fail the more generally liberty is established and knowledge diffused. But the facts by no means accord with their theory. There are certain populations in Europe whose unbelief is only equaled by their ignorance and debasement; while in America, one of the freest and most enlightened nations in the world, the people fulfill with fervor all the outward duties of religion.

The eighteenth-century philosophes have many indignant children in the West today, but time and again the facts of history stubbornly repel their prognostications. Those who have maintained that religion would evaporate as knowledge and liberties increase see that this is somehow not at all the case. The "God of the gaps" does in fact go away, but the true God of history only reveals himself the more.

But what is it about *American* religion that defies the predictions of the French Enlightenment secularists? What haven't they accounted for? In another place Tocqueville writes:

> The character of Anglo-American civilization . . . is the product . . . of two perfectly distinct elements that elsewhere have often made war with each other, but which, in America, they have succeeded in incorporating somehow into one another and combining marvelously. I mean to speak of the spirit of religion and the spirit of freedom.

But how is one a buttress to the other? For sure the main difference between how the founders saw faith and how most other societies saw faith had everything to do with what we in America call religious freedom or religious liberty. This did not exist in France, nor anywhere in Europe during this period. But in America, from the very beginning, it did. It was this that thwarted the predictions of the French Enlightenment philosophes and it is this that continues to thwart the predictions of modern secularists. Of course, Tocqueville saw it himself:

> The sects that exist in the United States are innumerable. They all differ in respect to the worship which is due to the Creator; but they all agree in respect to the duties which are due from man to man. Each sect adores the Deity in its own peculiar manner, but all sects preach the same moral law in the name of God. . . . Moreover, all the sects of the United States are comprised within the great unity of Christianity, and Christian morality is everywhere the same.

Since the Pilgrims came to our shores in 1620, religious freedom and religious tolerance have been the single most important principle of American life. This was the genius at the heart of it all. But tragically this linchpin of American liberty has been more misunderstood in recent years than at any time in our existence.

[1] Os Guinness spoke about this subject and his book *A Free People's Suicide* at Socrates in the City. That speech may be viewed at www.socratesinthecity.com.

[2] See John J. Pitney's article in *The Weekly Standard* titled "The Tocqueville Fraud," November 12, 1995. This explains the history behind the misattribution of the quote to Tocqueville.

[3] For further reading on Jefferson's faith, I recommend *Doubting Thomas: The Religious Life and Legacy of Thomas Jefferson* by Mark Beliles and Jerry Newcombe.

"The Golden Triangle of Freedom" Discussion Questions

1. **What is the Golden Triangle of Freedom?**

2. **Did the founding fathers believe and promote the idea that freedom requires virtue?**

3. **Was the role of religion in America encouraged or downplayed by our early political leaders?**

4. **Who was Alexis de Tocqueville, and what role did he play in American history?**

5. **Was the idea that faith and freedom could coexist generally accepted in the eighteenth century?**

“Political Animal” Video

Dr. Jeff Myers explores the *four myths* that keep Christians from getting involved in politics and exposes the fallacies behind these myths: 1) God doesn't care about politics; 2) It's not my problem; 3) Choosing between the lesser of two evils is evil; and 4) Politics just doesn't matter.

Dr. Myers goes on to examine the *five main views* about Christians and politics traditionally held by believers: 1) Christians should not be involved; 2) Society is not worth saving; 3) Political structures cannot change the human heart; 4) Christians should only be concerned about the church; and 5) Christians should get involved by following a party line. He concludes by asking and answering the question, “What are Christians to do?”

To access this video, go to www.summitu.com/utc and enter the passcode found in the back of your manual.

▶ "POLITICAL ANIMAL" VIDEO OUTLINE

Young people and evangelical Christians don't vote in great numbers. There are several factors why Christians don't participate in politics:

Four myths that keep Christians from getting involved in politics

1. *God doesn't care about* ____________________. God does care and is concerned with his glory (Psalm 57). This applies to Washington DC and every other seat of government. Politics is a form of discipleship. It honors God.
2. *It's not my problem.* In America, authority rests with the people. To refuse to participate in politics is to refuse to submit to authority, which is unbiblical.
3. *Choosing between the lesser of two evils is* ________________. All people have evil in their hearts but that doesn't exclude us from getting involved with politics. We are to overcome evil with good (Romans 12:21).
4. *Politics just doesn't matter.* Political policy set millions free in the Soviet Union, Taiwan, and South Korea. Political decisions affect our everyday lives.

Five main views Christians hold about politics

1. *Christian should not be involved.* Christianity is limited to the invisible and the devotional.
2. ____________________ *is not worth saving.* There's no point in trying to make anything better because it will be destroyed.
3. *Political structures cannot change the human heart.* Expecting anything to change the human heart is idolatry; still, God's sovereignty should be extended everywhere.
4. *Christian should only be concerned about* __________________. This is known as two-kingdom theology. Bible is for the church and politics is run by natural laws. The two shouldn't mix.
5. *Christian should get involved by following a party line.* Christians should try to take over and reclaim America for Christ. But this approach comes across as a raw grab for political power.

Christian theory of political involvement

Abraham Kuyper introduced the political theory of sphere sovereignty with three spheres:

- ____________________
- Church
- State

Society works best when each sphere handles what is appropriate to it. Problems arise when spheres improperly expand and squash other spheres. When faced with political questions, it is important to ask these questions:

1. Is it the proper domain of this sphere to take on this issue?
2. What is the effect on the other spheres?
3. Could this problem be solved in another way?

▶ "POLITICAL ANIMAL" DISCUSSION QUESTIONS

1. **What are the four myths that keep many Christians from getting involved in politics? Pick one and be ready to defend it as a valid reason for not voting.**

2. **Is it unbiblical for American Christians to refrain from voting or from getting involved in politics?**

3. **Why work to make society better when God is going to destroy this world anyway?**

4. **What is two-kingdoms theology? If you think it is valid, how would you defend it? If you think it is wrong, how would you refute it?**

5. **What is the theology of sphere sovereignty and how does it affect society?**

Chapter 12 Key Points

Key Questions:

1. What is the nature of government and politics?
2. What perspective do other worldviews have on civil government?
3. In what way should Christians be involved in politics?
4. How should Christians resist evil laws and evil government leaders?

Key Passages:

1. Genesis 2:15*
2. Romans 13:1–4*
3. Acts 5:29

Key Persons:

1. William Blackstone
2. Dietrich Bonhoeffer
3. Edmund Burke*
4. Abraham Kuyper

Key Terms:

1. Civil Disobedience
2. Communism
3. Democracy*
4. Dirigisme
5. Justice*
6. Legal Positivism
7. Mosaic Law
8. Natural law
9. Pan-Islam
10. Politics
11. Proletariat
12. Republic*
13. Sharia Law
14. Socialism
15. Sphere Sovereignty
16. Subsidiarity
17. Totalitarianism
18. Tort Law

**Short answer or essay question on the exam*

Chapter 12 Assignment

Answer the following questions with at least one paragraph.

1. **Why does a secular worldview seek to remove any discussion of religion from politics?**

2. **How does the perspective of leadership as a form of servanthood contrast with a worldly perspective of power?**

3. **What is the model of "sphere sovereignty"? What does it seek to balance and why?**

4. **Describe the principle of "subsidiarity" and what it seeks to protect or promote.**

UNIT
13

Religious Freedom and Persecution

Chapter 13 Learning Objectives

Students will be able to:

1. describe why religious freedom is under attack. [13.1]
2. identify past and present causes of religious persecution around the world. [13.2]
3. discuss ways the Bible shows that God cares for the oppressed and ways religious freedom is essential for sustaining a free and virtuous society. [13.3]
4. articulate why Christians should forsake a gospel of abandonment and advocate for religious freedom. [13.4]
5. conclude that persecution can foster the spread of the gospel and that there is a cost to following Christ. [13.5]

Chapter 13 Discussion Questions

1. **How are religious freedoms being restricted in the United States? [13.1]**

2. **What is religious freedom? [13.2]**

3. **What is religious persecution? [13.2]**

4. **How does the absence of tolerance lead to religious persecution? [13.2]**

5. **What caused religious persecution in the past? [13.2]**

6. **What events, historical or current, make you most embarrassed as a Christian? [13.2]**

7. **Who are the main victims of religious persecution today? [13.2]**

8. **How are Christians treated under Marxism? [13.2]**

9. How are Christians treated under Islam? [13.2]

10. Which Muslim countries are the most hostile toward Christians? [13.2]

11. What is the basis for religious freedom in America? [13.2]

12. How is the government attacking religious freedom in America? [13.2]

13. What are some examples of nongovernment attacks on religious freedom in America? [13.2]

14. How does the Bible show God's care for the oppressed? [13.3]

15. Why is religious freedom the key to a free society? [13.3]

16. Have you ever experienced religious persecution? [13.3]

17. Why is it important for Christians to forsake a "gospel of abandonment?" [13.4]

18. What is at stake when it comes to defending religious freedom? [13.5]

19. What is at stake when it comes to defending religious freedom? [13.5]

20. What is at stake when it comes to defending religious freedom? [13.5]

"A World Split Apart" Reading

This was Aleksandr Solzhenitsyn's first public address since arriving in the United States in 1976. Instead of a stern rebuke of communism, he spoke of the moral decline and spiritual weakness of the West. He accused the ruling and intellectual elites of being "passive, self-serving, weak, and cowardly."

As much as he disliked socialism and communism, they at least produced spiritual character in those forced to live under them. The West, with all its self-serving freedoms, was spiritually bankrupt and a poor role model for the rest of the world. The root problem, according to Solzhenitsyn, was the rationalistic humanism that sprang from the Age of Enlightenment. As he said, "The humanistic way of thinking, which had proclaimed itself our guide, did not admit the existence of intrinsic evil in man, nor did it see any task higher than the attainment of happiness on earth."

Finally, Solzhenitsyn charged, "We have placed too much hope in politics and social reforms, only to find out that we were being deprived of our most precious possession: our spiritual life."

A World Split Apart

by Aleksandr I. Solzhenitsyn

I am sincerely happy to be here with you on the occasion of the 327th commencement of this old and illustrious university. My congratulations and best wishes to all of today's graduates.

Harvard's motto is "VERITAS." Many of you have already found out and others will find out in the course of their lives that truth eludes us as soon as our concentration begins to flag, all the while leaving the illusion that we are continuing to pursue it. This is the source of much discord. Also, truth seldom is sweet; it is almost invariably bitter. A measure of truth is included in my speech today, but I offer it as a friend, not as an adversary.

Three years ago in the United States I said certain things that were rejected and appeared unacceptable. Today, however, many people agree with what I said. …

The split in today's world is perceptible even to a hasty glance. Any of our contemporaries readily identifies two world powers, each of them already capable of destroying each other. However, the understanding of the split too often is limited to this political conception: the illusion according to which danger may be abolished through successful diplomatic negotiations or by achieving a balance of armed forces. The truth is that the split is both more profound and more alienating, that the rifts are more numerous than one can see at first glance. These deep manifold splits bear the danger of equally manifold disaster for all of us, in accordance with the ancient truth that a kingdom—in this case, our Earth—divided against itself cannot stand.

There is the concept of the Third World: thus, we already have three worlds. Undoubtedly, however, the number is even greater; we are just too far away to see. Every ancient and deeply rooted self-contained culture, especially if it is spread over a wide part of the earth's surface, constitutes a self-contained world, full of riddles and surprises to Western thinking. As a minimum, we must include in this China, India, the Muslim world, and Africa, if indeed we accept the approximation of viewing the latter two as uniform.

For one thousand years Russia belonged to such a category, although Western thinking systematically committed the mistake of denying its special character and therefore never understood it, just as today the West does not understand Russia in Communist captivity. And while it may be that in past years Japan has increasingly become, in effect, a Far West, drawing ever closer to Western ways (I am no judge here), Israel, I think, should not be reckoned as part of the West, if only because of the decisive circumstance that its state system is fundamentally linked to its religion.

How short a time ago, relatively, the small world of modern Europe was easily seizing colonies all over the globe, not only without anticipating any real resistance, but usually with contempt for any possible values in the conquered people's approach to life. It all seemed an overwhelming success, with no geographic limits. Western society expanded in a triumph of human independence and power. And all of a sudden the twentieth century brought the clear realization of this society's fragility.

We now see that the conquests proved to be short lived and precarious (and this, in turn, points to defects in the Western view of the world which led to these conquests). Relations with the former colonial world now have switched to the opposite extreme and the Western world often exhibits an excess of obsequiousness, but it is difficult yet to estimate the size of the bill which former colonial countries will present to the West and it is difficult to predict whether the surrender not only of its last colonies, but of everything it owns, will be sufficient for the West to clear this account.

But the persisting blindness of superiority continues to hold the belief that all the vast regions of our planet should develop and mature to the level of contemporary Western systems, the best in theory and the most attractive in practice; that all those other worlds are but temporarily prevented (by wicked leaders or by severe crises or by their own barbarity and incomprehension) from pursuing Western pluralistic democracy and adopting the Western way of life. Countries are judged on the merit of their progress in that direction. But in fact such a conception is a fruit of Western incomprehension of the essence of other worlds, a result of mistakenly measuring them all with a Western yardstick. The real picture of our planet's development bears little resemblance to all this.

The anguish of a divided world gave birth to the theory of convergence between the leading Western countries and the Soviet Union. It is a soothing theory which overlooks the fact that these worlds are not evolving toward each other and that neither one can be transformed into the other without violence. Besides, convergence inevitably means acceptance of the other side's defects, too, and this can hardly suit anyone.

If I were today addressing an audience in my country, in my examination of the overall pattern of the world's rifts I would have concentrated on the calamities of the East. But since my forced exile in the West has now lasted four years and since my audience is a Western one, I think it may be of greater interest to concentrate on certain aspects of the contemporary West, such as I see them.

A decline in courage may be the most striking feature that an outside observer notices in the West today. The Western world has lost its civic courage, both as a whole and separately, in each country, in each government, in each political party, and, of course, in the United Nations. Such a decline in courage is particularly noticeable among the ruling and intellectual elites, causing an impression of a loss of courage by the entire society. There are many courageous individuals, but they have no determining influence on public life.

Political and intellectual functionaries exhibit this depression, passivity, and perplexity in their actions and in their statements, and even more so in their self-serving rationales as to how realistic, reasonable, and intellectually and even morally justified it is to base state policies on weakness and cowardice. And the decline in courage, at times attaining what could be termed a lack of manhood, is ironically emphasized by occasional outbursts and inflexibility on the part of those same functionaries when dealing with weak governments and with countries that lack support, or with doomed currents which clearly cannot offer resistance. But they get tongue-tied and paralyzed when they deal with powerful governments and threatening forces, with aggressors and international terrorists.

Must one point out that from ancient times a decline in courage has been considered the first symptom of the end?

When the modern Western states were being formed, it was proclaimed as a principle that governments are meant to serve man and that man lives in order to be free and pursue happiness. (See, for example, the American Declaration of Independence.) Now at last during past decades technical and social progress has permitted the realization of such aspirations: the welfare state.

Every citizen has been granted the desired freedom and material goods in such quantity and in such quality as to guarantee in theory the achievement of happiness, in the debased sense of the word which has come into being during those same decades. (In the process, however, one psychological detail has been overlooked: the constant desire to have still more things and a still better life and the struggle to this end imprint many Western faces with worry and even depression, though it is customary to carefully conceal such feelings. This active and tense competition comes to dominate all human thought and does not in the least open a way to free spiritual development.)

The individual's independence from many types of state pressure has been guaranteed; the majority of the people have been granted well-being to an extent their fathers and grandfathers could not even dream about; it has become possible to raise young people according to these ideals, preparing them for and summoning them toward physical bloom, happiness, and leisure, the possession of material goods, money, and leisure, toward an almost unlimited freedom in the choice of pleasures. So who should now renounce all this, why and for the sake of what should one risk one's precious life in defense of the common good and particularly in the nebulous case when the security of one's nation must be defended in an as yet distant land?

Even biology tells us that a high degree of habitual well-being is not advantageous to a living organism. Today, well-being in the life of Western society has begun to take off its pernicious mask.

Western society has chosen for itself the organization best suited to its purposes and one I might call legalistic. The limits of human rights and rightness are determined by a system of laws; such limits are very broad. People in the West have acquired considerable skill in using, interpreting, and manipulating law (though laws tend to be too complicated for an average person to understand without the help of an expert). Every conflict is solved according to the letter of the law and this is considered to be the ultimate solution.

If one is risen from a legal point of view, nothing more is required, nobody may mention that one could still not be right, and urge self-restraint or a renunciation of these rights, call for sacrifice and selfless risk: this would simply sound absurd. Voluntary self-restraint is almost unheard of: everybody strives toward further expansion to the extreme limit of the legal frames. (An oil company is legally blameless when it buys up an invention of a new type of energy in order to prevent its use. A food product manufacturer is legally blameless when he poisons his produce to make it last longer: after all, people are free not to purchase it.)

I have spent all my life under a Communist regime and I will tell you that a society without any objective legal scale is a terrible one indeed. But a society based on the letter of the law and never reaching any higher fails to take full advantage of the full range of human possibilities. The letter of the law is too cold and formal to have a beneficial influence on society. Whenever the tissue of life is woven of legalistic relationships, this creates an atmosphere of spiritual mediocrity that paralyzes man's noblest impulses.

And it will be simply impossible to bear up to the trials of this threatening century with nothing but the supports of a legalistic structure.

Today's Western society has revealed the inequality between the freedom for good deeds and the freedom for evil deeds. A statesman who wants to achieve something highly constructive for his country has to move cautiously and even timidly; thousands of hasty (and irresponsible) critics cling to him at all times; he is constantly rebuffed by parliament and the press. He has to prove that his every step is well founded and absolutely flawless. Indeed, an outstanding, truly great person who has unusual and unexpected initiatives in mind does not get any chance to assert himself; dozens of traps will be set for him from the beginning. Thus mediocrity triumphs under the guise of democratic restraints.

It is feasible and easy everywhere to undermine administrative power and it has in fact been drastically weakened in all Western countries. The defense of individual rights has reached such extremes as to make society as a whole defenseless against certain individuals. It is time, in the West, to defend not so much human rights as human obligations.

On the other hand, destructive and irresponsible freedom has been granted boundless space. Society has turned out to have scarce defense against the abyss of human decadence, for example against the misuse of liberty for moral violence against young people, such as motion pictures full of pornography, crime, and horror. This is all considered to be part of freedom and to be counterbalanced, in theory, by the young people's right not to look and not to accept. Life organized legalistically has thus shown its inability to defend itself against the corrosion of evil.

And what shall we say about the dark realms of overt criminality? Legal limits (especially in the United States) are broad enough to encourage not only individual freedom but also some misuse of such freedom. The culprit can go unpunished or obtain undeserved leniency—all with the support of thousands of defenders in the society. When a government earnestly undertakes to root out terrorism, public opinion immediately accuses it of violating the terrorist's civil rights. There is quite a number of such cases.

This tilt of freedom toward evil has come about gradually, but it evidently stems from a humanistic and benevolent concept according to which man—the master of the world—does not bear any evil within himself, and all the defects of life are caused by misguided social systems, which must therefore be corrected. Yet strangely enough, though the best social conditions have been achieved in the West, there still remains a great deal of crime; there even is considerably more of it than in the destitute and lawless Soviet society. (There is a multitude of prisoners in our camps who are termed criminals, but most of them never committed any crime; they merely tried to defend themselves against a lawless state by resorting to means outside the legal framework.)

The press, too, of course, enjoys the widest freedom. (I shall be using the word "press" to include all the media.) But what use does it make of it?

Here again, the overriding concern is not to infringe the letter of the law. There is no true moral responsibility for distortion or disproportion. What sort of responsibility does a journalist or a newspaper have to the readership or to history? If they have misled public opinion by inaccurate information or wrong conclusions, even if they have contributed to mistakes on a state level, do we know of any case of open regret voiced by the same journalist or the same newspaper? No; this would damage sales. A nation may be the worse for such a mistake, but the journalist always gets away with it. It is most likely that he will start writing the exact opposite to his previous statements with renewed aplomb.

Because instant and credible information is required, it becomes necessary to resort to guesswork, rumors, and suppositions to fill in the voids, and none of them will ever be refuted; they settle into the readers' memory. How many hasty, immature, superficial, and misleading judgments are expressed everyday, confusing readers, and then left hanging?

The press can act the role of public opinion or miseducate it. Thus we may see terrorists heroized, or secret matters pertaining to the nation's defense publicly revealed, or we may witness shameless intrusion into the privacy of well-known people according to the slogan "Everyone is entitled to know everything." (But this is a false slogan of a false era; far greater in value is the forfeited right of people not to know, not to have their divine souls stuffed with gossip, nonsense, vain talk. A person who works and leads a meaningful life has no need for this excessive and burdening flow of information.)

Hastiness and superficiality—these are the psychic diseases of the twentieth century and more than anywhere else this is manifested in the press. In-depth analysis of a problem is anathema to the press; it is contrary to its nature. The press merely picks out sensational formulas.

Such as it is, however, the press has become the greatest power within Western countries, exceeding that of the legislature, the executive, and the judiciary. Yet one would like to ask: According to what law has it been elected and to whom is it responsible? In the Communist East, a journalist is frankly appointed as a state official. But who has voted Western journalists into their positions of power, for how long a time, and with what prerogatives?

There is yet another surprise for someone coming from the totalitarian East with its rigorously unified press: One discovers a common trend of preferences within the Western press as a whole (the spirit of the time), generally accepted patterns of judgment, and maybe common corporate interests, the sum effect being not competition but unification. Unrestrained freedom exists for the press, but not for readership, because newspapers mostly transmit in a forceful and emphatic way those opinions which do not too openly contradict their own and that general trend.

Without any censorship in the West, fashionable trends of thought and ideas are fastidiously separated from those that are not fashionable, and the latter, without ever being forbidden have little chance of finding their way into periodicals or books or being heard in colleges. Your scholars are free in the legal sense, but they are hemmed in by the idols of the prevailing fad. There is no open violence, as in the East; however, a selection dictated by fashion and the need to accommodate mass standards frequently prevents the most independent-minded persons from contributing to public life and gives rise to dangerous herd instincts that block dangerous herd development.

In America, I have received letters from highly intelligent persons—maybe a teacher in a faraway small college who could do much for the renewal and salvation of his country, but the country cannot hear him because the media will not provide him with a forum. This gives birth to strong mass prejudices, to a blindness which is perilous in our dynamic era. An example is the self-deluding interpretation of the state of affairs in the contemporary world that functions as a sort of petrified armor around people's minds, to such a degree that human voices from seventeen countries of Eastern Europe and Eastern Asia cannot pierce it. It will be broken only by the inexorable crowbar of events.

I have mentioned a few traits of Western life which surprise and shock a new arrival to this world. The purpose and scope of this speech will not allow me to continue such a survey, in particular to look into the impact of these characteristics on important aspects of a nation's life, such as elementary education, advanced education in the humanities, and art.

It is almost universally recognized that the West shows all the world the way to successful economic development, even though in past years it has been sharply offset by chaotic inflation. However, many people living in the West are dissatisfied with their own society. They despise it or accuse it of no longer being up to the level of maturity by mankind. And this causes many to sway toward socialism, which is a false and dangerous current.

I hope that no one present will suspect me of expressing my partial criticism of the Western system in order to suggest socialism as an alternative. No; with the experience of a country where socialism has been realized, I shall not speak for such an alternative. The mathematician Igor Shafarevich, a member of the Soviet Academy of Science, has written a brilliantly argued book entitled Socialism; this is a penetrating historical analysis demonstrating that socialism of any type and shade leads to a total destruction of the human spirit and to a leveling of mankind into death. Shafarevich's book was published in France almost two years ago and so far no one has been found to refute it. It will shortly be published in English in the U.S.

But should I be asked, instead, whether I would propose the West, such as it is today, as a model to my country, I would frankly have to answer negatively. No, I could not recommend your society as an ideal for the transformation of ours. Through deep suffering, people in our own country have now achieved a spiritual development of such intensity that the Western system in its present state of spiritual exhaustion does not look attractive. Even those characteristics of your life which I have just enumerated are extremely saddening.

A fact which cannot be disputed is the weakening of human personality in the West while in the East it has become firmer and stronger. Six decades for our people and three decades for the people of Eastern Europe; during that time we have been through a spiritual training far in advance of Western experience. The complex and deadly crush of life has produced stronger, deeper, and more interesting personalities than those generated by standardized Western well-being. Therefore, if our society were to be transformed into yours, it would mean an improvement in certain aspects, but also a change for the worse on some particularly significant points.

Of course, a society cannot remain in an abyss of lawlessness, as is the case in our country. But it is also demeaning for it to stay on such a soulless and smooth plane of legalism, as is the case in yours. After the suffering of decades of violence and oppression, the human soul longs for things higher, warmer, and purer than those offered by today's mass living habits, introduced as by a calling card by the revolting invasion of commercial advertising, by TV stupor, and by intolerable music.

All this is visible to numerous observers from all the worlds of our planet. The Western way of life is less and less likely to become the leading model.

There are telltale symptoms by which history gives warning to a threatened or perishing society. Such are, for instance, a decline of the arts or a lack of great statesmen. Indeed, sometimes the warnings are quite explicit and concrete. The center of your democracy and of your culture is left without electric power for a few hours only, and all of a sudden crowds of American citizens start looting and creating havoc. The smooth surface film must be very thin, then, the social system quite unstable and unhealthy.

But the fight for our planet, physical and spiritual, a fight of cosmic proportions, is not a vague matter of the future; it has already started. The forces of Evil have begun their decisive offensive. You can feel their pressure, yet your screens and publications are full of prescribed smiles and raised glasses. What is the joy about?

How has this unfavorable relation of forces come about? How did the West decline from its triumphal march to its present debility? Have there been fatal turns and losses of direction in its development? It does not seem so. The West kept advancing steadily in accordance with its proclaimed social intentions, hand in hand with a dazzling progress in technology. And all of a sudden it found itself in its present state of weakness.

This means that the mistake must be at the root, at the very foundation of thought in modern times. I refer to the prevailing Western view of the world in modern times. I refer to the prevailing Western view of the world which was born in the Renaissance and has found political expression since the Age of Enlightenment. It became the basis for political and social doctrine and could be called rationalistic humanism or humanistic autonomy: the pro-claimed and practiced autonomy of man from any higher force above him. It could also be called anthropocentricity, with man seen as the center of all.

The turn introduced by the Renaissance was probably inevitable historically: the Middle Ages had come to a natural end by exhaustion, having become an intolerable despotic repression of man's physical nature in favor of the spiritual one. But then we recoiled from the spirit and embraced all that is material, excessively and incommensurately. The humanistic way of thinking, which had proclaimed itself our guide, did not admit the existence of intrinsic evil in man, nor did it see any task higher than the attainment of happiness on earth. It started modern Western civilization on the dangerous trend of worshiping man and his material needs.

Everything beyond physical well-being and the accumulation of material goods, all other human requirements and characteristics of a subtle and higher nature, were left outside the area of attention of state and social systems, as if human life did not have any higher meaning. Thus gaps were left open for evil, and its drafts blow freely today. Mere freedom per se does not in the least solve all the problems of human life and even adds a number of new ones.

And yet in early democracies, as in American democracy at the time of its birth, all individual human rights were granted on the ground that man is God's creature. That is, freedom was given to the individual conditionally, in the assumption of his constant religious responsibility. Such was the heritage of the preceding one thousand years. Two hundred or even fifty years ago, it would have seemed quite impossible, in

America, that an individual be granted boundless freedom with no purpose, simply for the satisfaction of his whims.

Subsequently, however, all such limitations were eroded everywhere in the West; a total emancipation occurred from the moral heritage of Christian centuries with their great reserves of mercy and sacrifice. State systems were becoming ever more materialistic. The West has finally achieved the rights of man, and even excess, but man's sense of responsibility to God and society has grown dimmer and dimmer. In the past decades, the legalistic selfishness of the Western approach to the world has reached its peak and the world has found itself in a harsh spiritual crisis and a political impasse. All the celebrated technological achievements of progress, including the conquest of outer space, do not redeem the twentieth century's moral poverty, which no one could have imagined even as late as the nineteenth century.

As humanism in its development was becoming more and more materialistic, it also increasingly allowed concepts to be used first by socialism and then by communism, so that Karl Marx was able to say, in 1844, that "communism is naturalized humanism."

This statement has proved to be not entirely unreasonable. One does not see the same stones in the foundations of an eroded humanism and of any type of socialism: boundless materialism; freedom from religion and religious responsibility (which under Communist regimes attains the stage of antireligious dictatorship); concentration on social structures with an allegedly scientific approach. (This last is typical of both the Age of Enlightenment and of Marxism.) It is no accident that all of communism's rhetorical vows revolve around Man (with a capital M) and his earthly happiness. At first glance it seems an ugly parallel: common traits in the thinking and way of life of today's West and today's East? But such is the logic of materialistic development.

The interrelationship is such, moreover, that the current of materialism which is farthest to the left, and is hence the most consistent, always proves to be stronger, more attractive, and victorious. Humanism which has lost its Christian heritage cannot prevail in this competition. Thus during the past centuries and especially in recent decades, as the process became more acute, the alignment of forces was as follows: Liberalism was inevitably pushed aside by radicalism, radicalism had to surrender to socialism, and socialism could not stand up to communism.

The communist regime in the East could endure and grow due to the enthusiastic support from an enormous number of Western intellectuals who (feeling the kinship!) refused to see communism's crimes, and when they no longer could do so, they tried to justify these crimes. The problem persists: In our Eastern countries, communism has suffered a complete ideological defeat; it is zero and less than zero. And yet Western intellectuals still look at it with considerable interest and empathy, and this is precisely what makes it so immensely difficult for the West to withstand the East.

I am not examining the case of a disaster brought on by a world war and the changes which it would produce in society. But as long as we wake up every morning under a peaceful sun, we must lead an everyday life. Yet there is a disaster which is already very much with us. I am referring to the calamity of an autonomous, irreligious humanistic consciousness.

It has made man the measure of all things on earth—imperfect man, who is never free of pride, self-interest, envy, vanity, and dozens of other defects. We are now paying for the mistakes which were not properly appraised at the beginning of the journey. On the way from the Renaissance to our days we have enriched our experience, but we have lost the concept of a Supreme Complete Entity which used to restrain our passions and our irresponsibility.

We have placed too much hope in politics and social reforms, only to find out that we were being deprived of our most precious possession: our spiritual life. It is trampled by the party mob in the East, by the commercial one in the West. This is the essence of the crisis: the split in the world is less terrifying than the similarity of the disease afflicting its main sections.

If, as claimed by humanism, man were born only to be happy, he would not be born to die. Since his body is doomed to death, his task on earth evidently must be more spiritual: not a total engrossment in everyday life, not the search for the best ways to obtain material goods and then their carefree consumption. It has to be the fulfillment of a permanent, earnest duty so that one's life journey may become above all an experience of moral growth: to leave life a better human being than one started it.

It is imperative to reappraise the scale of the usual human values; its present incorrectness is astounding. It is not possible that assessment of the President's performance should be reduced to the question of how much money one makes or to the availability of gasoline. Only by the voluntary nurturing in ourselves of freely accepted and serene self-restraint can mankind rise above the world stream of materialism.

Today it would be retrogressive to hold on to the ossified formulas of the Enlightenment. Such social dogmatism leaves us helpless before the trials of our times.

Even if we are spared destruction by war, life will have to change in order not to perish on its own. We cannot avoid reassessing the fundamental definitions of human life and society. Is it true that man is above everything? Is there no Superior Spirit above him? Is it right that man's life and society's activities should be ruled by material expansion above all? Is it permissible to promote such expansion to the detriment of our integral spiritual life?

If the world has not approached its end, it has reached a major watershed in history, equal in importance to the turn from the Middle Ages to the Renaissance. It will demand from us a spiritual blaze; we shall have to rise to a new height of vision, to a new level of life, where our physical nature will not be cursed, as in the Middle Ages, but even more importantly, our spiritual being will not be trampled upon, as in the Modern Era.

The ascension is similar to climbing onto the next anthropological stage. No one on earth has any other way left but—upward.

"A World Split Apart" Discussion Questions

1. **Who was Aleksandr I. Solzhenitsyn and why was he asked to speak at Harvard?**

2. **What did Solzhenitsyn see as the most striking feature in the West?**

3. **What did Solzhenitsyn think of the Western media?**

4. **Would Solzhenitsyn recommend the West as a model for the Soviet Union to follow?**

5. **To what factors did Solzhenitsyn attribute the decline of the West?**

“Religious Liberty” Video

Attorney Jeffery Ventrella expands on six threats to religious liberty and faithfully living the Christian life on secular campuses: 1) speech codes, 2) speech zones, 3) coerced speech, 4) nondiscrimination policies, 5) denial of equal access to fees and facilities, and 6) faculty censorship. He goes on to show how these ideologies and practices spread off campus and into society. He gives several real-life examples involving, firefighters, pharmacists, florists, bakers, and so on.

Ventrella insists the best way to combat these injustices is to exercise the religious freedoms guaranteed in the Constitution. Behind these cultural battles, there is a war going on between God and Satan; we must put on the armor of God and join the fight. Being salt and light requires us to engage the darkness.

To access this video, go to www.summitu.com/utc and enter the passcode found in the back of your manual.

"Religious Liberty" Video Outline

Attorney Jeffery Ventrella expands on six threats to religious liberty and faithfully living the Christian life on secular campuses:

1. **Speech ___________________**

   Attempts to codify what people can and cannot say in keeping with liberal ideas of political correctness. They often include vague terms like "civil" and "harassment," which are narrowly defined and seldom applied fairly.

2. **Speech ___________________**

   Attempts to define where and when students can exercise free speech. They are unconstitutional.

3. **___________________ speech**

   Forcing students into ideological conformity by requiring them to embrace a specific position, even if they don't believe in that position or it is against their personal or religious beliefs.

4. **___________________ policies**

   These are helpful in keeping students from being excluded on the basis of race, gender, age and religion. But nondiscrimination policies are harmful when used to erase valid distinctions based on free choice.

5. **Denial of equal access to fees and facilities**

   Restricting access to school space and resources unless organizations swear allegiance to school policies. This tactic is often used with religious groups but the Supreme Court has ruled that religious groups have to be treated the same as any other social groups on campus.

6. **Faculty censorship**

   Speech codes applied to professors. Students who are offended by what professors say can file complaints, which may lead to discipline or dismissal of the professors.

Cultural equivalents

What happens in universities goes on to influence the culture. Political correctness and speech codes are turned into ordinances and laws. People are coerced, put out of business, and threatened with jail if they choose not to provide a service with which they disagree, e.g., photography at same-sex weddings.

Spiritual warfare

Christians should be prepared for conflicts because there is a war going on between God and Satan; we must put on the armor of God and join the fight. Being salt and light requires us to engage the darkness.

"Religious Liberty" Discussion Questions

1. **What are speech codes and how are they used on college campuses?**

2. **Why is hate speech constitutional but speech codes and speech zones are unconstitutional?**

3. **When are nondiscrimination policies helpful and when are they harmful?**

4. **How does the battle over religious liberty on campus spill over into the culture?**

5. **What must Christians do to protect religious liberty?**

Chapter 13 Key Points

Key Questions:

1. What is religious freedom?
2. What causes religious persecution?
3. Why should Christians care about religious oppression?
4. What should Christians do about religious oppression?

Key Verses:

1. Luke 4:18

Key Players:

1. John Leland
2. Aleksandr Solzhenitsyn
3. Richard Wurmbrand

Key Works:

1. *The Gulag Archipelago* by Aleksandr Solzhenitsyn

Key Organizations:

1. Alliance Defending Freedom
2. Becket Fund
3. Voice of the Martyrs

Key Terms:

1. Atheism
2. Bourgeoisie
3. *Dhimmi*
4. Human Flourishing
5. Islamic Theocracy
6. Jihad
7. *Jizya*
8. Materialism
9. Medieval Inquisition
10. Pan-Islam
11. Proletariat
12. Proletariat Morality
13. Religious Freedom
14. Religious Persecution*
15. Salem Witch Trials
16. Sharia Law
17. Spanish Inquisition
18. Tolerance*

**Short answer or essay question on the exam*

Chapter 13 Assignment

Answer the following questions with at least one paragraph.

1. **Historically, how has a close connection between a religion and the power of the state shown itself to be dangerous, both in the persecution of people and in the corruption of the religion itself?**

2. **Why should Christians be concerned about the status of Christianity in the United States, even though American Christians do not face nearly the same level of persecution as those elsewhere?**

3. **How does the doctrine of *imago Dei* relate to issues of religious tolerance and persecution?**

4. **What can Christians do to stay clear about the real issue and avoid charges of bigotry or prejudice when arguing for the religious liberty to uphold their beliefs about marriage or oppose same-sex marriage?**

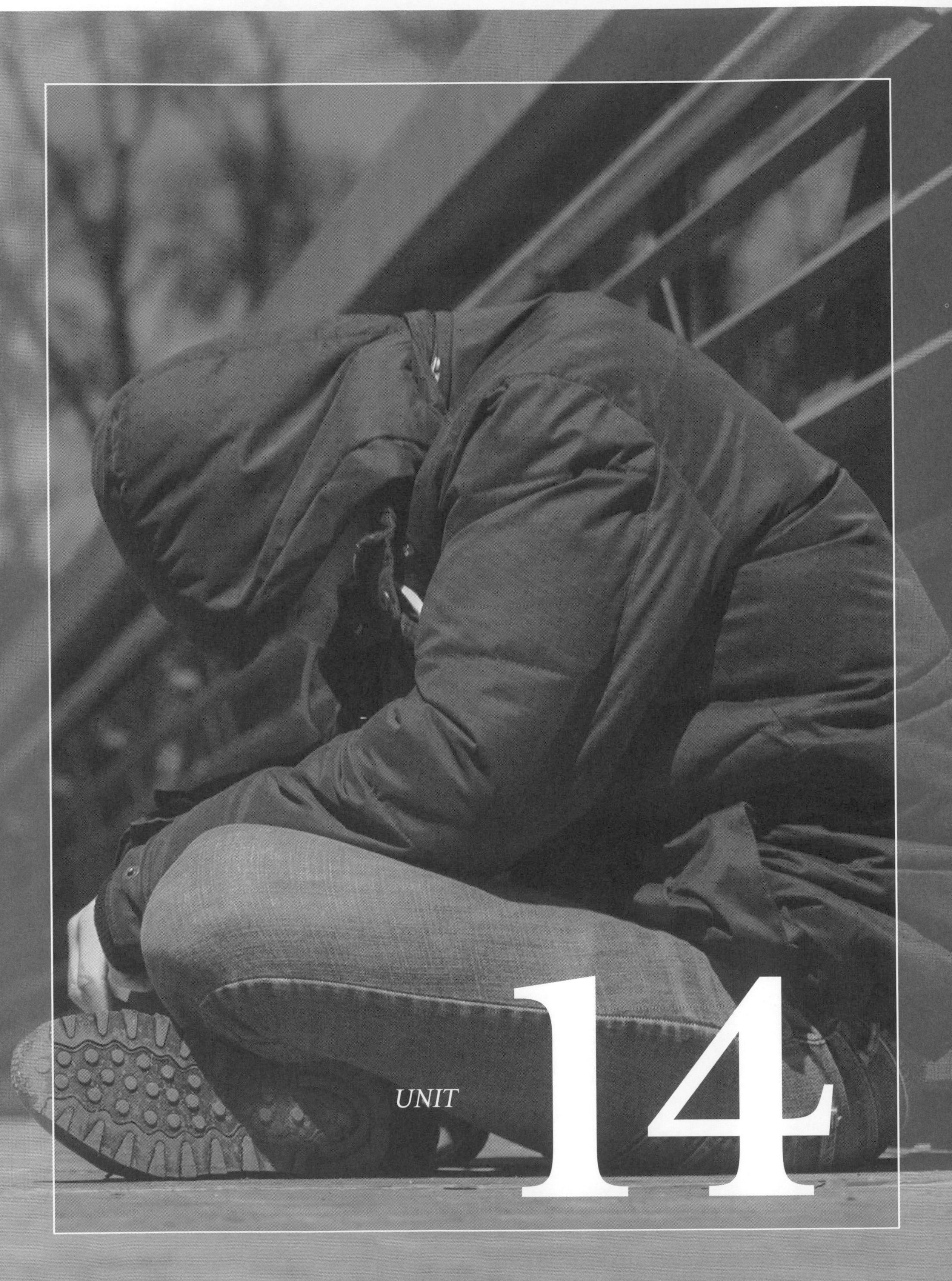

UNIT 14

Poverty Care, Poverty Cure

Chapter 14 Learning Objectives

Students will be able to:

1. explain how biblical principles such as stewardship, community, and creativity can help people move beyond poverty care to poverty cure. [14.1]
2. identify past and present causes of poverty. [14.2]
3. discuss ways the six worldviews attempt to solve the poverty problem. [14.3]
4. search Scripture to discover what God's Word says about poverty and examine how bearing God's image affects a Christian's relationship with the poor. [14.4]
5. describe ways Christians can be part of the solution to provide a cure for the problem of poverty. [14.5]
6. conclude that small steps can bring about a change that leads people out of poverty. [14.6]

Chapter 14 Discussion Questions

1. What is poverty? [14.2]

2. What are the main causes of poverty? [14.2]

3. How widespread was poverty in the past? [14.2]

4. What do you know about your family's financial history? Are you better off today than your parents were at your age? Your grandparents? Your great grandparents? Do you expect your children to be better off than you are?

5. **Can government intervention ensure prosperity? [14.2]**

6. **Can government programs ensure prosperity? [14.2]**

7. **Can government win the war on poverty? [14.2]**

8. **What is Secularism's approach to poverty? [14.3]**

9. What is Marxism's approach to poverty? [14.3]

10. What is Postmodernism's approach to poverty? [14.3]

11. What is Islam's approach to poverty? [14.3]

12. What is New Spirituality's approach to poverty? [14.3]

13. What does the Bible say about poverty? [14.4]

14. How does bearing God's image impact how we care for the poor? [14.4]

15. What does this proverb mean, "If you give a man a fish you feed him for a day. If you teach a man to fish, you feed him for a lifetime"? Can you give examples? [14.4]

16. What does it mean to "do justly"? [14.4]

17. What does it mean to "love kindness"? [14.4]

18. What does it mean to "walk humbly with God"? [14.4]

19. How will starting locally and giving generously help cure poverty? [14.5]

20. How will moving beyond aid to asset development help cure poverty? [14.5]

21. What's the difference between need-based community development and asset-based community development? [14.5]

22. How will moving beyond subsistence help cure poverty? [14.5]

“Living as if People Mattered” Reading

George Grant takes an in-depth look at serving people as the way to show them they really matter. He contrasts today’s “service economy” with the concept of biblical service, which is a priestly function of mercy. Because God is just and merciful, we are to be just and merciful. We are to serve others as he has served us; caring for the helpless, the hungry, the naked, the prisoner, and the innocent.

Grant shows that, starting in the New Testament and extending to our day, selfless service has been the primary power behind the gospel. He cites biblical teaching and historical examples to drive this point home. He concludes with the “Micah Mandate,” a call to repent from sinful and selfish behavior and to return to the path of righteousness and blessing.

> He has shown you, O mortal, what is good. And what does the Lord require of you? To act justly and to love mercy and to walk humbly with your God. (Micah 6:8 NIV)

Living as if People Mattered

by George Grant

Service

Service is a much ballyhooed concept these days. The literature of business success and personal management tosses it about rather profligately.

We are told, for instance, that our industrial economy has been almost completely transformed into a service economy by the advent of the information age. The service factor is the new by-word for success in the crowded global marketplace. Good service guarantees customer loyalty, management efficiency, and employee morale. It provides a competitive edge for companies in an increasingly cut-throat business environment. It is the means toward empowerment, flexibility, and innovation at a time when those qualities are essential for business survival. It prepares ordinary men and women to out-sell, out-manage, out-motivate, and out-negotiate their competition. It enables them to “swim with the sharks without being eaten alive.”[1]

According to Jack Eckerd and Chuck Colson, service on the job and in the workplace can mean many things: “Valuing workers. Managing from the trenches. Communicating. Inspiring excellence. Training. Using profits to motivate.”[2]

Virtually all the corporate prognosticators, strategic forecasters, motivational pundits, and management consultants agree—from Tom Peters, John Naisbitt, and Stephen Covey to Richard Foster, Michael Gerber, and Zig Ziglar. They all say that service is an indispensable key to success in business or success in life.

According to these analysts, service in business is essentially a complex combination of common courtesy, customer satisfaction, and the "spirit of enterprise." It is simply realizing that the customer is always right and then going the extra mile. It is a principle-centered approach to human relationships and community responsibilities. It is putting first things first.[3]

This new emphasis on service is not just confined to the corporate world. It has also suddenly reappeared as a stock-in-trade public virtue in the discourse of politics. Candidates now offer themselves for public service rather than to merely run for office. They invoke cheery images of community service, military service and civic service as evidence of their suitability to govern the affairs of state. Once in office they initiate vast federal programs for national service. They charge the lumbering government bureaucracy with the task of domestic service. And they offer special recognition for citizens who have performed exemplary volunteer service.

Again, service is defined rather broadly in a series of happy platitudes as an expansive sense of public-spiritedness, good neighborliness, community-mindedness, or big-hearted cooperativeness.

All of these things are certainly admirable. They are fine and good as far as they go. But they are not at all what the Bible has in mind when it speaks of service—as Francis Schaeffer would no doubt have readily attested.

Biblical service isn't a tactic designed to boost profit margins, protect market shares, keep customers happy, or improve employee relations. It isn't a strategy designed to inculcate patriotism, strengthen community relations, or attract more investments. It is not a technique to pad resumes, garner votes, or patronize constituents. It isn't a style of leadership, a personality bent, or a habit of highly effective people.

Instead, biblical service is a priestly function of mercy. The Hebrew word often used for service in the Old Testament is *sharath*. It literally means "to minister" or "to treat with affection." Similarly, in the New Testament the Greek word *diakoneo* is often used. It literally means "to care for" or to "offer relief." In both cases, the priestly connotations and the merciful intentions of service are quite evident. In both cases, the emphasis is on the interpersonal dimension rather than the institutional dimension, on mercy rather than management, on true righteousness rather than mere rightness. Biblical service is far more concerned about taking care of souls than about taking care of business.

This distinction between the ministry of service and the business of service is like the difference between faith in God and faith in faith.[4]

Doing Unto Others

God is merciful and just.

He works righteousness and justice for all. Morning by morning, He dispenses His justice without fail and without partiality. All his ways are just, so that injustice is an abomination to Him.

Thus, He is adamant about ensuring the cause of the abused, the meek, and the weak. Time after time, Scripture stresses this important attribute of God:

> The Lord abides forever; He has established His throne for judgment, and He will judge the world in righteousness; He will execute judgment for the peoples with equity. The Lord also will be a stronghold for the oppressed, a stronghold in times of trouble. (Psalm 9:7–9 NASB)
>
> "Because of the oppression of the weak and the groaning of the needy, I will now arise," says the Lord. I will protect them from those who malign them." (Psalm 12:5)
>
> A father to the fatherless, a defender of widows, is God in his holy dwelling. God sets the lonely in families, he leads forth the prisoners with singing; but the rebellious live in a sun-scorched land. (Psalm 68:5–6)

God cares for the needy. And His people are to do likewise. If God has comforted us, then we are to comfort others. If God has forgiven us, then we are to forgive others. If God has loved us, then we are to love others. If He has taught us, then we are to teach others. If He has borne witness to us, then we are to bear witness to others. If He has laid down His life for us, then we are to lay down our lives for one another.[5]

Whenever God commanded the priestly nation of Israel to imitate Him in ensuring justice for the wandering homeless, the alien, and the sojourner, He reminded them that they were once despised, rejected, and homeless themselves. It was only by the grace and mercy of God that they had been redeemed from that low estate. Thus they were to exercise compassion to the brokenhearted and the dispossessed. They were to serve.

Priestly privilege brings priestly responsibility. If Israel refused to take up that responsibility, then God would revoke their privilege. If they refused to exercise reciprocal mercy, then God would rise up in His anger to visit the land with His wrath and displeasure, expelling them into the howling wilderness once again. On the other hand, if they fulfilled their calling to live lives of merciful service, then they would ever be blessed.[6]

The principle still holds true. Those of us who have received the compassion of the Lord on High are to demonstrate tenderness in kind to all those around us. This is precisely the lesson Jesus was driving at in the parable of the unmerciful slave (Matthew 18:23–35).

The moral of the parable is clear. The needy around us are living symbols of our own former helplessness and privation. We are therefore to be living symbols of God's justice, mercy, and compassion. We are to do as He has done. God has set the pattern by His gracious working in our lives. We are to follow that pattern by serving others in the power of the indwelling Spirit.

In other words, the Gospel calls us to live daily as if people really matter. It calls us to live lives of selfless concern. We are to pay attention to the needs of others. In both word and deed, in both thought and action we are to weave ordinary kindness into the very fabric of our lives.

But this kind of ingrained mercy goes far beyond mere politeness. We are to demonstrate concern for the poor. We are to show pity toward the weak. We are to rescue the afflicted from violence. We are to familiarize ourselves with the case of the helpless, give of our wealth, and share of our sustenance. We are to put on "compassion, kindness, humility, gentleness and patience" (Colossians 3:12). We are to take up "the case of the stranger" (Job 29:16). We are to love our neighbors as ourselves (Mark 12:31) and "rescue those being led away to death" (Proverbs 24:11–12).

According to the Scriptures, this kind of comprehensive servanthood emphasis is, in fact, a primary indication of the authenticity of our faith: "Religion that God our Father accepts as pure and faultless is this: to look after orphans and widows in their distress and to keep oneself from being polluted by the world" (James 1:27).

We are called to do "righteousness and justice" (Genesis 18:19 NASB). We are to be ministers of God's peace, instruments of His love, and ambassadors of His kingdom. We are to care for the helpless, feed the hungry, clothe the naked, shelter the homeless, visit the prisoner, and protect the innocent. We are to live lives of merciful service.

Good Deeds

In writing to Titus, the young pastor of Crete's pioneer church, the apostle Paul pressed home this fundamental truth with a clear sense of persistence and urgency. The task before Titus was not an easy one. Cretan culture was terribly worldly. It was marked by deceit, ungodliness, sloth, and gluttony (Titus 1: 12). Thus, Paul's instructions were precise. Titus was to preach the glories of grace, but he was also to make good deeds evident. Priestly mercy and selfless servanthood were to be central priorities in his new work:

> For the grace of God has appeared, bringing salvation to all men, instructing us to deny ungodliness and worldly desires and to live sensibly, righteously and godly in the present age, looking for the blessed hope and the appearing of the glory of our great God and Savior, Christ Jesus; who gave Himself for us, that He might redeem us from every lawless deed and purify for Himself a people for His own possession, zealous for good deeds. (Titus 2:11–14 NASB)

Paul tells Titus he should build his entire fledgling ministry around works of mercy: He was to be an example of good deeds (Titus 2:7). He was to teach the people to watch for chances to do good (3:1). They were all to "learn to devote themselves to doing what is good, in order that they might provide for daily necessities and not live unproductive lives" (3:14). Some within the church professed to know God, "but by their actions they deny him. They are detestable, disobedient and unfit for doing anything good" (1:16). Titus was to "rebuke them sharply, so that they will be sound in the faith" (1:13).

As a pastor, Titus had innumerable tasks that he was responsible to fulfill. He had administrative duties, doctrinal duties, discipling duties, preaching duties, counseling duties, and arbitrating duties. But intertwined with them all, fundamental to them all, were his servanthood duties.

To the Uttermost

Paul called himself a servant (Galatians 1:10). Similarly, James, Peter, Epaphroditus, Timothy, Abraham, Moses, David, and Daniel were all called servants.[7] In fact, even before they were called "Christians," all of the first century believers were called "servants" (1 Corinthians 7:22).

Whenever and wherever the Gospel has gone out, the faithful have emphasized the priority of good works, especially works of compassion toward the needy. Every great revival in the history of the church, from Paul's missionary journeys to the Reformation, from the Alexandrian outreach of Athanasius to the Great Awakening in America, has been accompanied by an explosion of priestly service. Hospitals were established. Orphanages were founded. Rescue missions were started. Almshouses were built. Soup kitchens were begun. Charitable societies were incorporated. The hungry were fed, the naked clothed, and the unwanted rescued. Word was wed to deeds.[8]

This fact has always proven to be the bane of the church's enemies. Unbelievers can argue theology. They can dispute philosophy. They can subvert history. And they can undermine character. But they are helpless in the face of extraordinary feats of selfless compassion.[9]

Thus, Martin Luther said: "Where there are no good works, there is no faith. If works and love do not blossom forth, it is not genuine faith, the Gospel has not yet gained a foothold, and Christ is not yet rightly known."[10]

Likewise, the *Westminster Confession* asserted:

> Good works, done in obedience to God's commandments, are the fruits and evidences of a true and lively faith: and by them believers manifest their thankfulness, strengthen their assurance, edify their brethren, adorn the profession of the Gospel, stop the mouths of the adversaries, and glorify God whose workmanship they are.[11]

All too often in our own day though, we have tended to decline those priestly responsibilities—yielding the work of service to government bureaucrats or professional philanthropists. Grave societal dilemmas that have always busied the church before—like defending the sanctity of life, caring for the aged, and protecting the helpless—have been mentally and practically separated from our other "spiritual" responsibilities. They have been relegated to the status of "issues," even declared "political" and put on the other side of the fence from us in "the separation of church and state."

From a biblical perspective, though, these things are not "issues"; they cannot be separated from our tasks as believer-priests. They are our tasks as believer-priests. They *are* central to our purpose and calling in the world.

Many Christians have observed—only partly in jest—that if God doesn't judge America soon, He's probably going to have to apologize to Sodom and Gomorrah. That may well be true—but not for the reason that we think. God did not judge Sodom and Gomorrah because of their rampant greed, perversity, and corruption. He judged them because, those who were charged with serving didn't (Ezekiel

16:49–50). If God's wrath ever does utterly consume America, it will be for precisely the same reason. When biblical service is replaced by its worldly counterfeits, the effects go far beyond rising taxes, bloated bureaucracies, welfare graft, urban blight, and sundered families. When we fail to do the priestly work of mercy and compassion, judgment becomes inevitable.

Sava of Trnova, writing at the end of the seventh century, said:

> The chief spiritual works in the world are sevenfold: to admonish sinners, to instruct the ignorant, to counsel the doubtful, to comfort the sorrowful, to suffer wrongs patiently, to forgive injuries, and to pray for all men at all times. Thus, we are to feed the hungry, give drink to the thirsty, to clothe the naked, to ransom the captives, to shelter the homeless, to visit the sick, and to rescue the perishing, for only in these corporal acts of service may this world of carnality be guarded from the full consequences of judgment.[12]

The Bible tells us that if we will obey the command to be generous to the poor, we ourselves will taste joy. If we will serve the needy, God will preserve us. If we will offer priestly mercy to the afflicted, we ourselves will be spared. We will prosper, our desires will be satisfied, and we will even be raised up from beds of sorrow and suffering.[13] God will ordain peace for us, authenticate our faith, and bless our witness to the world.[14] But only if we will serve.

Charles Haddon Spurgeon, the great Victorian pastor, not only was a masterful pulpiteer, administrator, writer, and evangelist, he was a determined champion of the deprived and the rejected. He gave more than half of his incredibly busy schedule to one or another of the sixty organizations or institutions he founded for their care and comfort. Explaining his furious activity on behalf of the poor and needy, Spurgeon said:

> God's intent in endowing any person with more substance than he needs is that he may have the pleasurable office, or rather the delightful privilege, of relieving want and woe. Alas, how many there are who consider that store which God has put into their hands on purpose for the poor and needy, to be only so much provision for their excessive luxury, a luxury which pampers them but yields them neither benefit nor pleasure.[15]

Wherever committed Christians have gone, throughout Europe, into the darkest depths of Africa, to the outer reaches of China, along the edges of the American frontier, and beyond to the Australian outback, selfless care for the needy has been in evidence. In fact, most of the church's greatest heroes are those who willingly gave the best of their lives to the less fortunate. Service was their hallmark. Mercy was their emblem.

A Life of Service

According to the majority of eighteenth- and nineteenth-century historians, the most remarkable event during America's founding era did not take place on a battlefield. It did not occur during the course of the constitutional debates. It was not recorded during the great diplomatic negotiations with France, Spain, or Holland. It did not take place at sea, or in the assemblies of the states, or in the counsels of war.

In a humble demonstration of servanthood, the field commander of the continental armies surrendered his commission to the congressional authorities at Annapolis.

At the time, he was the idol of the country and his soldiers. The army was unpaid, and the veteran troops, well-armed and fresh from their victory at Yorktown, were eager to have him take control of the disordered country. Some wanted to crown him king. Others thought to make him a dictator—rather like Cromwell had been a century earlier in England.

With the loyal support of the army and the enthusiasm of the populace, it would have been easy enough for him to have made himself the ruler of the new nation. But instead, General George Washington resigned his officer's commission. He appeared before President Thomas Mifflin and his cabinet and submitted himself to their governance.

Though he had often wrangled in disagreement with his superiors over matters of military strategy, pay schedules, supply shipments, troop deployment, and the overlap of civil and martial responsibilities, there was never any question of his ultimate loyalty or allegiance. In the end, he always submitted himself to the authority God had placed over him.

And that was no mean feat.

Washington had faithfully served under eleven different American presidents at a time of severest crisis. The first two held office prior to the signing of the Declaration of Independence—Peyton Randolph of Virginia and Henry Middleton of South Carolina. The next six held office between the time of the Declaration and the ratification of the first constitution—John Hancock of Massachusetts, Henry Laurens of South Carolina, John Jay of New York, Samuel Huntington of Connecticut, Samuel Johnson of North Carolina, and Thomas McKean of Delaware. The last three held office under the Articles of Confederation—John Hanson of Maryland, Elias Budinot of New Jersey, and finally, Thomas Mifflin of Pennsylvania. Another four presidents would hold office during Washington's short interlude away from public life prior to the ratification of the current constitution—Richard Henry Lee of Virginia, Nathaniel Gorham of Massachusetts, Arthur St. Clair of Pennsylvania, and Cyrus Griffin of Virginia. During all those trying days, under each of those varied men, General Washington gave himself wholeheartedly to the loyal task of selfless service.

He obeyed orders. He rendered due respect. He yielded to the authority of lawful office and jurisdiction. He met the needs of the hour. He set aside personal ambition, preference, security, and at times, personal opinion in order to serve.

"His true greatness was evidenced," said the pundit Henry Adams, "in the fact that he never sought greatness, but rather service."[16] The dean of American historians, Francis Parkman, concurred that it was this "remarkable spirit of the servant" that ultimately "elevated him even higher in his countrymen's estimations than he already was."[17]

George Washington lived a life of service. He practiced what we today call servant-leadership. He would settle for nothing less. He would strive for nothing more. And he left the disposition of the matter of his life and fortune in the hands of God.

Though we generally think of mercy more in terms of charity or philanthropy, Washington's balanced and selfless perspective actually comes closer to the biblical ideal. Kindness, helpfulness, compassion, and care are the natural outgrowths of a servant's heart. Where personal ambition and a lust for self-fulfillment are subdued, true mercy is sure to follow.

Good Service

The prophet Micah condemned the people of his day for their heartless defrauding and victimizing of the needy (Micah 2:1–2). He asserted that the imminent judgment of their land was due to their tolerance of sin, their blatant selfishness, and their refusal to undertake their servanthood responsibilities (3:2–4). Instead, they were concerned only with their own comforts and pleasures (2:8–11). They were intent on their own personal peace and affluence, often at the cost of oppression and exploitation (3:5–11). They had thus violated the covenant (5:10–15).

Where there is no mercy there is no hope.

Thus, the Micah Mandate was not only a call to the people to repent and to return to the path of righteousness, it was a proclamation of reconciliation and healing. It was a promise of better things to come. The prophet asserted that the remnant would be regathered (Micah 4:6). The shame of affliction would be lifted (4:7). And the lost fortunes of the land would be restored (4:8).

Where there is mercy there is hope.

Therefore let us too be "zealous for good deeds" (Titus 2:14 NASB).

Zealous for Good Deeds

> "He has showed you, O man, what is good. And what does the Lord require of you? To act justly and to love mercy and to walk humbly with your God"(Micah 6:8).

Through the ages, the great heroes of the faith were notable as much for their charity and kindness as they were for their doctrinal fidelity. They were invariably men and women of mercy who lived lives of selfless service. Examples abound:

Not only did *John Wycliffe* (1329–84) revive interest in the Scriptures during a particularly dismal and degenerate era with his translation of the New Testament into English, he also unleashed a grassroots movement of lay preachers and relief workers that brought hope to the poor for the first time since the peasants' land had been taken more than two generations before. Those common Lollards—as they were most often called—carried Wycliffe's determined message of grace and mercy to the entire kingdom, laying the foundations for the Reformation in England more than a century and a half later.

John Calvin (1509–64) established Geneva as the epicenter of the Reformation with his profound theological insight and his rich devotional piety. His careful and systematic codification of the biblical foundations for Reform was like a magnet for the best and brightest throughout Christendom. The city quickly became an island of intellectual integrity and economic prosperity. In addition, though, it became renowned for its charitable compassion. It was a kind of safe haven for all of Europe's poor and persecuted, dispossessed and distressed. There they found that Calvin had not only instructed the people in such things as the providence of God, but he had also taught them the importance of mercy in balancing the Christian life.

Dwight L. Moody (1837–99) was America's foremost evangelist throughout the difficult days that immediately followed the cataclysm of the War Between the States and disruption of Reconstruction. Literally thousands came to know Christ because the former shoe salesman faithfully proclaimed the Gospel wherever and whenever he had opportunity—pioneering the methods of both modern crusade evangelism and Sunday-school outreach. But in addition to preaching to the masses, he cared for the masses. He was responsible for the establishment of some one hundred and fifty schools, street missions, soup kitchens, clinics, colportage societies, and other charitable organizations. He believed it was essential that Christians proclaim the Gospel in both word and deed. As a result, his impact on the nation is still felt through many of those institutions that continue their vital work—nearly a century after his death.

Dozens of others could be cited throughout the wide span of history: Polycarp (d. 155), Ambrose (d. 397), Angelica of Brescia (d. 1540), Edmund Arrowsmith (d. 1628) David Brainerd (d. 1747), George Mueller (d. 1898), and Florence Nightingale (d. 1910). Each made the priestly message of their lips manifest by the servanthood message of their hands. Thus, each became an emblem of mercy in this often merciless world.

Do a Good Turn Daily

> "He has showed you, O man, what is good. And what does the Lord require of you? To act justly and to love mercy and to walk humbly with your God"(Micah 6:8).[18]

An entire catalog of Scriptural exhorts us to act mercifully to those around us. Do a brief concordance study—looking up the verses that deal with mercy, kindness, and compassion—to get a good overview of the subject. Try to make a list—from memory, if possible—of all the saints and heroes of the past whose stories of mercy, service, and compassion you have heard in sermons, Sunday school, missions conferences, Bible studies, or devotions. What does your list tell you about the importance and impact of mercy ministry on the overall history of the church? There are needs all around us. It doesn't matter what section of the country we live in. It doesn't matter what kind of neighborhood we call home. Single mothers silently struggle to make ends meet. Elderly couples try to get by on fixed incomes. Young families are stymied by debt, underemployment, illiteracy, physical handicaps, or prejudice. There are undernourished and poorly clothed children, third- and fourth-generation welfare dependents. There are hurting, lonely, desperate people. They may be right next door, down the street, around the block, across the tracks, or on the other side of town. But they are there. Stop. Look. Listen. See if you can't develop new eyes to see those needs where they are. Now, get busy. You may not have abundant resources or even much time to spare, but none of us is too strapped to care about—and then do something about—the needs of others.

Exodus 22:25
Leviticus 19:10
Leviticus 23:22
Leviticus 25:35–37
Numbers 18:24
Deuteronomy 14:29
Deuteronomy 15:1–2
Deuteronomy 24:19–21
Ruth 2:1-23
Ruth 4:1-12
Psalm 41:1-3
Proverbs 11:25
Proverbs 14:21
Proverbs 14:31
Proverbs 17:5
Proverbs 21:13
Proverbs 22:9
Proverbs 28:27
Proverbs 29:7
Proverbs 31:8–9
Isaiah 1:10–17
Isaiah 10:1–2
Isaiah 32:6–8
Isaiah 58:1–12
Amos 5:1–27
Matthew 5:16
Matthew 7:12
Matthew 10:8
Matthew 25:31–46
Mark 12:44
Luke 3:11
Luke 6:38
Luke 9:48
Luke 10:30–37
Luke 11:41
Luke 12:33–34
Acts 20:35
Romans 12:8–20
2 Corinthians 1:3–4
2 Corinthians 8:1–24
2 Corinthians 9:7
Galatians 5:6
Galatians 6:2
Galatians 6:9–10
Ephesians 2:8–10
Ephesians 5:2
2 Thessalonians 3:6–10
1 Timothy 5:8
1 Timothy 6:18–19
Titus 2:11–14
Titus 3:1
Titus 3:8
Titus 3:14
Hebrews 13:16
James 2:14–26
1 John 3:17

The essay originally appeared as a chapter in George Grant, *The Micah Mandate* (Chicago: Moody Press, 1995), pp. 111–128. Reproduction Rights granted by Moody Press.

[1] *Houston Chronicle*, 18 May 1986; Forbes, 14 September 1992; Forbes, 9 September 1993; *Wall Street Journal*, 16 April 1992; Harvey Mackay, *Swim with the Sharks* (New York: William Morrow, 1988), 1.

[2] Chuck Colson and Jack Eckerd, *Why America Doesn't Work* (Dallas: Word, 1991), 168.

[3] George Gilder, *The Spirit of Enterprise* (New York: Simon and Schuster, 1984); Michael Gerber, *Power Point* (New York: HarperCollins, 1991); Tom Peters, *Thriving on Chaos* (New York: Knopf, 1987); Stephen Covey, Roger Merrill, and Rebecca Merrill, First Things First (New York: Simon and Schuster, 1994).

[4] Faith in God is personal and objective. Faith in faith is impersonal and subjective. Faith in God transcends self-interest and self-fulfillment. Faith in faith descends into self-reliance and self-assurance. Faith in God is a belief in Someone who has revealed Himself to man "at many times and in various ways" (Hebrews 1: 1). Faith in faith is simply "a belief" in something or any thing (James 2:19).

[5] To see these principles demonstrated in Scripture: 2 Corinthians 1:4; Ephesians 4:32; 1 John 4:11; Matthew 28:20; John 15:26–27; 1 John 3:16.

[6] See Isaiah 1:11-17; Exodus 22:24; Psalm 41:1–2.

[7] James 1:1; 2 Peter 1:1; Colossians 4:12; 2 Timothy 2:24; Psalm 105:42; Nehemiah 9:14; Psalm 89:3; Romans 6:20.

[8] George Grant, *Bringing in the Sheaves: Transforming Poverty into Productivity* (Brentwood, Tenn.: Wolgernuth and Hyatt, 1985).

[9] George Grant, *Third Time Around* (Brentwood, Tenn.: Wolgemuth and Hyatt, 1990).

[10] John Dillenberger, ed., *Martin Luther* (New York: Doubleday, 1961), 18.

[11] Confession, XVIII:2.

[12] Terra Ecalivat, VI: 82.

[13] Proverbs 14:21; Psalm 41:1-2; Proverbs 28:27; Proverbs 11:24; Proverbs 11:25; Psalm 41:3.

[14] Isaiah 26:12; James 2:14-26; Isaiah 58:6–12.

[15] George H. Neville, *Good Works* (Edinburgh, UK: McGavock, 1956), 202.

[16] B. L. Cartwright, *Washington* (Boston: Little, Brown, 1924), 166.

[17] Ibid.

[18] The following list is by no means comprehensive, but it may provide you with a good starting place for personal study. [Please refer to chart.]

"Living as if People Mattered" Discussion Questions

1. **What are some differences between worldly service and service as taught in the Bible?**

2. **How is our service to others connected to following God's example?**

3. **What was more stressed in the early church, good teaching or good deeds?**

4. What role did good deeds play in spreading the gospel?

5. What is the "Micah Mandate" and what impact should it have on Christians?

"Effective Compassion" Video

Jennifer Marshall points out the failures of the War on Poverty, despite more than $22 trillion in government spending over the past fifty years. Our financial and relational living standards have gone down, with more than 40 percent of children now being born to single moms and 80 percent of long-term poverty occurring in single parent homes.

Marshall maintains that helping people rise out of poverty begins with a right understanding of human nature. We are relational beings in need of God's shalom, which includes the ideas of justice, wholeness, and right relationships between individuals and the institutions we form, e.g., family, church, work/business, and government.

Effective compassion is expressed through private efforts and public policy. Both are important in helping more Americans overcome poverty and achieve self-sufficiency. The goal of effective compassion is to restore human dignity to all by bringing everyone into right relationship with God, themselves, and others.

To access this video, go to www.summitu.com/utc and enter the passcode found in the back of your manual.

"EFFECTIVE COMPASSION" VIDEO OUTLINE

The ________________ began in the mid-1960s. Fifty years later, the results:

- $22 trillion spent since 1964
- Eighty federal means-tested programs, e.g., food stamps, medical, housing
- Poverty rate as high as in the mid-1960s

Lessons from the War on Poverty: We won't win this war with more spending. The problem goes much deeper.

Relational living standards have gone down:

- Children born to single moms: eight percent in the 1960s, forty-plus percent today.
- Collapse of marriage related to poverty and welfare dependence.
- Eighty percent of long-term poverty occurs in single parent homes. Children born outside of marriage are five times more likely to experience poverty.

Two main causes of poverty:

- ________________: even in good economic times, the average poor family with children can be supported by only eight hundred hours of work per year.
- The collapse of ________________: if poor single mothers married the fathers of their children, two-thirds would be lifted out of poverty.

Relational flourishing—*shalom*:

Shalom means right relationships between individuals and institutions like family, church, work, and government. Each of these institutions has God-ordained roles and responsibilities.

1. *Family*. Family takes responsibility for the all-around care of individuals and meets a comprehensive range of needs. The family prepares ________________ to live in community when they grow up.
2. *Church*. The church can address all the relational dimensions for full human flourishing. The church strives to bring others into right relationship with God and one another through Jesus Christ.
3. *Work*. Work is essential for human ________________. It helps us pursue our creative potential as image bearers of God. It gives us an opportunity to use our gifts to earn a living and to help others in the process.
4. *Government*. According to the Bible, government has a limited role in society: to provide law and order, punish oppressors through the use of force, and preserve the space for other institutions to fulfill their roles and responsibilities.

What should helping look like?

- Private efforts: relational capital and creativity
- Policy reforms: right incentives in public assistance

Getting this combination right is the key to helping more Americans achieve self-sufficiency and overcome poverty and dependence on government. This can restore them to human dignity by being in right relationship with God, themselves, and others.

“Effective Compassion” Discussion Questions

1. **What have been the results of the War on Poverty declared by Lyndon Johnson in mid 1960s?**

2. **What are the two main causes of poverty in the United States?**

3. **What do we need to understand about people in order to alleviate poverty?**

4. What are the proper roles and responsibilities of the basic human institutions?

5. What does effective compassion look like?

Chapter 14 Key Points

Key Questions:

1. What is poverty?
2. How is poverty a worldview problem?
3. Can government win the war on poverty?
4. Why should Christians care about poverty?

Key Verses:

1. Leviticus 23:22
2. Micah 6:8
3. Philippians 2:4–8

Key Players:

1. Lyndon Johnson
2. John Maynard Keynes
3. Thomas Malthus
4. Franklin Roosevelt
5. Margaret Sanger
6. Muhammad Yunus*

Key Events:

1. Great Depression

Key Terms:

1. Asset-based community development
2. Communism
3. Elastic Good
4. Free-Market Economy
5. Government Subsidy
6. Government Redistribution
7. Impartiality
8. Inelastic Good
9. Microfinance
10. Need-Based Community Development
11. Poverty*
12. Social Safety Net
13. Socialism
14. Universal Enlightenment Production
15. War on Poverty
16. *Zakat*

Key Organizations:

1. Compassion International

**Short answer or essay question on the exam*

Chapter 14 Assignment

Answer the following questions with at least one paragraph.

1. **How can addressing poverty and material deprivation be a matter of one's worldview rather than simply an economic problem?**

2. **What is a major difference between Christianity and Islam in regard to caring for the poor?**

3. **Why should Christians try to end poverty when even Jesus said, "you always have the poor with you"?**

4. **Why does alleviating poverty require more than money—whether charity or wealth redistribution—to be truly effective?**

UNIT

15

The Use of Force

Chapter 15 Learning Objectives

Students will be able to:

1. explain that there is tension between Christianity and the use of force. [15.1]
2. discuss the point that Christianity is all about love and the question that asks if it is possible to be a Christian and a warrior at the same time. [15.2]
3. differentiate between the views of the Old and New Testament about the use of force. [15.3]
4. describe the four viewpoints: pacifism, nonresistance, just war, and crusade or preventive war. [15.4]
5. express ways to live Christianly in a world of evil and injustice. [15.5]

Chapter 15 Discussion Questions

1. **Why did Henry Gerecke agree to become chaplain to some of the worst mass murderers in history? [15.1]**

2. **Would you have taken the assignment Army chaplain Henry Gerecke was asked to do at Nuremberg? Explain why or why not. [15.1]**

3. **Is war the exception or the norm in human history? What makes it so? [15.2]**

4. **How did the early church feel about military service? [15.2]**

5. **What are the four most common views of war held by Christians? [15.2]**

6. **What is "force" and what kinds of force are there? [15.3]**

7. **In the Old Testament, what does God tell Israel about warfare and the use of force? [15.3]**

8. **According to the Old Testament, were individuals ever justified in using force? [15.3]**

9. Do you believe those convicted of capital crimes should be executed by the state? Give your arguments for and against the death penalty.

10. What does the New Testament say about the use of force by the state? [15.3]

11. Does the New Testament give individuals the right to use force? [15.3]

12. Before considering the four major viewpoints Christians have toward the use of force and warfare, what are some things upon which most Christians agree? [15.4]

13. What are the four main approaches to military service and warfare held by different Christian traditions? [15.4]

14. What is pacifism and how is it supported from Scripture? [15.4]

15. What is the pacifist view of military service and peace? [15.4]

16. What is nonresistance and how is it supported from Scripture? [15.4]

17. What is the nonresistance view of military service and peace? [15.4]

18. What is "just-war theory" and how is it supported from Scripture? [15.4]

19. What are the criteria a war must meet to be considered "just"? [15.4]

20. What is the "just war" view of military service and peace? [15.4]

21. What is "crusade or preventive war" and how is it supported from Scripture? [15.4]

22. What is the crusade or preventive war view of military service and peace? [15.4]

23. How can Christians pursue peace in a broken and violent world? [15.5]

"Just War Tradition" Reading

This article examines just-war tradition (JWT) as it was developed from the beginning of the church, through the Middle Ages, down to the present day. It is a Christian attempt to provide a comprehensive way to evaluate conflicts, as well as rules of engagement during war itself. The piece examines and explains six aspects of JWT:

1. The Developing Consensus—the history of the development of JWT from the church fathers to modern day.
2. When Is It Right To Fight?—five criteria to be met before engaging in war.
3. How Should We Then Fight?—two important criteria that keep war from escalating into savagery.
4. War and a Country's Character—what war reveals the about the hearts of men and the character of nations.
5. No Greater Love—we respect courage in battle because to risk one's life to save others is the ultimate act of sacrificial love (John 15:13).
6. Contemporary Issues of War—how does JWT address terrorism, nuclear weapons and landmines?

Just War Tradition

by Michael McKenzie

Summary

The just war tradition (JWT) arose from a desire to have the Christian faith influence the terrible necessity of warfare. Just War Tradition allows Christians to evaluate potential conflicts and to influence other conflicts once they have begun. It also allows Christians to see God as present and active even amid the violence and destruction of warfare. Although not a settled doctrine, JWT is a consensus of Christian and secular sources, and helps Christians to practice their faith in a responsible fashion in the public square.

When Bill Clinton was stumping for the presidency in 1992, his campaign centered almost exclusively on domestic policy, distilling all issues into his famous slogan, "It's the economy, Stupid." Since his inauguration in 1993, however, President Clinton has spent much time on foreign policy. He has kept U.S. troops wherever his predecessors had left them; and he has sent troops into other trouble spots around the globe. Clinton has discovered the two truths that every president this century has had to learn: the promise of American isolationism is an impossible myth, and the need for active and well-trained armed forces will not go away.

What is the place of the Christian faith in all this? How can Christians evaluate whether any proposed U.S. troop commitment is justified? How can the killing of human beings be squared with the Christian faith? Are Christians left with only three choices: complete pacifism, militaristic jingoism, or withdrawal from the political/military arena altogether?

This article will examine a fourth option, just war tradition (JWT). We will see how it gives Christians an intellectual and theological matrix through which to evaluate potential and actual conflicts, as well as guidelines for how wars ought to be fought. Just War Tradition is a broad consensus, not a settled doctrine. It was developed over centuries by theologians and jurists who desired to apply Scripture and moral wisdom even to the most brutal of human enterprises, and who wanted to bring Christian charity and justice even to warfare.[1] The tradition does not claim to remove all difficulties. Its broad consensus does, however, allow thoughtful people to bring their faith to bear on difficult issues in the secular political arena.

Just War Tradition—The Developing Consensus

Early Christian church fathers, speaking in behalf of a minority often persecuted for their faith, were substantially of one mind in their rejection of violence in general, and of military service for believers. Tertullian (ca. 155–240) was quite adamant in his advocacy of pacifism, claiming force was entirely out of place for the Christian. He stated that not only was violence at odds with the Christian faith, but the idolatry and emperor sacrifice required of the Roman military made army service doubly prohibitive for the Christian.[2] Later church fathers were not so sure.

Ambrose of Milan (ca. 339–397), the spiritual mentor of Augustine, argued that a secure peace may be won by a just war; and he insisted that the Christian faith should act to bring justice and compassion to the conduct of war.[3] This attitude almost certainly reflects the new role of the church as no longer the persecuted minority but an officially recognized religion of the state. It also reflects a more thorough exegesis of Scripture that was continued in the work of Augustine (354–430).

Augustine wondered why, if rejection of military force was so crucial to one's faith in God, men such as David, the Centurion of the Gospels (Luke 7), Cornelius (Acts 10), and the soldiers who came to John the Baptist (Luke 3) were not told to renounce their occupation, and in several cases were even held out as examples of faith. Augustine saw that Christianity was not incompatible with war, but was to influence it toward the proper methods and ends: "Peace should be the object of your desire; war should be waged only as a necessity."[4] Violence may be necessary in our fallen world to protect the innocent and to fulfill the command to love one's neighbor.

Augustine reasoned that what had been truly evil about war was not necessarily the deaths incurred, but that part of war which had been left too long without the influence of the faith: "The real evils in war are love of violence, revengeful cruelty, fierce and implacable enmity, wild resistance, and the lust of power, and such like; and it is generally to punish these things, when force is required to inflict the punishment, that, in obedience to God or some lawful authority, good men undertake wars, when they find themselves in such a position as regards the conduct of human affairs, that right conduct requires them to act, or to make others act in this way."[5]

In a world of sin, death, and misery, waging wars will always be necessary. Augustine did not doubt that this is so, but he was quick to acknowledge that these "stern and lasting necessities" were a "misery" to contemplate.[6] The universality of sin insured that there would always be insatiably evil men, who, unmoved by reason or tears, made certain that wars, like the poor, would always be with us.

During the Middle Ages and beyond, jurists and theologians continued to wrestle with how moral wisdom, compassion, and justice could be brought to bear on war and conflict. As a result, several broad streams of thought—both sacred and secular—came together to form the larger context of Just War Tradition. Scholars such as the Dutch jurist Hugo Grotius (1583–1645) were responsible for bringing Just War Tradition out of a purely church context, relying on the "laws of nations" and natural law, rather than theological reasons, on which to base their conclusions.[7] From traditions as varied as the early church fathers, the medieval church and knightly class, all the way to modern canon and secular lawyers, has come a surprising consensus of how just wars are to be fought.

Just War Tradition—When Is It Right to Fight?

Sending troops in harm's way is not something to be taken lightly. When President Clinton argued that the United States had a moral duty to send 20,000 ground troops to Bosnia, many Americans were unconvinced. Despite the triumph of the Gulf War, the specter of Vietnam was brought up again and again: Would U.S. troops once again become mired in a faraway country, fighting for a cause that was unclear at best, and lost at worst? Christians were particularly unsure. Could they support the president?

Just War Tradition has developed five criteria which ought to be satisfied before troops are sent into an arena of potential conflict.[8] Called the *jus ad bellum* (justice for war), these criteria serve to frame the discussion surrounding any potential war.

Just Cause. Wars designed for aggression against a neighbor, or those designed simply to increase a country's wealth or prestige cannot be justified. A just cause may be to *intervene* on behalf of an innocent third party, to *punish* an evil or aggressor nation, or to *defend* one's own nation against aggression or overthrow.[9]

Right Authority. This category is designed to ensure that the proper authorities are calling for the war. Just wars are not private revolutions. In the United States, the Congress has the power to declare war, thereby helping to ensure that there will be vigorous debate before the wholesale commitment of American ground forces.

Proportionality. Any potential conflict must be evaluated as to the cost and benefits. Are the potential gains worth the possible costs and sacrifice—both with regard to finances *and* human lives? Will the destructiveness of the proposed conflict outweigh any enhancement of other human values? Clearly, this category requires foresight; the difficulties involved do not absolve a country from this responsibility.[10] For example, there is more risk involved in committing ground troops than in utilizing air strikes. Is the risk of getting mired in a ground war worth the cost? As the Union troops in the Civil War battle for Fredericksburg found out, getting *in* may prove much harder than getting *out*.

The Goal of Peace. This criterion requires that just wars be fought with the final, *realizable* goal of peace in mind. Not only should there be a strategy to win; there should be a peace that can be achieved. It was this element that disturbed many Americans about the committing of U.S. ground troops to the conflict in Bosnia. They wondered if any "simple" one-year commitment of U.S. troops could do anything to bring a lasting peace to a conflict that had lasted centuries.

War as the Last Resort. Nonviolent means of persuasion should always be attempted for a *reasonable* amount of time before resorting to war. In the modern political climate, there are numerous means that can serve to achieve the desired end of peace: diplomacy, economic boycotts, and other tactics have all worked to achieve just ends. But, there are times when diplomacy fails. The "last resort" implies that the use of force may be legitimate.

Just War Tradition—How Should We Then Fight?

Once a decision has been reached that war is unavoidable, how should a nation conduct itself in warfare? Keeping in mind that wars are always "neater" on paper than in the field, Just War Tradition nevertheless has two important criteria that keep the violence of war from escalating into total mindless savagery. These criteria for *jus in bello* (justice in battle) are *proportionality* and *noncombatant immunity*.

Proportionality. In conducting a battle just as much as in determining to enter a war, likely goods must be weighed against likely evils. For example, in various campaigns in the South Pacific during World War II, Japanese-held islands were often bypassed and left "to wither on the vine" rather than be invaded. The cost in human lives was simply not worth any potential benefits. This was an example of proportionality in action.

Modern-day "smart weapons" are a huge advance over the weapons of 50 years ago, and can help in keeping violence proportional. As the Gulf War demonstrated, it is often possible to destroy a military target with a comparatively small load of explosives because of the pinpoint accuracy of the weapon. Not only does this advance in accuracy meet proportional goals, but it also provides better protection for civilians.

Noncombatant Immunity. This criterion requires that civilians not be directly and intentionally targeted. While it is true that wars inevitably kill some civilians, such killing must be an unintended and indirect product of attacks on the military.

Modern-day terrorists and guerrilla fighters pose grave threats to the doctrine of noncombatant immunity. Intentionally locating their command headquarters or military targets within civilian areas, these groups use civilians as human shields for their acts of terror. Ironically, when they hide behind civilians in this way, terrorists are paying those nations that adhere to JWT a compliment, acknowledging that such nations do not make it a practice to kill civilians intentionally. Saddam Hussein repeatedly hid military targets in the middle of residential neighborhoods. Tomahawk Cruise missiles, however, often proved more than a match for such tactics, flying *around* hospitals and schools in order to destroy legitimate targets.

Just War Tradition—War and a Country's Character

There is nothing like warfare to reveal what is in the heart of man. As Joshua Lawrence Chamberlain, hero of the Battle of Gettysburg, said, "War makes bad men worse and good men better."[11] War also reveals the driving philosophy of the nations fighting the conflict.

During the early years of World War II, the Japanese plane most feared by allied pilots was the Zero. Nimble, quick, tight-turning, the Zero was a scourge for the Americans and British who faced it. But the plane's agility came at a price. The Japanese government constructed the plane of paper-thin aluminum, with neither armor for the pilot nor self-sealing gas tanks—the Japanese were willing to sacrifice such pilot protection to make a lighter plane. Later on, such calculations came back to haunt them. American Air Corps P-38 Lightnings and Navy Corsairs—both heavily armored—could take massive punishment and then turn the Zeros into fireballs. In addition, the Japanese pilots often were not provided with parachutes. Such "luxuries" were thought to disgrace the warrior code of *Bushido*. Neglecting the most basic measures of safety for one's own pilots was flouting the spirit of JWT.

This disregard for the individual was also characteristic of the Soviet Union during World War II. General Dwight (Ike) Eisenhower was astonished when the Soviet commander, Marshal Zhukov, related the Soviet "strategy" for clearing a minefield: "Our infantry attacks exactly as if it were not there."[12] This tactic of using men as human fodder later caused Ike to remark dryly: "I had a vivid picture of what would happen to any American or British commander if he pursued such tactics."[13] The Russians cared little about individual human lives, but only, as Ike put it, "for the overall drain on the nation."[14]

An even more horrible example of Soviet indifference toward suffering in war was their attitude toward their own men who had been captured by the Germans. Zhukov expressed disbelief that the United States fed German prisoners the same rations as American G.I.'s. When Ike explained that it was best to treat German prisoners well because of the Geneva standards of decency and because ill-treatment would doubtlessly inspire Hitler to treat Allied prisoners even more harshly, Zhukov was astounded: "Why do you care about men the Germans have captured? They have surrendered and cannot fight any more."[15] In other words, once a Russian soldier had been captured, he was of no further use to "the Motherland." Such callousness was in flagrant disregard of just war traditions of prisoner treatment and human decency. As Chamberlain might remind us, "Evil men had become worse."

Just War Tradition—No Greater Love

On July 31, 1943, Roger Young was pinned down with the rest of his reconnaissance patrol by a Japanese machine gun on New Georgia, one of the Solomon Islands.[16] The cleverly laid ambush had already killed four soldiers and, since there was virtually no hope of rescue, it appeared that the rest of the patrol would soon be cut to pieces. Young, who had recently requested a demotion to private because he was losing his hearing, began to inch forward toward the machine gun nest. His lieutenant barked at him to stay put. Young kept going, jerking himself out of the officer's grasp. He soon came under withering fire that nearly cut off his legs. In extreme agony, Young kept crawling within five yards of the machine gun, where he found a small depression that sheltered him from the rain of bullets. With his last gasp of strength, Young pulled out a grenade, then reared up and back, bringing himself out of the protection of the ground. A blast of machine gun fire caught him full in the face, killing him just as he released the grenade. But his aim was true. The grenade landed squarely in the middle of the machine gun nest, killing every enemy soldier. The thin, pale, bespectacled Young had saved his patrol.

On February 7, 1943, submarine skipper Howard Gilmore was on routine patrol in the South Pacific. After ramming a Japanese ship, his submarine suffered heavy damage and was being destroyed by the ship's machine gun fire. Two seamen were killed and Gilmore was badly wounded on the conning (observation) tower. Unable to make it to the hatch, Gilmore did the only thing he thought he could to save his crew. Despite the protests of his officers and crew, he ordered the sub to dive, leaving himself to die on the surface. Howard Gilmore had died in order to save his 69 men.[17]

Young and Gilmore both received the Congressional Medal of Honor, America's highest military honor. Criteria for the Medal are "unquestionably strict." The act in question must be reported by at least two eyewitnesses, distinguishable above other acts of gallantry, and involve the risk of one's own life. In fact, nearly two of every three men who so far have received the medal did not live to see their award.[18] According to a revered military custom, every officer—generals included—must rise and salute any winner of the Medal. The salute shows the endearing respect for "the man, the medal, the deed."[19]

But why do we respect such heroism and self-sacrifice? Why is it so moving to read the story of a Roger Young or a Howard Gilmore? I believe that God's creating humanity in His image includes a connection between that image and the ultimate act of giving one's life. We respect such courage because we know that to give all one has, to give all that a person holds dear in this world, is to act outside oneself. It is a pointer, however humanly expressed, toward God, who expressed Himself in the ultimate act of self-sacrifice on Calvary. This is a courage that transcends even the horrible carnage of war.

Jesus said, "Greater love [*agape*] has no one than this, that one lay down his life for his friends" (John 15:13). The Lord is speaking in the immediate context of His own coming death on the cross. But there is no need to restrict His saying to that context. Jesus is pointing out that self-sacrifice is the indication of *agape* in action. His own sacrifice would be the ultimate fulfillment of that.

Paul's comments in Romans 5:7 likewise point to the connection between *agape* and self-sacrifice. In the Greek text, there is an insertion that Paul seemingly added to admit that men do indeed sometimes "die for a good man." Paul's main point is to compare that sort of self-sacrifice with Christ, who died for us "while we were yet sinners" (5:8). The apostle uplifts Christ's death not to disparage the human sacrifice, but to point out the greatness of the divine sacrifice: the dying and *agape* occurred while we were opposed to God.

Human awe in the face of bravery is nearly universal. Despite the killing, the terror, the horror of war, there can emerge an inexplicable, yet undeniable, transcendence. This transcendence is not simply a function of zealous patriotism. Rather, it remains a pointer to the God whom even stark tragedy cannot drive away. It is also, at the very least, an acknowledgment of God's providence. "Fighting and destruction are terrible," wrote Joshua Lawrence Chamberlain, "but are sometimes agencies of heavenly rather than hellish powers."[20]

Just War Tradition—Contemporary Issues of War

Several contemporary issues pose special problems for JWT. The likelihood is that terrorists and guerrillas will continue to press the limits of noncombatant immunity, threatening to bring as many people as possible into the circle of war in order to achieve their ends. Such concerns are particularly significant in light of the collapse of the former Soviet Union, the internal discord within the various former Soviet republics, and the danger of "black-market" sales of nuclear weapons. Any country that desires to adhere to Just War Tradition must not return terror for terror. Instead, despite temptations to the contrary, it must strive as much as possible to adhere to the *jus in bello* criterion of noncombatant immunity.

Other moral concerns involve nuclear weapons themselves. Not long after the destruction of Hiroshima in 1945, debate began on the morality of nuclear weapons. Such debate has focused on two main issues that are seen by some to overturn the *concept* of just war altogether: the enormous power of nuclear weapons and the strategies employed by the nuclear powers to prevent war (deterrence).

Some scholars are convinced that the tremendous destructive capacity of nuclear weapons places them entirely outside the scope of JWT. They are simply *too* destructive, *too* powerful to categorize in the traditional categories of *jus in bello*.[21] Yet, there has been a significant progress in nuclear weapons technology. To cite just one example, "miniaturized fusion bombs" (commonly called "neutron bombs") can now be delivered to military targets with far less collateral damage and long-term radiation effects.[22] These developments in so-called "smart weaponry" should be viewed as significant moral improvements over strategies such as delivering megatonnage bombs over general, less specific targets. Thus, advancement in military technology toward greater accuracy and precision has given the U.S. an opportunity to shift its strategic emphasis from general targets with large civilian populations where accuracy wasn't needed to specific, detailed military targets where accuracy is at a premium.

Some argue that nuclear weapons are so destructive that even their *nonuse* is immoral. Such thinkers are convinced that their awful destructive capacity, combined with the immoral nuclear deterrent doctrine of "mutually assured destruction," insures that even the *threat* to use such weapons is wrong. How can it be moral to threaten to destroy another country's cities after one's own country has been leveled?[23]

Such arguments, however, are directed at the policy of "counter-city" nuclear attack, complete with inaccurate, megatonnage nuclear weapons delivered over or near cities, insuring that civilian deaths would be disproportionate. Because of the evolution of weapons technology, targeting doctrine is now likewise open to evolve in the direction of "counter-force." The JWT would welcome such a change. In the past decade, the accuracy of weapons delivery systems has improved to the extent that it is now possible to reduce the size of the warhead. Because of this increase in accuracy, it may even be possible at times to substitute conventional warheads for nuclear, thus eliminating the danger of radiation.[24] It also must be acknowledged that nuclear weapons *do* deter. During the Gulf War, one of the biggest concerns of both the American military intelligence and the general public, was that Saddam Hussein would unleash his biological and chemical arsenal upon American soldiers. He had shown in the past against the Kurds that he had no qualms about using such weapons, and many people were fearful that he would do the same in Kuwait against American troops and in Scud missiles fired into Israel. It turned out that the only reason he did not was that he feared a nuclear retaliation by either Israel or the United States. According to General Wafic Al Samar'ai, the then military advisor to Hussein and former chief of Iraqi military intelligence, "Some of the Scud missiles were loaded with chemical warheads, but they were not used. . . . We didn't use them because the other side had a deterrent force."[25] In my opinion there is a legitimate place for nuclear deterrence in modern Just War Tradition, but it should avail itself of every proven advance that allows nuclear deterrent to be focused on military, not civilian, targets. (This is not to deny the importance of negotiations among nations that result in reductions in nuclear arsenals and nuclear test ban treaties. However, since such negotiations are not directly a part of JWT, I have not expounded on them in this article.)

If nuclear weapons are the crisis of the wealthier powers, then the epidemic of military mines is the crisis of poorer nations. The criteria of *jus in bello* dictate, "Weapons of war should be, by design, highly controllable and relatively limited in their destructive effects."[26] The eight to ten *million* mines still buried in Cambodia, on the other hand, are primarily designed to injure horribly whoever might stumble onto them.[27] And since their destructive power can last for a century or more, hundreds and thousands of civilians will be maimed and killed long after the related conflicts are forgotten.

Mines have traditionally been used to block or slow military advances, halt enemy infiltration, or help protect defensive positions. In southeast Asia, however, mines are often scattered anonymously with no regard for marking their location or for any military purpose. Hidden in agricultural or residential areas, those mines are used primarily to cause terror among the civilian population.[28]

Military technology has not been of much help in reducing this horror. So-called "smart mines," designed to self-destruct after a certain amount of time in the ground, have a 10 to 20 percent failure rate, insuring that live mines will remain a danger long after the war is over. Additionally, most of the mines do not come from countries that have manufactured smart weapons and are too primitive to self-destruct.[29]

Although JWT can support a regulated use of land mines in military operations, Christians and other thoughtful people have a responsibility to support legislation that attempts to place international controls and restrictions on the manufacture, sale, and use of land mines. The maiming and killing of civilians—men, women, and children—is continuing at a horrific pace in southeast Asia. Such atrocities fly in the face of the just war tradition.

Just War Tradition—Dual Citizens

Christians have long recognized that they hold dual citizenship. As citizens of the kingdom of God and ambassadors of Christ, they strive to let their light shine everywhere (Matt. 5:16). JWT is an invaluable moral matrix for Christians so that their faith may influence even the most horrible of humanity's enterprises. Given the intractability of sin, Jesus says that wars will be with us until He returns (Matt. 24:7). To ignore that fact is to ignore reality. To ignore our moral responsibility is to invite conflicts to continue without the mediating influence of thoughtful Christians. The just war tradition provides no easy answers, but it can help to mediate Christ's grace in a fallen and tragic world.

This essay originally appeared as an article on http://www.equip.org/article/just-war-tradition/. It is reproduced here with the permission of its author.

[1] See the excellent discussion of the background of the JWT in James Turner Johnson's *Can Modern War Be Just?* (New Haven: Yale University Press, 1984), 12–16.

[2] See Arthur F. Holmes, ed., *War and Christian Ethics* (Grand Rapids: Baker Book House, 1975), 37–47.

[3] Ibid., 55.

[4] Ibid., 62–63.

[5] Ibid., 64.

[6] Ibid., 64.

[7] Johnson, 12–16.

[8] See the discussion of these categories in Johnson, 18–29.

[9] Ibid., 19.

[10] Ibid., 25.

[11] Joshua Lawrence Chamberlain, *The Passing of the Armies* (New York: Bantam Books, 1993 edition of the 1915 Putnam book), 295.

[12] Dwight Eisenhower, *Crusade in Europe* (Garden City, NJ: Doubleday & Company, 1948), 468.

[13] Ibid.

[14] Ibid.

[15] Ibid., 469.

[16] The entire Roger Young story appears in *World War II* 8, no. 4, 66–72.

[17] *Medal of Honor: True Stories of America's Greatest War Heroes* (Washington, D.C.: *U.S. News & World Report*, 1991), 22.

[18] Ibid., 5.

[19] Ibid.

[20] Chamberlain, 295.

[21] Such is the opinion of many of the writers in Todd Whitmore, ed., *Ethics in the Nuclear Age: Strategy, Religious Studies, and the Churches* (Dallas: Southern Methodist Press, 1989).

[22] See James Turner Johnson's essay in *Ethics in the Nuclear Age,* especially 108–9.

[23] Such is the position, for example, of John Howard Yoder in *Ethics in the Nuclear Age* (79–92).

[24] See Johnson, *Ethics in the Nuclear Age*, 113.

[25] Transcript of *Frontline,* 9 January 1996 (Denver: Journal Graphics, 1996), 19. United Nations Inspector David Kay agrees: "I think the Iraqis were genuinely afraid that if they used biological or chemical weapons, the United States—or if not the United States, the Israelis—would reply with nuclear weapons. And it was really the deterrent power of U.S. weapons, primarily, that prevented the use of it." See transcript of *CBS Reports: The Gulf War + 5*, 18 January 1996 (Livingston, N.J.: Burrell's Information Services, 1996), 12.

[26] Johnson, *Ethics in the Nuclear Age*, 110.

[27] It is actually estimated that there are nearly 100 million armed land mines in over 60 countries. See transcript of *Terror in the Minefields*, aired on *Nova*, 9 January 1996 (Denver: Journal Graphics, 1996), 1.

[28] *See Terror in the Minefields*, 6.

[29] Ibid., 3.

“Just-War Theory” Discussion Questions

1. **According to just-war theory, when it is right to fight?**

2. **How should a nation conduct itself in warfare?**

3. **Why do we respect the heroism and self-sacrifice acknowledged by the Congressional Medal of Honor?**

4. **What contemporary issues pose special problems for just-war theory?**

5. **How does the deployment of military mines violate the criteria of just-war theory?**

“The Rules of the Game” Video

“Thou shalt not kill.” This is perhaps the most famous moral commandment in the Western world. And yet Judeo-Christian religious leaders have also created a doctrine that can justify killing—commonly known as just-war doctrine. What sort of military action does just-war doctrine permit and what does it proscribe? Is America’s campaign against terrorism a just war?

These questions, and others, are addressed by the moderator Peter Robinson and panel members: Reverend William McLennan, Dean of Religious Life at Stanford University; Rabbi Daniel Lapin, President of Toward Tradition; and Father Robert Sirico, President of the Acton Institute for the Study of Religion and Liberty.

To access this video, go to www.summitu.com/utc and enter the passcode found in the back of your manual.

"THE RULES OF THE GAME" VIDEO OUTLINE

Is the United States War on Terror a just war?

President Bush declared a war on terrorism after the 9/11 attacks on the United States. ______________________ allows a government to use warfare to protect its citizens, at home or abroad.

The War on Terror isn't "an eye for an eye." Just-war doctrine requires a commitment to minimize civilian causalities, while ____________________ deliberately targets civilians to create the maximum amount of terror.

Does the Bible allow for a just war?

The Ten Commandments include the command not to kill (Exodus 20:13). The Hebrew word translated "kill" also means "murder" and includes other destructive activities. The imperative not to kill is in the context of unlawful killing resulting in bloodguilt.

The Bible does allow for the taking of human life (Ecclesiastes 3:3) in the case of warfare, capital punishment, and ____________________. God has also given governments (not individuals) the right to use the sword to promote justice (Romans 13:1–7).

Also note that soldiers who convert to Christianity are allowed to remain in their vocations, which includes killing.

Christian pacifism

Christian pacifism is the theological and ethical position that any form of ____________ is incompatible with Christianity. It is based on the example of Jesus and on his teachings, e.g., the Sermon on the Mount.

Christian denominations known for their pacifism include Mennonites, Quakers, and some Catholic monastic orders.

Just-war doctrine allows for pacifism; it just deals with those situations where pacifism doesn't work.

Criteria for entering into a just war

The main reason for going to war is to protect ______________________ people against aggression. This type of war is defensive and must be undertaken

- with the intent that the means employed will be proportionate to the ends sought;
- only as a last resort;
- only when there is a reasonable probability of success; and
- only when affirmed as legitimate by the international community.

Criteria for waging a just war

The main criteria for waging a just war are using only the amount of force necessary to achieve the just end and avoiding the intentional killing of innocent civilians.

The panel discussed whetherAmerica's use of atomic bombs to end World War II was acceptable according to the criteria for waging a just war. They also asked if there are certain kinds of weapons that are unjust in and of themselves—e.g., nuclear and biological weapons—and made a distinction regarding weapons with the capacity to destroy the entire earth.

"The Rules of the Game" Discussion Questions

1. **Is the current United States war on terror an example of a just war? Why or why not?**

2. **Is there a contradiction between the biblical command not to kill (Exodus 20:13) and the statement that there is a time to kill (Ecclesiastes 3:3)?**

3. **What is Christian pacifism and what has been its place in the church?**

4. What are the criteria for entering into a just war?

5. What are the criteria for waging a just war?

Chapter 15 Key Points

Key Questions:

1. Are Christians ever justified in taking the life of another human being?
2. Should the church ever have anything to do with war?
3. Should Christians ever serve in the military?
4. Should Christians ever use force to protect others?

Key Verses:

1. Isaiah 2:4
2. Matthew 5:38–44
3. Mark 12:31
4. John 13:34–35
5. Ephesians 6:10–18

Key Terms:

1. Force
2. *Jus ad Bellum*
3. *Jus in Bello*
4. Just Peacemaking
5. Just-War Theory*
6. *Lex Talionis*
7. Nonresistance*
8. Pacifism*
9. Preemptive War
10. Preventive War
11. *Shalom*

Key Players:

1. Augustine
2. Thomas Aquinas

**Short answer or essay question on the exam*

Chapter 15 Assignment

Answer the following questions with at least one paragraph.

1. **How does the Christian worldview provide a more profound definition or purpose for peace than a secular worldview can?**

2. **Explain the distinction that this chapter draws between the Bible's prohibition of murder and a legitimate application of the death sentence.**

3. **On matters regarding authority, earthly power, and the use of force, what is theologically significant about the differences between Old Testament Israel and the New Testament church?**

4. **How does the principle of nonresistance distinguish between who may and may not participate in war or use force?**

UNIT 16

JUSTICE

CHAPTER 16 LEARNING OBJECTIVES

Students will be able to:

1. explain how Martin Luther King Jr.'s involvement with protesting against segregation led him to make the statement about the cup of endurance runs over. [16.1]

2. answer these questions: What is the basis of justice? What is the government's role? [16.2]

3. identify three aspects of justice that emerge from Scripture. [16.3]

4. describe ways reform has been taking place through restorative justice and prison reform. [16.4]

5. express ways that transformation is taking place as justice is being established. [16.5]

Chapter 16 Discussion Questions

1. **What was Martin Luther King Jr.'s concept of justice and do you think he was right? [16.1]**

2. **How do our understanding of liberty and law affect our definition of justice? [16.2]**

3. **What are the two dominant views of law and how do they impact one's view of justice? [16.2]**

4. **What are the two dominant views of justice and how do they differ? [16.2]**

5. **What is retributive justice and how does it work? [16.2]**

6. **What are some of the long-term costs of being tough on crime? [16.2]**

7. **What is distributive justice and how does it work? [16.2]**

8. **What role does redistribution play in distributive justice? [16.2]**

9. **Is equality or liberty more important to distributive-justice advocates? [16.2]**

10. **According to the Bible, why should we care about justice? [16.3]**

11. **What can the Old Testament teach us about justice and law? [16.3]**

12. **What are some things emphasized in the Mosaic law that should be foundational for any judicial system? [16.3]**

13. What is restorative justice and how does it work? [16.4]

14. What are some ways to increase the pace of the judicial system? [16.4]

15. What are some effective programs to take better care of the victims of crime and injustice? [16.4]

16. Why is the United States prison population so large? [16.4]

17. What are some reforms that would help reduce prison overpopulation? [16.4]

18. What role should rehabilitation play in our prison system? [16.4]

19. How does the Christian worldview see justice? [16.5]

"Letter from Birmingham Jail" Reading

Dr. Martin Luther King Jr., president of the Southern Christian Leadership Conference (SCLS), saw Birmingham, Alabama as the most segregated city in the country. In April 1963 he joined the protests against segregation and was jailed. He wrote this letter to answer his critics who branded him as an "outside agitator" trying to stir up trouble.

Dr. King outlined the four steps in a nonviolent campaign: 1) collection of the facts, 2) negotiation, 3) self-purification, and 4) direct action. He cited biblical and historical precedence for disobeying unjust laws. He wanted to stir to action "the white moderate who is more devoted to 'order' than to justice; who prefers a negative peace which is the absence of tension to a positive peace which is the presence of justice."

Despite the rough treatment and harsh circumstances, Dr. King's hope was "to meet each of you, not as an integrationist or a civil rights leader, but as a fellow clergyman and a Christian brother."

Letter from a Birmingham Jail

by Martin Luther King, Jr.

My Dear Fellow Clergymen,

While confined here in the Birmingham City Jail, I came across your recent statement calling our present activities "unwise and untimely." Seldom, if ever, do I pause to answer criticism of my work and ideas. ... But since I feel that you are men of genuine good will and your criticisms are sincerely set forth, I would like to answer your statement in what I hope will be patient and reasonable terms.

I think I should give the reason for my being in Birmingham, since you have been influenced by the argument of "outsiders coming in." I have the honor of serving as president of the Southern Christian Leadership Conference, an organization operating in every Southern state with headquarters in Atlanta, Georgia. We have some 85 affiliate organizations all across the South. ... Several months ago our local affiliate here in Birmingham invited us to be on call to engage in a nonviolent direct action program if such were deemed necessary. We readily consented. ...

But more basically, I am in Birmingham because injustice is here. Just as the prophets of the eighth century B.C. left their villages and carried their "thus saith the Lord" far beyond the boundaries of their home towns, and just as the Apostle Paul left his village of Tarsus and carried the gospel of Jesus Christ to the far corners of the Greco-Roman world, so am I compelled to carry the gospel of freedom beyond my own home town. Like Paul, I must constantly respond to the Macedonian call for aid.

Moreover, I am cognizant of the interrelatedness of all communities and states. I cannot sit idly by in Atlanta and not be concerned about what happens in Birmingham. Injustice anywhere is a threat to justice everywhere. We are caught in an inescapable network of mutuality, tied in a single garment of destiny. Whatever affects one directly, affects all indirectly. Never again can we afford to live with the narrow, provincial "outside agitator" idea. Anyone who lives inside the United States can never be considered an outsider anywhere within its bounds. …

In any nonviolent campaign there are four basic steps: 1) collection of the facts to determine whether injustices are alive; 2) negotiation; 3) self-purification; and 4) direct action. We have gone through all of these steps in Birmingham. … Birmingham is probably the most thoroughly segregated city in the United States. Its ugly record of police brutality is known in every section of the country. Its unjust treatment of Negroes in the courts is a notorious reality. There have been more unsolved bombings of Negro homes and churches in Birmingham than in any city in this nation. These are the hard, brutal, and unbelievable facts. On the basis of these conditions Negro leaders sought to negotiate with the city fathers. But the political leaders consistently refused to engage in good faith negotiation.

Then came the opportunity last September to talk with some of the leaders of the economic community. In these negotiating sessions certain promises were made by the merchants—such as the promise to remove the humiliating racial signs from the stores. On the basis of these promises Reverend Shuttlesworth and the leaders of the Alabama Christian Movement for Human Rights agreed to call a moratorium on any type of demonstrations. As the weeks and months unfolded we realized that we were the victims of a broken promise. The signs remained. As in so many experiences in the past, we were confronted with blasted hopes, and the dark shadow of a deep disappointment settled upon us. So we had no alternative except that of preparing for direct action, whereby we would present our very bodies as a means of laying our case before the conscience of the local and national community. We were not unmindful of the difficulties involved. So we decided to go through the process of self-purification. We started having workshops on nonviolence and repeatedly asked ourselves the questions, "are you able to accept the blows without retaliating?" "Are you able to endure the ordeals of jail?" …

You may well ask, "Why direct action? Why sit ins, marches, and so forth? Isn't negotiation a better path?" You are exactly right in your call for negotiation. Indeed, this is the purpose of direct action. Nonviolent direct action seeks to create such a crisis and establish such creative tension that a community that has constantly refused to negotiate is forced to confront the issue. … Just as Socrates felt that it was necessary to create a tension in the mind so that individuals could rise from the bondage of myths and half-truths to the unfettered realm of creative analysis and objective appraisal, we must we see the need for nonviolent gadflies to create the kind of tension in society that will help men rise from the dark depths of prejudice and racism to the majestic heights of understanding and brotherhood. …

My friends, I must say to you that we have not made a single gain in civil rights without legal and nonviolent pressure. History is the long and tragic story of the fact that privileged groups seldom give up their privileges voluntarily. Individuals may see the moral light and give up their unjust posture; but as Reinhold Niebuhr has reminded us, groups are more immoral than individuals.

We know through painful experience that freedom is never voluntarily given by the oppressor; it must be demanded by the oppressed. Frankly I have never yet engaged in a direct action movement that was "well timed," according to the timetable of those who have not suffered unduly from the disease of segregation. For years now I have heard the word "Wait!" It rings in the ear of every Negro with a piercing familiarity. This "wait" has almost always meant "never." It has been a tranquilizing Thalidomide, relieving the emotional stress for a moment, only to give birth to an illformed infant of frustration. We must come to see with the distinguished jurist of yesterday that "justice too long delayed is justice denied." We have waited for more than 340 years for our constitutional and God-given rights. The nations of Asia and Africa are moving with jetlike speed toward the goal of political independence, and we still creep at horse and buggy pace toward the gaining of a cup of coffee at a lunch counter.

Perhaps it is easy for those who have never felt the stinging darts of segregation to say wait. But when you have seen vicious mobs lynch your mothers and fathers at will and drown your sisters and brothers at whim; when you have seen hate-filled policemen curse, kick, brutalize, and even kill your black brothers and sisters with impunity; when you see the vast majority of your twenty million Negro brothers smothering in an airtight cage of poverty in the midst of an affluent society; when you suddenly find your tongue twisted and your speech stammering as you seek to explain to your six-year-old daughter why she can't go to the public amusement park that has just been advertised on television, and see the tears welling up in her little eyes when she is told that Funtown is closed to colored children, and see the depressing clouds of inferiority begin to form in her little mental sky, and see her begin to distort her little personality by unconsciously developing a bitterness toward white people; when you have to concoct an answer for a five-year-old son who is asking in agonizing pathos: "Daddy, why do white people treat colored people so mean?" when you take a cross country drive and find it necessary to sleep night after night in the uncomfortable corners of your automobile because no motel will accept you; when you are humiliated day in and day out by nagging signs reading "white" men and "colored" when your first name becomes "nigger" and your middle name becomes "boy" (however old you are) and your last name becomes "John," and when your wife and mother are never given the respected title of "Mrs." when you are harried by day and haunted by night by the fact that you are a Negro, living constantly at tip-toe stance, never quite knowing what to expect next, and plagued with inner fears and outer resentments; when you are forever fighting a degenerating sense of "nobodiness"—then you will understand why we find it difficult to wait. There comes a time when the cup of endurance runs over, and men are no longer willing to be plunged into an abyss of injustice where they experience the bleakness of corroding despair. I hope, sirs, you can understand our legitimate and unavoidable impatience.

You express a great deal of anxiety over our willingness to break laws. This is certainly a legitimate concern. Since we so diligently urge people to obey the Supreme Court's decision of 1954 outlawing segregation in the public schools, at first glance it may seem rather paradoxical for us consciously to break laws. One may won ask: "How can you advocate breaking some laws and obeying others?" The answer lies in the fact that there fire two types of laws: just and unjust. I would be the Brat to advocate obeying just laws. One has not only a legal but a moral responsibility to obey just laws. Conversely, one has a moral responsibility to disobey unjust laws. I would agree with St. Augustine that "an unjust law is no law at all."

Now, what is the difference between the two? How does one determine whether a law is just or unjust? A just law is a man-made code that squares with the moral law or the law of God. An unjust law is a code that is out of harmony with the moral law. To put it in the terms of St. Thomas Aquinas: An unjust law is a human law that is not rooted in eternal law and natural law. Any law that uplifts human personality is just. Any law that degrades human personality is unjust. All segregation statutes are unjust because segregation distort the soul and damages the personality. It gives the segregator a false sense of superiority and the segregated a false sense of inferiority. Segregation, to use the terminology of the Jewish philosopher Martin Buber, substitutes an "I-it" relationship for an "I-thou" relationship and ends up relegating persons to the status of things. Hence segregation is not only politically, economically and sociologically unsound, it is morally wrong and awful. ...

I hope you are able to see the distinction I am trying to point out. In no sense do I advocate evading or defying the law, as would the rabid segregationist. That would lead to anarchy. One who breaks an unjust law must do so openly, lovingly, and with a willingness to accept the penalty. I submit that an individual who breaks a law that conscience tells him is unjust and who willingly accepts the penalty of imprisonment in order to arouse the conscience of the community over its injustice, is in reality expressing the highest respect for law.

Of course, there is nothing new about this kind of civil disobedience. It was evidenced sublimely in the refusal of Shadrach, Meshach and Abednego to obey the laws of Nebuchadnezzar, on the ground that a higher moral law was at stake. It was practiced superbly by the early Christians, who were willing to face hungry lions and the excruciating pain of chopping blocks rather than submit to certain unjust laws of the Roman Empire. To a degree, academic freedom is a reality today because Socrates practiced civil disobedience. In our own nation, the Boston Tea Party represented a massive act of civil disobedience.

We should never forget that everything Adolf Hitler did in Germany was "legal" and everything the Hungarian freedom fighters did in Hungary was "illegal." It was "illegal" to aid and comfort a Jew in Hitler's Germany. Even so, I am sure that, had I lived in German at the time, I would have aided and comforted my Jewish brothers. If today I lived in a Communist country where certain principles dear to the Christian faith are suppressed, I would openly advocate disobeying that country's antireligious laws.

I must make two honest confessions to you, my Christian and Jewish brothers. First, I must confess that over the last few years I have been gravely disappointed with the white moderate. I have almost reached the regrettable conclusion that the Negro's great stumbling block in the stride toward freedom is not the White citizens' "Councilor" or the Ku Klux Klanner, but the white moderate who is more devoted to "order" than to justice; who prefers a negative peace which is the absence of tension to a positive peace which is the presence of justice; who constantly says "I agree with you in the goal you seek, but I can't agree with your methods of direst action" who paternistically feels that he can set the timetable for another man's freedom; who lives by the myth of time and who constantly advises the Negro to wait until a "more convenient season." Shallow understanding from people of good will is more frustrating than absolute misunderstanding from people of ill will. Lukewarm acceptance is much more bewildering than outright rejection. …

You spoke of our activity in Birmingham as extreme. At first I was rather disappointed that fellow clergymen would see my nonviolent efforts as those of an extremist. I started thinking about the fact that I stand in the middle of two opposing forces in the Negro community. One is a force of complacency made up of Negroes who, as a result of long years of oppression, have been so completely drained of self-respect and a sense of "somebodiness" that they have adjusted to segregation, and a few Negroes in the middle class who, because of a degree of academic and economic security, and at points they profit from segregation, have unconsciously become insensitive to the problems of the masses. The other force is one of bitterness and hatred and comes perilously close to advocating violence. It is expressed in the various black nationalist groups that are springing up over the nation, the largest and best known being Elijah Muhammad's Muslim movement. This movement is nourished by the contemporary frustration over the continued existence of racial discrimination. It is made up of people who have lost faith in America, who have absolutely repudiated Christianity, and who have concluded that the white man in an incurable "devil." …

The Negro has many pent-up resentments and latent frustrations. He has to get them out. So let him march sometime; let him have his prayer pilgrimages to the city hall; understand why he must have sit-ins and freedom rides. If his repressed emotions do not come out in these nonviolent ways, they will come out in ominous expressions of violence. This is not a threat; it is a fact of history. So I have not said to my people, "Get rid of your discontent." But I have tried to say that this normal and healthy discontent can be channeled through the creative outlet of nonviolent direct action. …

In spite of my shattered dreams of the past, I came to Birmingham with the hope that the white religious leadership in the community would see the justice of our cause and, with deep moral concern, serve as the channel through which our just grievances could get to the power structure. I had hoped that each of you would understand. But again I have been disappointed.

I have heard numerous religious leaders of the South call upon their worshippers to comply with a desegregation decision because it is the law, but I have longed to hear white ministers declare: "Follow this decree because integration is morally right and the Negro is your brother." In the midst of blatant injustices inflicted upon the Negro, I have watched white churchmen stand on the sideline and merely mouth pious irrelevancies and sanctimonious trivialities. In the midst of a mighty struggle to rid our nation of racial and economic injustice, I have heard so many ministers say, "Those are social issues with which the Gospel has no real concern," and I have watched so many churches commit themselves to a completely other-worldly religion which made a strange distinction between body and soul, the sacred and the secular. …

I hope this letter finds you strong in the faith. I also hope that circumstances will soon make it possible for me to meet each of you, not as an integrationist or a civil rights leader, but as a fellow clergyman and a Christian brother. Let us all hope that the dark clouds of racial prejudice will soon pass away and the deep fog of misunderstanding will be lifted from our fear-drenched communities and in some not too distant tomorrow the radiant stars of love and brotherhood will shine over our great nation with all of their scintillating beauty.

Yours for the cause of Peace and Brotherhood,

M. L. King, Jr.

This open letter was written on April 16, 1963 by Dr Martin Luther King, Jr. from his jail cell in Birmingham, AL. It is in the public domain.

"Letter from Birmingham Jail" Discussion Questions

1. **Why was Dr. King in Birmingham and why was he jailed?**

2. **What plan of action did the SCLC employ in the Birmingham campaign?**

3. **How did Dr. King answer the charge that he was breaking the law and encouraging others to do so?**

4. **What did Dr. King see as the greatest stumbling block to the success of the civil rights movement? Do you agree with his assessment?**

5. **Did you realize the civil rights movement had such deep Christian roots? How many biblical references can you find in the letter?**

"The Struggle for Equality" Video Summary

Michael Sherrard examines two different approaches to equality, dignity, value and human rights. The functionist view maintains that human beings have value because of characteristics we can acquire or things we can do. The substantist view says that we have value simply because of who we are—human.

The functionist view is held by secular materialists, who see humans as merely matter in motion. There is nothing special about us and our dignity and value can vary or even disappear. The substantist view is based on the Christian worldview. It insists all humans have inherent value by virtue of being made in the image of God. Sherrard goes on to explain how the Christian perspective on human value is the only view that leads to equality, freedom, clarity, and hope.

To access this video, go to www.summitu.com/utc and enter the passcode found in the back of your manual.

"The Struggle for Equality" Video Outline

There are two different approaches to understanding equality, dignity, value and human rights:

The functionist view:

The functionist view holds that humans are valuable because of what we can ___________ or what characteristics we can acquire. We get value from properties or characteristics such as self-awareness, the ability to feel pleasure and pain, the ability to think, and so on.

The substantist view:

The substantist view insists humans are valuable because of who we are—____________. This approach is based on the Christian worldview, which says we are valuable because we are valued by God, who made us in his image. This is the only view that leads to true equality and inalienable human rights.

The main problems with the functionist view:

1. It leads to inequality because humans have different properties and characteristics.
2. Those in power get to decide what gives value. Since there is no absolute value and dignity, there are no absolute ________________ .

The main benefits of the substantist view:

The substantist/Christian view of human dignity is superior to the functionist/secularist view and does a better job explaining things:

Equality: humans are made in the image of God and that gives us inestimable value.

This is the only thing we all share equally, hence we are equally valuable.

Freedom: we are free to pursue life, liberty, and the pursuit of happiness. We are free to work, not as a way to define our value, but because we already have value.

Ethical Clarity: this view brings clarity to pressing ethical issues:

1. All humans deserve equal _______________ because we are equally valuable in our nature, even if we are unequal in our abilities or circumstances.
2. Humans aren't defined by the characteristics we possess, nor should our dignity and rights be based on our attributes and abilities.
3. Being human is an end, not a _______________ to an end. Existence has value all by itself. We don't have to earn value by what we acquire and accomplish.
4. Our destinies aren't determined by the laws of nature and genetics. We are embodied souls with the ability to exercise free choice.

Hope: we all make mistakes and experience failure. We struggle with our sense of worth at such times. But mistakes and success don't change our value. Christ died for us while we were sinners and reconciled us to God. His death and resurrection show just how valuable we are.

"The Struggle for Equality" Discussion Questions

1. **What is dignity and what does it have to do with human rights?**

2. **What is the functionist view of human value?**

3. **What is the substantist view of human value?**

4. **What do these different views teach about freedom?**

5. **How do the implications of the substantist view of human value bring clarity to many of the ethical questions we face?**

Chapter 16 Key Points

Key Questions:

1. What is justice?
2. What is the government's role in securing justice?
3. How can Christians help promote justice?

Key Verses:

1. Psalm 33:5
2. Deuteronomy 1:17a

Key Players:

1. Martin Luther King, Jr.
2. John Rawls

Key Organizations:

1. Prison Fellowship

Key Events:

1. Nuremberg Trials

Key Terms:

1. Distributive Justice
2. Doctrine of Original Sin
3. Human Trafficking
4. Inherent Rights View of Justice
5. Justice*
6. Law
7. Legal Positivism*
8. Liberty*
9. Natural Law*
10. Negative Liberty*
11. Minimum Mandatory Sentencing
12. Mosaic Law
13. Plea Bargaining
14. Positive Liberty*
15. Rehabilitation
16. Restorative Justice*
17. Retributive Justice
18. Right-Ordering View of Justice
19. Sex Trafficking
20. Tort Law

**Short answer or essay question on the exam*

Chapter 16 Assignment

Answer the following questions with at least one paragraph.

1. **Explain the difference between negative and positive liberty as described in this chapter.**

2. **Contrast the natural law theory's philosophy of law with that of legal positivism.**

3. **Christians, more than any others, ought to care about the poor and about justice. Therefore, might they have a problem with the notion of social justice?**

4. **List and explain briefly the four principles of a just and humane legal system that we can find in the law of Moses.**

UNIT 17

17

Community Renewal

Chapter 17 Learning Objectives

Students will be able to:

1. explain how the Clapham Sect used a "grasstops" movement to change the world. [17.1]
2. describe why city populations are increasing. [17.2]
3. describe why the brokenness of sin affects communities. [17.2]
4. explain why the church is God's choice to bring reform to a community. [17.3]
5. identify ways Christians can focus on human flourishing and bringing change to communities. [17.4]
6. discuss the three steps to community renewal and reformation. [17.5]

Chapter 17 Discussion Questions

1. **What lessons can we learn from the Clapham Sect about how to transform society? [17.1]**

2. **Why is it important to focus on cities when working toward community renewal? [17.2]**

3. **How can city governments and local churches work together to bring about community renewal? [17.2]**

4. **What is the forming process God is carrying out in creation? [17.3]**

5. **How does the Protestant Reformation illustrate God's forming process?** [17.3]

6. **How are cities central to God's plan?** [17.3]

7. **What role does the church play in God's plan to reform society?** [17.3]

8. **In what ways does the Christian view of reform differ from the materialistic view of reform?** [17.3]

9. **How can we help people flourish and reach their God-given potential? [17.4]**

10. **How does the biblical idea of *shalom* relate to human flourishing? [17.4]**

11. **What lessons about helping society flourish can be learned from the life of William Carey? [17.4]**

12. **What did Jesus mean when he told us to love our neighbors? [17.4]**

13. What are some modern examples of Christians loving their neighbors by being present in their pain? [17.4]

14. What are some ministries you have personally seen in action that meet people at the point of their pain and make a healing difference in their lives? If you were going to participate in or start such a ministry, what would it be? [17.4]

15. What is the difference between need-based community development (NBCD) and asset-based community development (ABCD)? [17.4]

16. What are some of the assets we can tap into for community development? [17.4]

17. Do governments or individuals have the right to take someone's goods, even if it's for good of the community? [17.4]

18. Is self-interest always bad? [17.4]

19. Should Christians be involved in redeeming entertainment? [17.4]

20. What are some steps to bring renewal and reformation in our communities? [17.5]

“A Theology of Cities” Reading

Timothy Keller, pastor of Redeemer Presbyterian Church in Manhattan, draws on biblical truth and personal experience to develop a theology of cities. He begins with the revelation that the “city” is God’s idea. He designed it with the power to draw out the resources of creation and to build civilization. “The city is not to be regarded as an evil invention of ungodly fallen man,” Keller insists. “The ultimate goal set before humanity at the very beginning was that human-culture should take city-form.” He goes on to explain *why* cities develop culture, and *how* they do it.

The city brings out the very best and absolute worst of human nature and capabilities, which Keller briefly outlines. Then he focuses on the struggle for control of every city being waged between the city of Satan and the city of God. In this ongoing battle, churches adopt models of ministry based on how they see themselves and the city around them. Keller explains how Christians are to see the city as something to love and win by seeking its *shalom* (peace), and gives practical examples of how this can be done.

A Theology of Cities

by Timothy Keller

As more and more people become city-dwellers it is imperative that the church understands how to reach out to the expanding cities of the 21st century. Here Tim Keller shares some biblical insights.

The Meaning of the City

God designed the city with the power to draw out the resources of creation (of the natural order and the human soul) and thus to build civilization.

A. God’s Invention

God’s future redeemed world and universe is depicted as a “city.” Abraham sought the city “whose builder and maker is God” (Hebrews 11.10). Revelation 21 describes and depicts the apex of God’s redemption, as a city! His redemption is building us a city—the new Jerusalem.

In fact, when we look at the New Jerusalem, we discover something strange. In the midst of the city is a crystal river, and on each side of the river is the Tree of Life, bearing fruit and leaves which heal the nations of all their wounds and the effects of the divine covenant curse. This city is the Garden of Eden, remade. The City is the fulfillment of the purposes of the Eden of God. We began in a garden but will end in a city; God’s purpose for humanity is urban! Why?

So the city is God's invention and design, not just a sociological phenomenon or invention of humankind.

B. Why Cities Develop Culture

"The city is not to be regarded as an evil invention of ungodly fallen man... The ultimate goal set before humanity at the very beginning was that human-culture should take city-form... there should be an urban structuring of human historical existence... The cultural mandate given at creation was a mandate to build the city. Now, after the fall, the city is still a benefit, serving humankind as refuge from the howling wilderness condition into which the fallen human race, exiled from paradise, has been driven... The common grace city has remedial benefits even in a fallen world. It becomes the drawing together of resources, strength and talent no longer just for mutual complementation in the task of developing the resources of the created world, but now a pooling of power for defense against attack, and as an administrative community of welfare for the relief of those destitute by reason of the cursing of the ground" (Meredith G. Kline, "Kingdom Prologue").

It is widely understood that when God tells Adam and Eve to "have dominion" and "fill the earth" he is directing them to build a God-honoring civilization. They are to bring forth the riches that God put into creation by developing science, art, architecture, human society. Kline reveals, however, that since Revelation reveals that the "end" of creation (the climax of the work of the "Second Adam" Jesus Christ) is a city—that therefore God was calling Adam and Eve to be city builders. City building is an ordinance of God just like work and marriage. And indeed, cities draw together human talent and resources and tap the human potential for cultural development as nothing else does.

There is no absolute way to define a "city." A human settlement becomes more "urban" as it becomes more a) dense and b) diverse in its population. God made the city to be a developmental tool, a form of cultural "gardening," designed to draw out the riches he put into the earth, nature and the human soul at creation. Even after the fall, cities are places of "common grace" though each factor also now can be used (and is!) for evil purposes.

C. How It Does It

1. First, the city (as the Garden) is a place of refuge and safety. It has always been a place where people come who are too weak to live in other places. In the earliest days, cities provided refuge from wild animals and marauding tribes and criminals. When Israel moved into the promised land, the first cities were built by God's direction as "cities of refuge," where the accused person could flee for safety and civil justice. Thus God invented cities to be a sign of divine, not self, protection. Even today, people like the homeless, or new immigrants, or the poor, or people with "deviant" lifestyles, must live in the city. The city is always a more merciful place for minorities of all kinds. Why? The density of the city creates the possibility of strong minority communities. Density creates diversity. The dominant majorities often dislike cities, but the weak and powerless need them. They cannot survive in the suburbs and

small towns. Cain built his cities for self-protection from God and the vengeance of others. So the refuge of the city can be misused, as when people with sinful lifestyles find refuge in the city from the disapproval of the broader culture.

Practical note: It is hard for middle-class families to live in the cities, and thus the cities are seen as hostile places. But for anyone who is not part of the dominant culture (singles, the poor, ethnic minorities, etc.) the city has great advantages over non-urban areas.

2. Second, the city as a cultural mining/development center. Even the description of the wicked city of Babylon shows the power of the city to draw out the resources of creation—of the physical world and the human soul. In Revelation 18 we see that the city is a place of 1) music and the arts (v. 22a), 2) crafts and works of all arts and manufacturing (v. 22b), 3) trade and retailing (v. 23c), 4) technological advance (v. 23a), and 5) family building (v. 23b). This is what the city was designed by God to do, as an instrument of glorifying him by "mining" the riches of creation and building a God-honoring civilization.

Practical note: The city, then, has a powerful magnifying glass effect. Since God invented it as a "cultural mine," it brings out whatever is in the human heart. Why? The density and therefore diversity of the city brings out the best (and the worst—see below) in the human heart. How does it do so? The divinely-given ability of the city to do "culture-making" can be discerned at the most practical level by the urban resident.

- The city puts me together with unique numbers of people unlike me.
- The city attracts the minorities of any society who can band together for mutual support. Thus the city is deeply merciful to those with less power, creating safe enclaves for singles vs. families, the poor (and even the rich!) vs. the bourgeois, immigrants vs. longer-term residents, racial minorities vs. majorities. Thus the city will always be the most diverse human-life structure.
- Because I am put together (by its density) with unique numbers of diverse people, all my thinking and views are radically challenged. I am confronted with creative new ways to think about things, and
- I must abandon my traditional ways or become far more knowledgeable and committed to them than
- I was before. Thus I become vastly more creative, committed, skillful in all I am or do.
- Sin takes this divine-strength—the diversity of the city—and turns it into a place of conflict and strife. The gospel is needed to resist the dark side of this gift.
- The city puts me together with unique numbers of people like me.
- The city also attracts the strongest as well as the weakest (see above). The challenge of the city attracts the most talented, ambitious (and restless, see below). Thus, whoever you are, when you come to the city you are confronted by far more people who are far better than you at whatever you do.
- Because I am put together with unique numbers of like-but-extremely-skilled people in my field, I am radically challenged to "reach down deep" and do my very best. More than that, I feel driven and pressed by the intensity of the density to realize every ounce of my potential.

- Sin takes this divine strength—the culture-forming intensity—and turns it into a place (also) of both deadly hubris and burn-out. The gospel is needed to resist the dark side of this gift.

Cities draw and gather together human resources and tap their potential for cultural development as no other human-life organization structure can.

It is quite wrong to see the city as intrinsically evil! It was designed by God to "draw out" and to "mine" what God made. We should appreciate the power of the city and realize that the tremendous evil has been brought to it by us!

3. Third, the city as the place to meet God. Ancient cities were religious institutions. They were usually built around a "ziggurat"—the original skyscrapers! They were temples where a particular god was thought to "come down." The cities were seen to be the royal residences of the god, and the city was dedicated to him/her. The city was where the cultus for that god was centered, and where you went if you wanted to serve him or her. All of this was probably a twisted "memory trace" of the original design of God, that the Edenic city, the new Jerusalem, would be the place where people would meet him, where his temple/presence would be.

After Eden was lost to us (temporarily) through sin, God creates a new city in the desert, by dwelling among his people in the tabernacle, and around his Tent is a city of tents. The city of God will be his dwelling place. Later, the earthly city of Jerusalem becomes a symbol and sign to the future city of God. In the earthly Jerusalem, God's dwelling place, the temple, stands as the central integrating point of the city's architecture and as apex of its art and science and technology. As a result, Jerusalem is "the joy of the whole earth" (Psalm 48.2). But she is only a sign of the city of God which is heavenly and which is to come. All true believers even now have as their mother, "the Jerusalem that is above, is free" (Galatians 4.26).

Why are cities always "religious hotbeds" where people are spiritually seeking and restless? The density and diversity of the city—the same dynamics that produce cultural development—also keep people spiritually "off balance" and restless. Cities, therefore, are the key to evangelism in any area. Paul's missionary journeys essentially ignored the countryside. When he entered a new region, he planted churches in the biggest city, and then left!

- Why? The reason for ministry in cities mirrors what we've seen about the nature of cities.
- Cultural cruciality. In the village, you might win the one or two lawyers to Christ, but if you wanted to win the legal profession, you need to go to the city where you have the law schools, the law journals published, etc.
- Global cruciality. In the village, you can win only the single people group that is there, but if you want to spread the gospel into 10-20 new national groups and languages at once, you go to the city where they can all be reached through the lingua franca of the place.
- Personal cruciality. In the village little changes and people live in very stable environments. Thus they are suspicious of any major change. Because of the diversity and intensity of the cities, urbanites are much more open to radically

new ideas—like the gospel! Because they are surrounded by so many people like and unlike themselves (see above), and so much more mobile and subject to change, urbanites are far more open to change/conversion than any other kind of resident. They may have moved to the city out of a searching restlessness. But even if not, once they get to the city, the pressure and diversity makes even the most traditional and hostile people open to the gospel.

- Result? By year 300 AD, 50% of the urban populations of the Roman empire were Christian, while over 90% of the countryside was still pagan.
- (Note: Some believe that the very word "pagan" comes from the Greek paganus meaning a farmer or man of the country.) Because Christianity captured the cities, it eventually captured the society, as must always be the case. What captivates the cities also captivates the arts, media, scholarship and the professions. Cities are the "culture-forming wombs" of the society, made by God to be so.

D. How Sin Breaks the City

1. The diversity of the city under sin creates a place of racism, classism, and violence. Also the city becomes a refuge, not from the wilderness or persecution, but from God and his law.

For example, people have gone to the cities to engage in sexual practices that are proscribed by many places in society, but the natural "tolerance of diversity" that cities inherently have is twisted into a place where "anything goes." People go to the city to create their own moralities.

Second, while cities still do attract and sustain enormous race and cultural diversity, human sin makes cities places of constant racial strife, class warfare, crime and violence. This can be seen perfectly in Genesis 11 and Babel. The Babel-builders specifically sought to build a city that would gather people for their own glory (see below). (Many scholars believe that, since Genesis 9 and 10 indicates God wanted human spread and cultural differentiation, Babel may have actually been built in resistance to cultural diversity. See Vos.) In any case, the result of the sin of Babel is confusion. People cannot communicate. Any human effort at unity based on common defiance of God resulted in fragmentation and greater disunity. So today, cities built on human defiance of God and for "making a name" for the human builders find enormous strife and confusion and violence between diverse groups of people.

Practical note: Many people hate cities because of the diversity of cultures, people "not like us," but we see that God enjoys and wills the diversity of cultures as bringing forth the richness of his creation. Christians should rejoice and enjoy diversity of cultures, recognizing that they all stand judged by God's Word.

2. The cultural-development power of the city under sin creates a place of pride, arrogance, excess, over-work, and exhaustion. The quintessential City of Rebellion is Babel. "Come, let us build ourselves a city, with a tower that reaches to the heavens, so that we may make a name for ourselves and not be scattered over the face of the whole earth" (Genesis 11.4).

The first skyscraper is built in clear defiance of God. The original mandate of God to humankind was to be "miners" of all the riches of creation. They were to turn to the natural resources of the physical universe and the personal resources of their own creation in the image of God. They were thus to be culture builders, developing science and art and civic life, building civilization that glorified God as its source and ground. Now we have a city dedicated to "mining cultural riches" for human glorification and to show its independence of God.

Since the human heart is made in the image of God and is totally depraved, therefore the city brings out the very, very best and worst of human capabilities. Adam would have developed a city of God and all the potentialities of creation (physical nature and human spirit) would have been untainted and thus the city would be glorious. Today, however, art and science and technology and education serve to both bring out the best and worst. We can all feel it. Nothing challenges and presses you to excellence like the city. But nothing drives you to reach down deep and do well. In sin that all becomes tainted and idolatrous and exhausting, of course. The purpose of the City of Rebellion is "to make a name for ourselves." This is still a deep drive and engine in the building of any human city. It is a spirituality of darkness of enormous force, it is a motivation moving many or most people who move toward the city.

3. The spiritual restlessness of the city under sin makes the city a hotbed of cults and false belief. Cities are always the hotbed of religious cults. They are inveterately religious. Every city is dedicated to a god—even if it is the secular "religion." In cities, ordinarily, the Christian churches can be found with the best ministries, theological resources, churches, etc. Until recently, that is. Protestant Christians abandoning the city inevitably make it easier for the city to turn to false gods. Because God invented cities to be religious centers, human idolatries are enhanced in the city. It is not surprising that cities were the places in which the "new" ideas of the Enlightenment first took place and where irreligion first became rampant in Western society. Cities are always places that are "ahead of the curve." But it stands to reason that these would be the first places where secular people who are steeped in the unbelief of their culture would be the most open to Christianity as a new idea. Cities would be the place where any new vision of Christianity would take shape and begin to capture the culture's imagination again.

Summary

- Reach the city to reach the culture. Protestant (evangelical) Christians are the least urban religious group and thus have the least impact culturally. Three kinds of people here affect the future: a) elites, b) new immigrants, c) the poor. The single most effective way for Christians to "reach" the US would be for 25% of them to move to two or three of the largest cities and stay there for three generations.
- Reach the city to reach your region and the world. a) Region. You can't reach the city from the suburbs, but can reach all the metro area from the city. b) World. The return of the "city-state." The cities of the world are now linked more to one another than to their own states and countries. Each major city is a "portal" to the other major cities of the world.

- Reach the city to reach your own heart with the gospel.
- In the city you'll find a) people that seem "hopeless" spiritually, and b) people of other religions or no religion and of deeply non-Christian lifestyles that are wiser, kinder, and deeper than you. This will shock you out of your moralism and force you to either finally believe the gospel of sheer grace, or give it up altogether. You may get top marks on justification by faith alone, but functionally, believe salvation by works. The city will show this to you as nothing else will.
- In the city you will find that the poor and the broken are often much, much more open to the idea of gospel grace and much more dedicated to its practical outworkings than you are.
- You should eventually come to see that you need the city more than the city needs you.

How to Live in the City

A. Models of Life in the City

In every earthly city, there are two "kingdoms" present, two "cities" vying for control. They are the City of Baal (or Satan or the god of this world) and the City of God.

- The city of Satan deifies power and wealth and human culture itself (making art, technology, business an end in itself instead of a way of glorifying God).
- The city of God is marked by God shalom (Jerusalem)—his peace. His peace is a place where stewardship of God, creation, justice, compassion and righteousness lead to harmony and family building and cultural development under God.
- Christians are to see the earthly city as something to love and win. They are to win it by seeking its shalom (Jeremiah 29) and seeking to spread the city of God within it, and to battle the city of Satan within it.
- We are to see that, though the fight between these two kingdoms happens everywhere in the world, earthly cities are the flashpoints on the battlelines, the places where the fighting is most intense, where the war can be won.

Models of urban ministry are then:

- We despise the city. Church as fortress. (Forgetting the city as Jerusalem).
- We are the city. Church as mirror. (Forgetting the city as Babylon).
- We use the city. Church as space capsule. (Forgetting the city as battleground).
- We love the city. Church as leaven. Jeremiah 29.

Any theological model of the city will fail if one or more of these three biblical themes of the city is neglected, omitted, or over-emphasized.

B. Basic Methods/Ministries

WORD (Ezra). Ezra recovered the Word for the people. Preaching, discipling, teaching. evangelizing in a way contextualized to the concerns and capacities of the people of the city.

DEED (Nehemiah). Nehemiah made the city safe and functional. Mercy and Justice! Holistic ministry. Safe streets, good jobs, decent housing, good schools.

WORK (Esther). Esther rose high in a pagan society but then used her position at great risk to work for justice in society and for her people. A key part of city ministry is to equip Christians to work distinctively as Christians in their vocation.

COMMUNITY (Jeremiah). Jeremiah's letter (chapter 29) told the exiles to neither assimilate nor separate but live out their lives as a community "seeking the peace of the city." So we are not only to be "witnesses" by our individual lives, but by the beauty of our communal life. a) Generosity with money and simplicity of life, b) races and classes loving together over barriers, c) sexual purity and respect shown by men/women to one another in relationships.

C. Getting the Power

Jesus went down to the city, and was crucified "outside the gate:" sent into howling wilderness, the biblical metaphor for forsakenness—losing the city! Jesus lost the city that was, so we can be citizens of the city to come, making us salt and light in the city that is! Our citizenship in the City-to-come, by his grace, equips us for the city that is.

This essay originally appeared as a piece in the 2012 issue of CRU Press Green. It is used here with the permission of its author.

"A Theology of Cities" Discussion Questions

1. **Is the idea of "city" a divine concept or a human invention?**

2. **What are some of the major strengths of the city?**

3. **What are some of the major weaknesses of the city?**

4. What two kingdoms are in conflict for the heart of the city?

5. What are some basic strategies Old Testament leaders used to reach their cities?

“Christianity in Community” Video

Jizmejian looks at the importance of community at college and throughout life. He notes the negative impact of technology on social relationships in the past thirty years and discusses three pitfalls to Christian community related to human sinfulness.

Jizmejian moves on to trace the biblical timeline of community, from *creation* and the *fall* through *redemption* and *consummation*. Then he closely examines how Jesus built community, putting his disciples before his natural family (Luke 14:26), and setting up a new community (the church) with himself at the center and everyone gathered as family around a table (Communion). Our identity in Christ is the most important thing in life, connecting us at the deepest level to God and one another.

To access this video, go to www.summitu.com/utc and enter the passcode found in the back of your manual.

"Christianity in Community" Video Outline

Importance of Community in College

Three things help college students thrive, according to *Fabric of Faithfulness:*

- ______________________: having a solid worldview
- Character: finding a mentor or teacher who embodies this worldview
- ______________________: choosing to live out their worldview with mutually committed people

Technology and Community

1985–2004: Social isolation

- The average number of confidants per person was reduced from three to two.
- Three times as many people said they have no one to talk to in 2004, compared to 1985.

2011–2015: Impact of media

- Screen time went from 11:11 hours to 12:04 hours a day.
- The average person checks his or her phone ______________ times a day.
- The average teenager sends 111 texts a day.
- The average person touches their phone more than one million times a year

Pitfalls to Christian Community

We long for the intimacy of Christian community, but our sinful tendencies pull us in ways that destroy community:

- Inner ring: we desire to be part of the inner circle; when we make it, we exclude others.
- Selfish desires: others can never fill the void; it's not about them meeting our individual needs.
- Human love: it can never fully satisfy; it can turn to hatred if rebuffed.

Biblical Timeline of Community

***Creation*:** Adam and Eve were naked and unashamed. They were created for ______________ with God, with others, and with the world.

***Fall*:** Adam and Eve were hiding and fearful. They abused and abandoned their responsibilities and relationships.

***Redemption*:** God's answer to the fall was redemption through the cross of Christ.

***Consummation*:** Christ restores broken relationships and invites us into community "naked and unashamed" as God originally intended.

How Jesus Built Community

Jesus upset the social order by putting his __________ before his natural family (Luke 14:26). He is the center of this new community and our fellowship with him and one another centers around a family meal—communion.

Americans don't spend much time together around the table. According to *Tablets to the Table*:

- Twenty percent of Americans eat meals in cars.
- Twenty-five percent of meals are eaten at restaurants or fast food franchises.
- In 1955 the average meal took 90 minutes; today it is 13 minutes.

The gospel of Luke shows Jesus spending a lot of time at the table. Christ set up the local __________ around a table (communion). Our identity in Christ is the most important thing. It connects us at the deepest level to God and one another.

"Christianity in Community" Discussion Questions

1. **According to Steven Garber in *Fabric of Faithfulness*, what three things help college students thrive at university and beyond?**

2. **What are some of the impacts technology has on community?**

3. **What are some of the main pitfalls to Christian community?**

4. What were we created for and what happened at the fall?

5. How did Jesus build community?

Chapter 17 Key Points

Key Questions:

1. What type of communities experience transformation?
2. Why should Christians care about community renewal?
3. How can Christians help renew communities?

Key Verses:

1. 2 Chronicles 7:14
2. Jeremiah 29:4–7
3. Luke 10:25–37
4. Revelation 21:1–4

Key Players:

1. John Calvin
2. William Carey
3. William Wilberforce

Key Events:

1. Protestant Reformation
2. First Great Awakening

Key Terms:

1. Asset-Based Community Development*
2. Caste System
3. Capital
4. Capitalism
5. Community Discipleship
6. Community Renewal
7. Free-Market Economy
8. Grassroots Movement
9. Grasstops Movement
10. Human Flourishing
11. Materialism
12. Mosaic Law
13. Needs-Based Community Development*
14. *Imago Dei*
15. Right
16. *Shalom*
17. *Suttee*

Key Organizations:

1. Clapham Sect

**Short answer or essay question on the exam*

Chapter 17 Assignment

Answer the following questions with at least one paragraph.

1. **How can Christianity's doctrine of the Trinity give believers a unique understanding of relationships, communities, and the meaning of *shalom*?**

2. **How does a nonmaterialistic worldview (like Christianity) that sees people as a community's most important resource offer more possibilities for social change than a secular, materialistic view of life?**

3. **How does the power of the market undermine the materialistic understanding of wealth as a zero-sum game?**

4. **How can Christians, who are called to abstain from greed, participate in a free-market system that depends on self-interest? Stated differently, how does Christian stewardship work alongside self-interest?**

UNIT

18

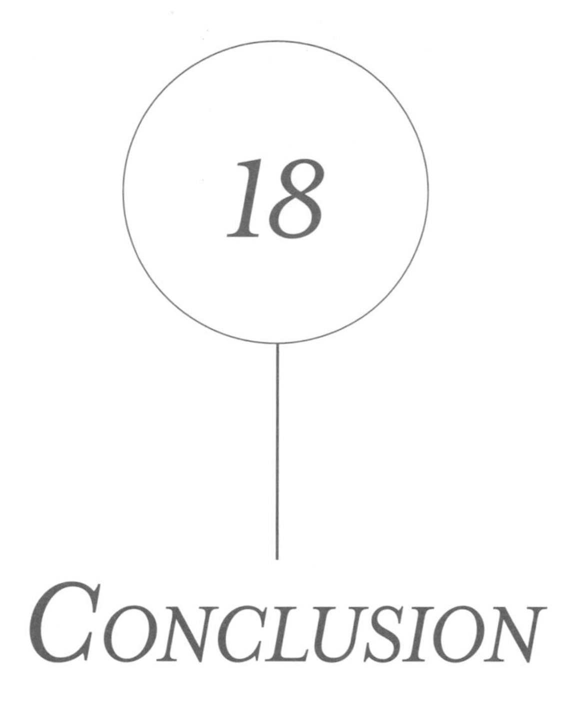

Conclusion

Chapter 18 Learning Objectives

Students will be able to:

1. articulate why Christians should make a difference. [18.1]
2. define what culture is. [18.2]
3. describe how Christians have been culture shapers throughout history. [18.3]
4. identify the two actions that Christians can use to make a difference: posture of engagement and direction of engagement. [18.4]
5. explain why thinking and speaking clearly are important elements for Christians to use effectively to engage the culture. [18.5]
6. discuss why technology is in dire need of shifting its focus from a non-Christian worldview to a Christian worldview. [18.6]
7. express the Christian worldview's answer to the idea of using entertainment to escape from reality. [18.7]
8. explain why Christians should care about the value of human life. [18.8]
9. describe how sexual brokenness has become an epidemic and how the Christian worldview views intimacy with God as the basis of sexual wholeness. [18.9]
10. identify why the state of marriage is a key indicator of a society's state of health and what the Christian worldview says about marriage. [18.10]
11. explain that a Christian worldview cares for creation and Christians bear God's image by being good stewards of what he has entrusted to us. [18.11]
12. discuss why Christians involved in politics can help ensure that people are treated justly, that society is orderly, and that leaders do what they're supposed to do. [18.12]
13. explain why a Christian worldview protects religious freedom not only for itself but also for those who disagree with it. [18.13]
14. describe why the goal of a Christian worldview is not just caring for the poor but curing poverty itself. [18.14]
15. differentiate between the four views of force and what the Bible says about the use of force. [18.15]
16. explain that there is tension between Christianity and the use of force. [18.16]
17. identify why the Christian worldview favors restorative justice. [18.17]
18. explain why the gospel renews communities. [18.18]

Chapter 18 Discussion Questions

1. **For what purpose was this book written? [18.1]**

2. **What is a worldview and what's different about the Christian worldview? [18.1]**

3. **How can we move beyond understanding culture to changing it? [18.2]**

4. **While many religions have much in common, what makes Christianity different? [18.3]**

5. **What does it mean to have a posture of engagement with culture? [18.4]**

6. **Why are good arguments essential for good living? [18.5]**

7. **How does the Christian worldview seek to balance technology and wisdom? [18.6]**

8. **What is the Christian view of the arts and entertainment? [18.7]**

9. **What are the three main views of the value of human life? [18.8]**

10. **How did the sexual revolution change our view of sexuality and was the change for the better? [18.9]**

11. **What does the Christian worldview have to say about marriage? [18.10]**

12. **What are the main approaches to caring for the environment? [18.11]**

13. Should Christians be involved in politics? [18.12]

14. Is there greater religious freedom in the world today due to the progress of civilization? [18.13]

15. How does the Christian view of poverty differ from other worldviews? [18.14]

16. What are some practical ways Christians can work to alleviate poverty? [18.14]

17. How does the Christian worldview understand warfare and the use of force? [18.15]

18. What are the three dominant views of justice? [18.16]

19. What is the biblical approach to community renewal? [18.17]

20. What does it mean for Christians to be the church in a broken world? [18.18]

Chapter 18 Key Points

Key Questions:

1. How should Christians try to understand our culture?
2. How should Christians go about changing our culture for the better?

Key Verses:

1. Psalm 24:1
2. Jeremiah 29:4–7
3. Matthew 22:37–40
4. Matthew 25:35–40
5. Luke 4:18
6. Luke 10:25–37
7. Romans 12:2
8. Colossians 2:8
9. James 1:27

Key Players:

1. Martin Luther King, Jr.
2. William Wilberforce

Key Terms:

1. Abortion
2. Active Euthanasia
3. Age of Enlightenment
4. Amusement
5. Appeal to Ignorance
6. Argument
7. Community Renewal
8. Cultural Anthropologist
9. Culture
10. Cyberculture
11. Endowment View of Human Life
12. Entertainment
13. Environmentalism
14. Euthanasia
15. Fallacy
16. Government Redistribution
17. Grass-tops Movement
18. Human Flourishing
19. *Imago Dei*
20. Inherent Rights View of Justice
21. Inappropriate Appeal to Authority
22. Jihad
23. Just-War Theory
24. Justice
25. Marriage
26. Natural Law
27. Pacifism
28. Passive Euthanasia
29. Performance View of Human Life
30. Politics
31. Pornography
32. Poverty
33. Propaganda
34. Religious Freedom
35. Restorative Justice
36. Right-Ordering View of Justice
37. Sexual Revolution
38. Sexual Purity
39. *Shalom*
40. Shariah Law
41. Stewardship
42. Technology
43. Tolerance
44. *Tzedek*
45. Utilitarianism View of Human Life
46. Valid Argument
47. Wisdom
48. Worldview

**Short answer or essay question on the exam*